MW01234682

DATE TO WIN

*How to Have More Dates, Find That
Lasting Relationship, Or Meet Your
Ideal Marriage Partner*

Rick Mater & Kathy Wing

A Laurel Canyon Book

ISBN: 0-9643444-0-8
Library of Congress Catalog Card Number: 94-96386
Printed in the United States of America
10 9 8 7 6 5 4 3 2 1

This book is dedicated to the magnificent efforts on behalf of Joshua Whitworth Wing Mater by the entire staff of the NICU unit at St. Joseph's Hospital, Burbank, California.

About the Authors

Rick Mater is a television executive and a freelance writer. Kathy Wing, his collaborator, is a pediatric bone marrow transplant nurse. *Date To Win* is the product of a year-and-a-half of extensive national research, combined with the authors' own successful experience dating to win. They met through the *LA Weekly* personal ads in September of 1991, were married in May of 1993, and live in Los Angeles with their newborn baby boy, Joshua.

CONTENTS

PART IV: MATCHMAKERS AND DATING INTRODUCTION SERVICES

PART V: VIDEODATING

PART VI: FOLLOWING THROUGH FOR SUCCESS

PART VII: THE NATIONAL DATING DIRECTORY

Introduction: Dating To Win

Would you like to have more dates? How about more dates with *compatible* people? How would you like to be able to target a dating or relationship goal - whether it's having more dates, or finding that special lasting relationship, or your ideal marriage partner - and then take immediate action to achieve it? You can do it dating to win, and you can do it starting right now.

A Unique Book

Most books about dating and relationships skip over the practical mechanics of how to actually find your candidate for a lasting relationship and/or marriage partner in the first place. *Date to Win* picks up where the other books leave off, and focuses solely on meeting people to date - *viable* candidates for that special lasting relationship or marriage partner.

If you are a woman, dating to win gives you the option of avoiding the traditional male-dominated dating selection process. You can select the men *you* are interested in meeting. Whether you are a man *or* a woman, dating to win is a way to take real control over achieving personal happiness. After all, finding that special relationship - and the dating leading up to it - is perhaps the single most important set of decisions you will make in your lifetime.

Dating and Relationship Success

Goal, Gameplan, Action!   1

Normally when you want to accomplish something in life,

1) you set a goal,

2) you figure out a gameplan,

3) you take action and go for it!

This is how successful people operate. Actually this is what *all* of us do much of the time, often without consciously thinking about it. We especially do it when we want something important, like buying a house, or getting a new job. In fact, we do it in virtually all areas of our lives except one: dating, love and marriage.

Waiting For Love
We stumble through the dating process, hoping that through the everyday happy accidents of life we will find: a) enough people to date, b) the right people to date, and c) eventually the future partner to share the rest of our life with. One day (when "fate" or "chance" leads them to us) that special someone will magically drop into our lives, and we will live happily ever after.

Is this how you would run any *other* area of your life and expect to get results? Compared with the goal/gameplan/action method we apply to the rest of our lives, our dating and relationship search is an erratic, unfocused process, lacking the correlation we normally can get between effort applied and results achieved.

Maybe *you* are dating regularly and pretty successfully, but you just can't seem to find that special person, or even the right *type* of person for a serious relationship. Maybe your job makes it hard to find time to meet members of the opposite sex. Maybe you find the bar scene depressing. Maybe you'd like to be dating more, but can't find enough people you really want to go out with. Or, maybe you hit periodic dating slumps when you have trouble meeting enough people who want to date *you* (!).

Dating To Win
Dating to win changes everything. Dating to win is a way to target dating and relationship goals and then take systematic action to achieve them. It's a way to take the bull by the horns using the same goal/gameplan/action formula you apply to the *rest* of your life, to take charge of your own dating and relationship success. You do so by using the New Dating Options available in the 90's: 1) *personal ads,* 2) *organized singles activities,* 3) *video-dating,* or 4) *matchmakers and dating introduction services.*

The New Dating Options
1) Personal Ads
The personal ads have exploded into a bonafide national phenomenon. Once relegated to singles publications, personal ads now appear in hundreds of mainstream newspapers and magazines, from *New York* magazine to the Little Rock, Arkansas *Democrat-Gazette,* and *USA Today* to the *New York Review of Books.* The *Los Angeles Times* carries *1,500* personals a *week,* triple what they ran just three years ago. While major urban centers like New York, Chicago, Los Angeles, Philadelphia, Boston, Houston, Atlanta, and San Francisco offer the widest variety of

publications carrying personals, ads can also be found in most smaller cities and towns, from Bakersfield to Oshkosh.

2) Organized Singles Activities

It began with a few dozen members in 1991. Now *California Singles* sends a newsletter to 3,000 people, and sponsors functions ranging from singles dinners to moonlight hikes, and white water rafting trips to introductory mixers held in local cafes and restaurants. The fact is singles activities are a growth industry. There are *Sierra Club Singles* hikes, singles dinners, dances, parties, white water rafting and ski trips. For single restaurant aficionados there's *Single Gourmet* in Los Angeles. For the athletically minded there's *Singles Outdoor Adventures* in Atlanta. Parties and dances are available across the country, sponsored by *The Dr. Kate Relationship Center* in Chicago, *Jewish Singles News* in New York City, the *Post Club* in Boston, *The Network* in Pittsburgh, *Young Unattached Professionals* (*Y.U.P.S.*) in the San Francisco Bay Area, and many more groups like them.

3) Videodating

Great Expectations reports over 100,000 members, and more than 40 branches in major cities around the country, including Baltimore, Boston, Chicago, Dallas, Denver, Houston, Los Angeles, Philadelphia, Pittsburgh, Seattle and St. Louis. There are also dozens of non-*Great Expectations* local videodating services, like *Video Introductions* in San Francisco, *Single Attractions* in Milwaukee, *Visual Choice International* in Columbus, *New Beginnings* in Omaha, and *Videodates* in Nashua, New Hampshire. Videodating is especially popular with people who place a premium on eliminating blind dating, and thoroughly pre-screening their dates in advance.

4) Matchmakers And Dating Introduction Services

Dating services are thriving, from lunchtime matchmaking services like *It's Just Lunch* in New York and Chicago, to national chains like *Together Dating Service* and *MatchMaker International* (each advertising over 90 outlets around the country, and more than 100,000 members). Dating introduction services blanket the nation, from smaller cities like Rochester, N.Y., and Greensboro, North Carolina, to larger ones like Memphis, Boston, Los Angeles, Chicago and Phoenix. The more affluent can also use upscale matchmakers like Denise Winston in New York, Debra Winkler in Los Angeles, and Page Greytok in Chicago.

Why The New Dating Options?

The explosive growth of singles options in the 90's reflects the practical demands and realities of our ever-changing, more mobile society. Most people no longer marry straight out of high school, or even college. They often don't live and work where they grew up. Instead, as adults men and women find themselves living in a new town or city, where they lack the old support network of family, friends, community groups and churches or synagogues "back home."

Women have also established themselves in careers, and no longer need to rush into marriage for financial support. Both men and women stay single longer, or find themselves single again (and back in the dating world) as the result of our high divorce rate, or the breakup of a relationship. According to the U.S. Census Bureau *39%* of all adults in the U.S. are now single. That's *78 million* people. Since 1970 the percentage of single Americans age 25 to 45 has more than *doubled*. The percentage of single 30 to 34 year olds has *tripled*.

Most of these people are looking for a lasting relationship, and eventually marriage, and would like to be dating actively and successfully. There's a demand for alternative - and better - ways for people who are single to meet. The New Dating Options provide an avenue for single people to target dating and relationship goals; then effectively focus their time and energy to achieve them.

A Universal Dating And Relationship Solution
You can date to win in as little as a few hours a week, and you can do it anywhere in the country. Dating to win works from age 18 to 80, although if you're in your mid-20's through your 40's, you're in the age range of the majority of the other people using the New Dating Options. However, don't give up if you're older or younger. There are many people in their 50's, 60's, and older participating, as well as many under 25.

But Who Are These People?
Just who places and responds to personal ads, uses videodating, matchmakers and dating introduction services, or attends singles activities? Well, it's a cross section of people who *just happen to be single*. People like you: secretaries, corporate vice presidents, doctors, lawyers, social workers, teachers, self-employed business people, etc.

Many are upscale professionals. For example, in one issue of *New York* magazine the men placing personal ads include: two doctors, a dentist, a lawyer, a journalist, and a banker. The women include: two doctors, a CEO, and a Ph.D. These are career-oriented professionals who likely have neither the time nor the inclination to hang out in bars.

Our Own Date To Win Success Story
RICK: In 1990 I was 42-years-old and never married. I wanted to find a way to get past long dating "dry spells" and fleeting inconsequential affairs. I wanted to find a way to meet the opposite sex which would jump-start my social life. Most of all, I wanted to be able to take *concrete action* to find something which was feeling both increasingly elusive and important in my life - a *longterm relationship leading to marriage.* Here I was finally ready to settle down with the right woman, but things were so slow I was worried about finding a half-decent relationship, much less anything resembling a marriage possibility.

Then I tried two of the date to win options. First I used videodating, and when it didn't produce a serious relationship I tried the personal ads. I began by responding to some personals placed by women in the largest Los Angeles "alternative" publication; but soon decided to run my own ad. With my first *LA Weekly* personal my social life changed dramatically: 18 women responded. I called back 15, met 10 in person, and had a short relationship with one.

I ran five more ads in the next year, two more in the *LA Weekly*, and three in upscale *Los Angeles* magazine. *The results got better with each personal ad as I became more comfortable with the process, and learned how to write an ad that really worked.* My second *LA Weekly* personal generated 40 replies, my third 46. My three *Los Angeles* magazine personals resulted in a total of about 95 responses. That's almost *200* responses altogether for six ads (talk about jump-starting your social life!).

A wide array of women responded to my personals, including a social worker, a real estate broker, several lawyers, a doctor, an artist, a former beauty queen, a record company A & R person, a stock broker, a speech therapist, a college professor, and several nurses.

There is a misconception among some people that only "losers" would run (or respond to) a personal ad, use a matchmaker or a dating introduction service, sign up for videodating, or go to a singles dance. But throughout my date to win experience I met many smart, successful, attractive women - and then I married one.

When I ran my third, and what turned out to be my final *LA Weekly* personal, I received 46 mostly high quality responses. Kathy was one of them: 32-years-old, very smart, very appealing, and with a challenging career as a pediatric bone marrow transplant nurse. What started out as "just dating" steadily escalated into a very serious, romantic relationship. I'll let her complete the story, but first let me underscore that finding Kathy was no accident. It was the result of using the practical, effective dating system described in this book.

KATHY: I moved to Los Angeles from Maine in 1989. Recently divorced, 30-years-old, I initially just wanted to date, not find a relationship. Soon I had a busy social life and dated frequently, but I eventually found myself increasingly restless and dissatisfied with my dating experiences. I'd begun to think about having a serious relationship again, but was having difficulty meeting the right "type" of man. I found myself turning down dates rather than going out Saturday night just to go out. I decided to break out of my existing circle of friends and acquaintances to meet new relationship possibilities, and to do so by answering some personal ads.

I discovered the personals were a way to meet and date interesting, nice guys. At first no longterm relationship resulted, but then in September of 1991 I answered Rick's ad. Our meeting wasn't love at first sight - I'll go into that a little more later! - but it quickly became very romantic and very serious. A year later on the first anniversary of our initial meeting for a drink, Rick proposed to me over dinner at one of the nicest (and most romantic) restaurants in Los Angeles.

Eight months later on May 8th, 1993, we were married. It was a beautiful wedding ceremony in the mountains above Malibu, California attended by over 100 friends and relatives. Afterwards we left for a romantic, once-in-a-lifetime three week honeymoon to Europe. All this from a personal ad!

Women And Personal Safety
If you're a woman concerned about the safety of the New Dating Options, dating to win requires exercising the same common sense precautions you need to be use in *all* dating nowadays - no more no less. This book features a chapter covering women and personal safety called Women, Men, Singles and Safety, and pays special attention throughout to how women can protect their privacy and safety when dating to win.

Women's Dating Liberation
For women, dating to win avoids the traditional male dominated dating selection process. It levels the playing field between the sexes. The New Dating Options allow women to easily *initiate* the dating process, and pick the men *they* are interested in dating.

The National Dating Directory
The exclusive *National Dating Directory* at the end of the book will help you participate in the date to win process *wherever* you may live. It includes more than

1,000 entries: publications carrying personal ads, organized singles activities, videodating outlets, matchmakers and dating introduction services.   This unique national dating reference resource is organized by state and by city, and includes all 50 states, plus the District of Columbia.

The Sky Is The Limit
Dating to win can work for you and this book will show you how. If you follow the guidelines, you are going to get results. At minimum, you will get out and meet more people, and do more dating. Very likely a *lot* more dating. What's the best thing that can happen? Simply put: the sky is the limit. If you want a great social life, you can have it. If you want a relationship, it can happen. If you want marriage and maybe kids, well, we are happily living that result now. It worked for us, and it can work for you.

Dating to Win   2

CHOOSING YOUR DATE TO WIN OPTION
Goal/Gameplan/Action
The first step in dating to win is to set a dating and relationship *goal*, whether it's having more dates, finding a serious relationship, or meeting your future marriage partner. Next, you formulate a *gameplan*, choosing the New Dating Option you feel is right for you. Then you take *action* and participate in the process.

While your goal should be the most important factor in your decision, there is also the question of option availability in your area, as well as option cost. We will cover these subjects in the section of the book devoted to each option, but a quick scan of the *National Dating Directory* will give you an indication of options in your town or city. Generally speaking, availability is greatest in cities and their surrounding suburbs, and more limited in smaller outlying towns.

Your Goal And Time Frame
If your goal is a serious relationship - even marriage - the best course of action is choosing a *contact-intensive* option. These involve in-depth, one-on-one contact with the opposite sex. Except for some singles activities, *all* the New Dating Options are contact-intensive. The more you desire a serious relationship, the more important this fact is to you.

If on the other hand you are looking for dates as opposed to a serious relationship, all singles activities - from white water rafting trips to singles parties and dances - should be considered. You can also use the personal ads, videodating and dating introduction services. Matchmakers, however, usually attract only people seeking a serious relationship or marriage.

The Comfort Factor
Regardless of how comfortable (or uncomfortable) you might feel with any particular New Dating Option prior to using it, this should *not* be the primary basis for making your option choice. The option you *think* you will feel the most comfortable using, and which appeals to you the most at the outset, may actually be the one that is merely the least threatening. It's the easiest to choose, but not necessarily the one that will be the most effective for achieving your goal.

Making a video for videodating, or placing a personal ad, can be an intimidating and unappealing prospect. But keep in mind that nervousness and skepticism (and embarrassment!) is the reaction *most* of us have at the beginning, including those who go on to use the New Dating Options very successfully. Finding out about each option in detail in its own section of the book should help you feel more at ease, more knowledgeable, and more in control of the situation when you place that personal ad, call *Great Expectations* to find out more about videodating, attend a progressive singles dinner, visit a dating introduction service, or consult with a matchmaker.

Your Personality
For the person who isn't usually aggressive about meeting people - and that can include many of us in a·strange new situation - certain options are better than others. For

example, a singles dance might not be the best activity for a non-assertive guy to try, because he might not be willing to approach women in that environment. A woman might also feel reluctant to approach a guy she is interested in at a dance. However, they might both feel more comfortable doing so via a third party, such as through videodating, or a dating introduction service.

APPROACHING PEOPLE MADE EASY

Normally when you see someone you're interested in, whether at a party, in a supermarket, at a bar, on a subway, at a night school class - wherever - the first thing you have to do is approach them, find out if they're single, and then ascertain whether they are interested in *you*. For example, suppose you meet someone at a party. First you have to find out if they're single and available (or waste your time finding out they're not), and then you have to get them to consider you for dating.

At its worst, trying to create this dating connection can be a frustrating, time-consuming and rejection-filled process. You can get shot down when your potential date rejects your invitation for dinner, lunch, or coffee (or even just staying in touch!); or your flirtatious attempts at eliciting a positive response from them go absolutely nowhere. In the process your hoped-for date-to-be never has to acknowledge, even for a second, that you are potential dating material.

When you date to win with the New Dating Options, however, you *already* know the people you will meet are *single, available* and *actively looking to meet other single people to date*. They've gone so far as to make themselves available to being approached; they *want* to be approached. When you meet your cards are already on the table. It's a *given* that you're both single and looking for dates and/or a relationship, and you're meeting each other in that context.

THE IMPORTANCE OF ATTITUDE, FLEXIBILITY AND PERSISTENCE

1) Attitude

Before we move on to choosing your date to win option, there's one more important area of preparation to cover. Simply put, it's not always easy to start dating to win with the right *attitude* - to jump right into the process with a smile and open mind. These options are new to most of us, and we may not be comfortable with them initially. However, your attitude going into the date to win process is *extremely* important.

At minimum, you need to be ready to be convinced dating to win can work for you. Ideally, you go in with the feeling that this will be a positive experience, one of your life's adventures. After all, you are doing something very good for yourself, and you need to avoid undercutting success with a negative attitude.

2) Flexibility

Another major component for a positive date to win experience is *flexibility.* Not only flexibility in being willing to try a New Dating Option, but also flexibility about what you're looking for in the opposite sex. Too often we won't even consider people for dating who don't fit our preconceived picture of what we *think* we are looking for. Unfortunately, this not only limits who we approach across the proverbial crowded room of life, but can lead to involvement with some of the very worst choices for us (as we repeat the same unsuccessful dating and relationship patterns some of us have been doing for years).

During the date to win process you will talk to and meet

people you normally wouldn't consider "dating material." This will happen regardless of whether you are using the personals, videodating, trying a dating introduction service or matchmaker, or are approached by an aggressive member of the opposite sex while attending a singles activity. Work with it! Dating to win is as good a time as any (actually better than most) to be willing to break with your past dating patterns, and to open up and experiment a bit. If you give people more of a chance than you may have in the past (even if they don't fit your initial expectations exactly), you may be pleasantly surprised by the results.

3) Persistence

A third component of a successful date to win experience is *persistence*. It counts in everything we do in life, and dating is no exception. Dating to win works, but you have to put energy and effort into it - and *stick with it*. If one New Dating Option doesn't work for you, try another one. If running one personal ad is unsuccessful, try another one (maybe in a different publication). If you go to a singles dinner and it's a bust, don't drop out of the date to win process - try another singles activity; maybe even another singles dinner.

A Lesson In Attitude And Flexibility

RICK: I had my own attitude problem to overcome when I first started dating to win. Before I ran my first personal ad I responded to about a half-dozen women's 900 number personals. I left my recorded "hello" phone message for each. A couple of days later, a woman called me back. Instead of sounding glad to hear from her, I was uptight and defensive. "What have I gotten myself into now?!" was my first thought.

As we talked I was very conscious that I was on the verge

of meeting a member of the opposite sex by way of that social scourge, the blind date. I hated blind dates so much that I had never actually been on one! Sure enough, as we talked on the phone she suggested we get together for lunch. Despite the fact that she worked only a few blocks from me, was the right age (mid-30's), and sounded smart and nice, I told her I needed to see a photo of her first - even though a 900 number phone personal doesn't normally include a photo exchange. She paused, obviously somewhat taken aback. A bit reluctantly she said "okay." Then she asked me to send her a photo of myself (touche!). "Sure," I said gamely.

The Photo
Her photo arrived a few days later, and she was a pleasant looking, even pretty, brunette. Relieved, I sent her my own picture, and then a few days later called her. I left a message on her answering machine, but she didn't return my call. I tried one more time and still didn't hear anything back. Then I realized I would never hear from her. My lack of enthusiasm, and my general unwillingness to just jump into the process and say "hello" in person - not to mention my insistence on imposing a photo exchange - had no doubt turned her off. Or else, two can play the photo game, and maybe *my* photo hadn't met *her* standards!

Deja Vu
A few months later - and by now much more comfortable with the personals process - I called a psychiatrist who'd responded by letter to a personal ad I ran in *Los Angeles* magazine. Once on the phone, she almost immediately balked, and sounded defensive and uptight. She confessed it was the first time she'd answered a personal ad, and she said she wasn't ready to go through with actually meeting anyone.

As she back-pedaled furiously from her original good intentions of responding to personals to get out there and meet men - to look for that special relationship she no doubt sought in her heart of hearts - I suddenly flashed back on how much she sounded like *I* had just a few months earlier. With the roles now reversed, I remembered my own earlier phone conversation with embarrassment.

I also realized my new found attitude of openness to the date to win process - including going on blind dates - was being rewarded by meeting many interesting, appealing women. I was giving myself a real chance of achieving my goal of finding that special lasting relationship.

BLIND DATING

With 900 number phone personal ads, virtually all matchmakers, and most introduction services (the ones not using photos), you will be blind dating when you date to win (in that you will not have actually *seen* the person, but you will have almost always talked on the phone). You can also choose *not* to blind date by selecting as your option videodating, note and *photo* personal ads, organized singles activities, or those dating introduction services and matchmakers who *do* use photos.

The Blind Date Advantage

Let's go back for a moment to our discussion earlier in this chapter mentioning meeting someone at a party. In a party pickup scenario you often have only a few minutes to try to "sell" yourself. Unless the other person is *immediately* attracted to your *appearance* on some level, you're often quickly rejected on some very superficial basis, without the person knowing the "real you." They just might not *initially* respond to your appearance: your looks, your hair, your clothes, your body, whatever. But "initially" is the only chance you get.

Rejection can be ego crushing and frustrating - especially if it comes from someone you're sure you would have had more of a chance with, *if only they got to know you better.* With most of the New Dating Options you meet on the phone *before* you meet in person. There is no intrusion of looks, clothes, and other visual cues. Personality, compatibility and how you come across verbally are the key factors determining your success over the phone, *not* appearance. In fact, this phone process sometimes actually works *against* many very attractive people, because they're not used to having to "sell" themselves without trading on their looks.

Because the phone conversation precedes meeting in person, and lasts anywhere from 20 minutes to an hour (or more), you have a much longer period of time to "sell" yourself, *before* appearance comes into play. You have a real opportunity to establish a rapport with each other *first.* When you go on to meet in person, you have, at minimum - even under the most limited of circumstances - an additional half-hour to an hour to further introduce yourselves to each other.

If you're average looking (*RICK:* like myself), or you're sometimes nervous and not your best in the first moments of meeting someone new, this extra time helps. The personals, for example, present a terrific opportunity. A well-done personal ad, and a positive first phone conversation, creates consideration for dating where - due to initial visual rejection (because you're not someone's usual "type" - or they're not yours - not necessarily because someone is "unattractive") - there would otherwise have been none.

This kind of blind dating thus helps you successfully date to win by "forcing" you to at a minimum meet people on the phone, without dismissing them prematurely on the basis of appearance (or they you). It keeps you from being your own worst dating enemy, and aids you in meeting good people you otherwise might have overlooked.

Our Own First Blind Date

RICK: Kathy didn't match my preconceived visual picture of what I was looking for in a woman. When we first met in person, neither one of us was initially all that sexually attracted to the other. But our first phone conversation had gone well, and when we met for a blind date drink and talked, we discovered we enjoyed each other's company and shared an amazing commonality of values and outlook on life. Romance and passion soon followed.

KATHY: Though I had a list of qualifications for "Mr. Right" (under 40, full head of hair, gym enthusiast) I read Rick's ad with an open mind, because he sounded interesting, and let go of much of my list. However, had I seen a photo first I don't know that I would have agreed to meet! That we ended up getting married is a testimony to the good fortune of being "forced" to get to know each other as blind dates.

Pre-screening

Pre-screening via a well done personal ad, or by effectively using a dating introduction service or matchmaker (and then by correctly sizing up the person during the introductory phone call) can still prevent most in-person meetings of the blind date total disaster variety. As noted, if you still want to see what your dates look like before hand, you can do so by using note and photo personals, videodating, organized singles activities, or those matchmakers and introduction services which use photos.

Let's Date To Win

We recommend that you read each section of this book in sequence. You may very well start out trying one date to win option, and later come back to try another because of something that stuck with you after your first reading.

Part II is devoted to Personal Ads, Part III Organized Singles Activities, Part IV Matchmakers And Dating Introduction Services, and Part V Videodating. Each section is introduced by a real couple's success story (with names changed to preserve privacy), and then covers how the option works, how to use it successfully; plus information about cost, and also how to find out more about option availability in your own area.

The next to last section of the book, Part VI Following Through For Success, will cover meeting on the phone and in person, women and personal safety, and troubleshooting your option choice if things aren't working out to your satisfaction. It's followed by the *National Dating Directory*, which has at its end a Personals Glossary of Terms covering common abbreviations used in personal ads.

The Personals

Part II, the Personals Ads section, is the longest in the book for several reasons. When using the personal ads you're in a very real sense acting as your *own* matchmaker and dating introduction service, so there is more information to cover. The personals are also the New Dating Option most universally available around the country, and since they are usually the *least expensive* (along with certain singles activities), they're likely to be the option of the most interest to the largest number of readers.

Additionally, in discussing the personals we will go over

in detail the kind of information about yourself to include in a personal ad, as well as what to say about what you're looking for in another person. This is the same information you'll also need to think about and give when videodating, or using a matchmaker or dating introduction service.

Now let's date to win!

Personal Ads

11

Introducing The Personals Explosion   3

Albany, New York: Joe and Barbara
Barbara sits inside the Ginger Man restaurant sipping mineral water and reading a copy of *Metroland*, Albany's local "alternative" paper. She's wearing her favorite purple dress, matching shoes, and black tights. Barbara's 30-years-old, a social worker, and has never been married.

Tonight she's awaiting the arrival of her personal ad date, Joe #2. She's dubbed him Joe #2 because she met another guy named Joe earlier in the day for lunch. That Joe - Joe #1 - had been a nice enough guy, but she felt he was "too nerdy," and "too short" (unfortunately they'd never gotten around to discussing height on the phone, and she hadn't mentioned her's in her personal ad). Frankly, lunch with Joe #1 had basically been a waste of time. However, Barbara's very much anticipating the arrival of Joe #2 - they'd really hit it off on the phone.

While Barbara has had some serious relationships with men, she pretty much sat out the past two years. Only recently did she decide to actively work on her personal life. In addition to her personal ad, she recently attended some local organized singles activities. Barbara wants to meet a nice Jewish guy, and running a personal in the *Albany Jewish World* pre-screens for that (and as a subscriber to the paper the ad was *free*).

About 18 guys responded with letters (it was a by-mail personal rather than a 900 number phone ad). While she could have asked for a photo, she decided not to, feeling other things were more important than looks. But it means she doesn't really have any idea what her date Joe #2 looks like, other than (thankfully) "tall." Periodically she peeks up from the paper and out the restaurant windows.

Suddenly a guy walks into the Ginger Man. He's tall, and she thinks "kinda cute." He's wearing a sharp looking teal green shirt and jeans. He looks around, comes over to her and asks if she's Barbara, and they spend the next hour-and-a-half talking. Joe #2 is 37, never married, a musician, and owns his own business. Their time together at the restaurant is fun for both of them, and most of all they will later remember how "comfortable" they immediately felt with each other. After their get acquainted session, they part outside the Ginger Man without a kiss - but they trade last names and agree to see each other again. Barbara is smitten.

Joe calls two days later. Barbara spends the first few minutes of the conversation trying to figure out if it's Joe #1 or Joe #2. When she finally realizes it's her no-go lunch date Joe #1, she politely declines his request to see her again. When Joe #2 calls later they make a brunch date for the following weekend.

Brunch is a very successful follow up to their first meeting, and they begin to date steadily. Meanwhile, however, Barbara is still meeting some of the other respondents to her personal ad - something she feels a little awkward about since she likes Joe so much. Soon she makes some "thank you for responding to my personal but I met someone" calls to the rest of the guys who answered her ad.

After a year of dating Barbara and Joe move in together. While both say neither one used the personals with the intention of getting married, after three years together they are married in June of 1994.

THE PERSONALS EXPLOSION
Everyone, regardless of where they live, can participate in the personals explosion. Ads are often inexpensive, occasionally free, and can be found in hundreds of newspapers and magazines, including some national publications. The *National Dating Directory* at the back of this book lists more than *700* publications carrying personals.

An effective, well constructed personal ad will do wonders for your dating (not to mention your self-confidence) when 10, 20, 30, 60 or even a *100* or more people respond. A 1993 TV news story in Los Angeles featured a woman who received 130 responses, and another one *200* responses, to *one* personal ad.

Your Location
While personals can be successfully used anywhere in the country, some places are better than others. Major metropolitan areas have the greatest diversity of choice, and have pioneered the acceptance of personals as a legitimate way for people to meet. The Los Angeles area alone offers *several thousand* personals each week. Many are in just two publications: the *Los Angeles Times* and the *LA Weekly*. *Los Angeles* magazine is also an excellent source. More than two dozen *other* Los Angeles area publications carrying personals are also listed in the *National Dating Directory.*

Other metropolitan areas also feature a variety of publication choices. Chicago has two major newspapers which carry personals, the *Sun-Times* and the *Tribune*, plus two city-named magazines, *Chicago* and *Chicago Life*. There is also a major alternative paper, the *Chicago Reader*, with several hundred of the best ads in town each week; and *Singles Choice*, a singles magazine with over 400 personals an issue. Even in conservative Salt Lake City the *Salt Lake Tribune* carries about 600 personals a week. Other urban centers such as New York, San Francisco, Boston, Baltimore, Altanta, Philadelphia, Denver, Phoenix, etc., offer a variety of excellent personals choices. Personals are also available in most smaller cities, and many towns.

Types Of Personals Publications
There are five types of publications to look for personal ads in:
1) Newspapers
2) City-named magazines
3) Alternative newspapers
4) Singles publications
5) Classifieds-only publications and shoppers guides

1) Newspapers
From the *San Francisco Chronicle* to the *Miami Herald*, and the *Baltimore Sun* to the *Philadelphia Inquirer*, using the personals is as easy as looking in the classifieds section of your Sunday paper. Since personals are in hundreds of newspapers, there is ready access to ads - even in smaller cities, such as Pueblo, Colorado (the *Chieftan*) and Bridgeport, Connecticut (the *Post*). If your local paper is not listed in the *National Dating Directory*, you should still check the paper yourself, or give their classifieds department a call. Even with the over 700 personals publications listed in the *Directory* it is impossible to include all the newspapers with personals.

2) City-Named Magazines

Upscale magazines named after their city, like *New York, Chicago, Boston, Baltimore, Philadelphia,* and *Los Angeles* are an excellent source for personal ads. Look for the personals at the back in the classifieds section. Personals in these city-named publications are usually fairly expensive: for example, *New York* magazine charges $34.50 per line. But people who use them find them worth the extra cost because of the quality environment for their ad. Additionally, they are often primarily *note and photo* by-mail ads, not 900 number blind date phone ads (we will cover the distinction between the two types in detail in the next chapter).

Check the *National Dating Directory* to find the city-named magazine in your area. If it's not listed, as with newspapers take a firsthand look at your local magazine anyway. Some city-named magazines which don't yet carry personals report they are considering it, and may have indeed started since we checked.

Another source for personals are special interest publications. This includes the Sierra Club *Southern Sierran* newsletter, sent monthly to members in Southern California; and Jewish publications nationwide. Joe and Barbara met when he answered her personal in Albany, New York's *Jewish World.* In Los Angeles, the local *Jewish Journal* is a popular source for personal ads. The *Boston Jewish Advocate* features up to 200 personals a week. If you are of a literary bent, there are even national personals in the back of the *New York Review of Books.* The politically oriented can check *The Nation* magazine, and *The New Republic.*

The advantage of using special interest publications like these is that readers already have something in common with each other, whether it be ethnic heritage, the environmental concerns of fellow Sierra Club members, or literature, or politics. Take a look for personals in any such publications you might already be receiving.

3) Alternative Newspapers

Some of the very best publications carrying personals are the dozens of alternative weekly newspapers in cities across the country. They include *New Times* in Phoenix, *Westword* in Denver, *Creative Loafing* in Atlanta, Tampa, and Charlotte, *SF Weekly* and the *Bay Guardian* in San Francisco, *The Village Voice* in New York, and many more.

Most alternative publications carry a healthy dose of music and movie reviews and topical articles. They usually come out once a week, and can almost always be picked up for free. Use the *National Dating Directory* to find your nearest alternative publication, or look at your local music store, book store or newsstand. Like newspapers, alternative publications often offer inexpensive personals. As with newspapers and magazines you can usually subscribe to them, even if you live outside their immediate distribution area.

4) Singles Publications

There are many singles publications, from the *National Singles Register* and *Single Connections* magazine in Los Angeles, to *Single Scene* in Scottsdale, Arizona, and *Dateline New England* in New Hampshire, and New York City's *Jewish Singles News* (an excellent source for singles event information). Virtually *all* carry personal ads. There has been a move underway in the singles magazine field to make publications more upscale: glossy paper instead of newsprint, quality graphics, avoiding sleazy advertisements, etc. Publications like *Atlanta Singles*, *Houston Singles File*, Milwaukee's *SingleLife* and Michigan's straightforward *Sincere Singles* and *Singles Network* are some of the very best examples of quality singles magazines.

Singles publications are usually the best source of information about singles activities in your area, and often carry ads and listings for videodating, and matchmakers and dating introduction services. Their personals are also some of the least expensive around. A 35 word personal in San Diego's *Single Magazine* costs only $10. However, with the tremendous personals activity that can now be found in other magazines and newspapers, singles publications have generally lost some of their uniqueness as a source for personals.

5) Classifieds-Only/Shoppers Guides
Personals appear nationwide in free *Penny Saver* and *Thrifty Nickel* shopping giveaways, and in classifieds-only publications such as the *Recycler* in Los Angeles. These publications may, or may not, be appropriate for reaching the type of people you want to find (their ads tend to appeal to those who want the cheapest personals available).

If Your Area Does *Not* Have Personals
If you live in a town without personals, you still have several options:
   1) use the nearest major city personals publication,
   2) use regional or national publications,
   3) do your own creative local personal.

We will go into more detail about all three of these options in Chapter 17, Dating to Win in Oshkosh.

Your Local Newsstand
To research your town or city for personals, there is no substitute for a trip to the local newsstand, in tandem with a look at your state and city in the *National Dating*

Directory. The bigger the newsstand the better - not just the magazine and newspaper rack in your local 7-11. At the newsstand, you can check for local or regional singles publications, newspapers, a glossy city-named magazine, and national publications.

Local Publications Are Superior
When you look for publications, remember that local publications are superior to regional or national ones. Why? Because 100 local personals in your immediate area will be more of an effective resource for you than 100 ads scattered throughout a number of states in a regional or national singles publication (such as the *Bachelor Book* or *Single Gentlemen & Women* magazine - which are listed under the National heading at the end of the *National Dating Directory*, and will be discussed in the next chapter under the subheading Photo Personals).

You only need to use national or regional publications if you live in an area *not* served by personals in your local newspapers and magazines. However, if your results with local publications aren't as good as you'd like, you can augment your search with an additional statewide, regional or national personals outlet.

Your Publication
Which publication is right for you? Look at the publication's personal ads - how do they strike you? Do they sound like people you want to meet? You can also call some of the 900 number ads you think look promising, and listen to the taped message the person placing the ad left for you to hear.

Remember that each publication has a different readership. For example, alternative weekly newspapers (such as the *Sacramento News & Review* and Philadelphia's *City*

Paper) - tend to attract a "hipper" crowd. City-named magazines like *Washingtonian, New York, Chicago* and *Los Angeles* generally go after a more upscale audience. Alternative publications also carry more personals from people in their 30's and under, while many singles publications skew older. Newspapers can reach a cross section of people.

PLACING AND ANSWERING PERSONAL ADS

Placing A Personal

Placing a personal ad is simply a matter of following the written instructions in your publication of choice. Don't hesitate to call the newspaper or magazine directly with any questions. The classifieds department should be only too happy to help you. You can usually place an ad by phone, fax, mail, or bring it by in person. Ads that require calling a free 800 number to place the personal mean you will dictate your ad to a personals operator over the phone. In all cases, charging by credit card is standard.

Answering Ads

Before actually running your own ad, you can *respond* to some personals first. This will get you comfortable with the process of leaving phone messages, sending notes and photos, and screening people by a telephone conversation to decide whether to meet in person. It will also help you see what makes an effective personal from the perspective of the ad *reader* - which will then make you more prepared to write your own personal. Answering ads also gives you a better idea what type of people are using a given publication before you run your personal.

KATHY: A lot of people, however, never run their own personal, preferring instead to only answer other people's ads. For me this worked just fine, and I felt in control of choosing who I was interested in talking to and potentially meeting. It's like looking through a menu and picking what you want. It also means you avoid the time-consuming process of 1) composing your own personal, 2) wading through numerous responses, and 3) dealing with the people who are questionable prospects. In addition to responding to Rick's personal, I responded to only one other ad in that issue of the *LA Weekly.* In fact, I only responded to about a *dozen* personals *ever.* Not a bad investment of time and effort to find love and marriage. By the way, Joe (from our personals success story) says he only answered *one* ad ever - Barbara's.

RICK: On the other hand I found just the opposite. Running my *own* ad gave me better results and more of a feeling of being in control of the process. If your initial results *answering* ads are mediocre, don't let it sour you on the personals. Stick with it. I found the odds change dramatically when you have people (perhaps dozens) responding to your own personal. In fact, if you want, you can skip the tryout stage and just jump in and place your own ad.

MAINSTREAM ADS ONLY
In this book we are dealing only with *mainstream* legitimate personal ads. Most major newspapers and magazines are adamant about not running "sleazy" ads - the kind which have given personals a somewhat mixed reputation in the past. Frankly, the advent of 900 number phone technology has made personal ads so financially lucrative that most publications don't want to risk alienating readers with off-color ads. Such ads would also be at odds with the public image of most major newspapers and magazines.

But...

Some alternative publications have very liberal ad content policies. For example, the *SF Weekly* allows some really off-the-wall ads in the Wild Side section of their personals (if you aren't offended, they can be a hoot to read). On the other hand, the *LA Weekly* is relatively content-strict (the *LA Reader* being the Los Angeles more "anything goes" alternative publication).

The personals content of singles publications can be anything from very liberal to very conservative. Alabama's *Connections Flyer* is very strict and does not, for example, permit gay and lesbian personals. But gay and lesbian personals are standard fare in alternative publications and in most major papers, from the *San Francisco Chronicle* to the *Chicago Sun-Times*. (Gay and lesbian personals are placed in their own section, under "alternate lifestyles," or "men seeking men," or "women seeking women").

Professionals At Work

However, even in publications with mainstream personals you will sometimes find ads which include come-ons, like "be my sugar daddy," or "beautiful young blonde seeks generous older gentleman." They may just have money on their minds, or they may be from "professionals." Some publications also run advertisements for 976 phone sex lines near their regular personals (*The Village Voice* seems to hold the record for sheer numbers in this regard), surrounding their legitimate ads with an unfortunate air of tackiness.

Use Common Sense

Always read *all* personal ads with basic common sense smarts, regardless of *what* publication they are in. Remember publications seldom screen the people placing ads. On the other hand, don't be paranoid. Meeting someone through the personals should be approached like meeting *any* new person, whether at a party, club, or the supermarket check-out line. As mentioned earlier, in Part VI's Women, Men, Singles and Safety chapter, we will give safety tips for women using the personals and the other date to win options. It's a chapter men should read too, if only to be aware of how to help women feel more comfortable with the date to win process, and increase the chances for *both* of you to have an enjoyable and successful experience.

How To Use The Personals   **4**

There are two main types of personal ads:

1)   **Note and photo ads:** people respond by *mailing* in a *note* with their phone number and usually a *photo*.

2)   **900 number ads:** people respond by *calling* in and leaving a taped phone message with their name and phone number.

At the end of the chapter we will also touch on **photo personals**, and **computer bulletin boards**.

1) NOTE AND PHOTO ADS
How The Ad Works
This is the more traditional personal ad. It gives some descriptive information about the person running the ad, and requests that the reader send a note, his or her phone number and usually a photo. Assuming the reader does send a photo, for the person who *placed* the personal it's *not* a blind date situation.

Advertising with this kind of ad can be especially appealing to someone using the personals for the first time, since note and photo ads allow for receiving a photo, and can be found in quality city-named magazines like *Washingtonian, New York, Chicago, Chicago Life, Balti-*

more, Boston, Philadelphia, Cleveland, Pittsburgh, and *Los Angeles.*

A note and photo ad also allows you as a personals advertiser to leisurely peruse your respondent's notes and photos, taking your time deciding which ones to respond back to. By using the notes and photos you can effectively pre-screen people to decide who you're interested in enough to phone for a possible meeting. You can exclude anyone who sends you a note written in crayon or a neurosis-ridden five page life story letter - or a photo that makes it obvious this could never work.

Cost
A note and photo ad in a city-named magazine can be fairly expensive. In addition to the cost of the ad itself, note and photo ads in some publications can also include a handling charge of $2, or $3 (or even $5) per letter forwarded to you.

RICK: My three note and photo personals - each running in one monthly issue of *Los Angeles* magazine - cost $152, $221, and $207 for a fairly long (about a 40 word) ad. That's the upper limit of cost, however; other publications can be *much* less expensive, including singles magazines (which along with city-named magazines are the other primary location for note and photo personals).

Photos
When you run a note and photo ad, you will probably receive photos from about half your respondents, although this is a figure which can vary greatly. You can increase this percentage if you insist in your ad that a photo is a *"must,"* or *"required."* However, this insistence is also likely to reduce your number of respondents, costing you some of those who were going to contact you without

sending a photo.

Insisting on a photo will likely also keep some people from responding, because it may sound to them like the only thing you care about is physical appearance. Or, sending a photo may intimidate them if they worry they aren't attractive enough. A good alternative is to ask for a photo by using less dogmatic terms than "must" or "required." At the end of your personal simply write "photo requested," or "photo please," or "photo appreciated," or simply "note, photo, phone." Some people also specify that it be a "recent" photo.

Don't Judge Photos Too Harshly

Up to a point, a photo used properly is a valuable tool for deciding who to phone and potentially meet in person. But some people will pleasantly surprise you by being a lot more appealing in person than in their picture - that is, if you give them a chance and call them anyway, even if their photo doesn't knock your socks off.

The fact is because you *do* have a photo, it's easy to find fault with people and not call them. This is especially true if you're looking for a serious relationship and/or marriage, and immediately subject every photo to the laser-intense scrutiny of, "could I see spending the rest of my life with this person?" If every photo is viewed through the standard of being a future marriage partner you might never call anyone!

Remember the name of this book: *Date to Win*. Dating comes first, *before* considering a relationship or marriage. It helps to think of respondents at this point only as potential *casual dates*. Try to use photos as a disqualifier only if it is clear that this person is a definite *no-way-ever*. If you are on the fence, call them anyway. Decide whether to go on and meet in person on the basis of the *phone conversation*, not their photo. Try to be loose, take some chances, and be *flexible*.

RICK: Don't toss out those notes just yet from people who *didn't* send a photo. Once a woman sent me a little card, a very short note, and no photo. Noticing from her phone number that she must live very near me, I eventually called her anyway, and we went on to meet in person. She turned out to be very smart, very classy, and the most attractive woman I met from that personal ad.

RESPONDING TO A NOTE AND PHOTO PERSONAL
The Mechanics
When responding to a note and phone ad, follow the mailing directions in the magazine or newspaper carefully, and call the publication if you have any questions. Commonly publications use a coded numbering system for their personal ads. When you respond to the ad it's by number, and in the case of note and photo personals often by using the magazine as a go-between. Address your response letter to the coded ad number, put it inside another envelope addressed to the publication, and mail it. The publication then forwards it to the person who ran the ad. This way *neither the respondent or advertiser has the other's home address.* When the person who placed the ad receives the letter, they then contact the respondent back by phone.

Using this system means if you are a woman *running* a note and photo ad, men can only contact you through the magazine - then wait for you to respond back to them if *you* choose to. *You will be in full control of the situation, with your privacy protected.*

Send A Photo?
When responding to a note and photo personal, the first thing you need to decide is whether or not to send a photo (assuming the ad requested one since some don't, like Barbara's in our success story). If you *don't* include a photo, the person running the ad may not call you. If you *do* include one, and they don't like the way you look, they also may not call you. If you start out sending a photo when answering ads and you are not getting called back, you might want to experiment a bit and answer some ads *without* supplying a photo. See if it improves your response rate.

Get A Photo Taken
Don't mail in the only copy of your favorite snapshot and request that the person return it. You can, however, get prints made of that favorite snapshot. Even better is to simply go to an inexpensive photo store/studio that takes pictures (use the *Yellow Pages*).

RICK: I went to a discount photo chain store, and it cost me about $20 to get 20 black and white photos taken in five minutes. I picked out the one I liked the best (choose one with a nice smile), had them make a bunch of prints, and used them to respond to personals.

The Note
In the note you send in to respond to an ad, you want to give some of the same kind of information about yourself you would put in a personal if you were writing one. At minimum that means your age, some indication of your weight, your height, something about your interests, why the ad you are answering appeals to you, your first name, and your phone number. There is no reason to send a long letter with the story of your life to a total stranger (and it's rather bizarre to be on the other end of receiving

one). Instead, keep it short, and put in some basic information to pique their interest. Less is more. Save the rest for when they call you.

Rather than send a note or letter, you can instead make it a card with just a paragraph about yourself. A card is more original and casual than a letter. Put a little effort into selecting it, and let the artwork or illustration say something about you and your personality. Unless your handwriting is abysmal, try to write by hand. It's a nice personal touch that pays off. Avoid word processors and typewriters if possible. Above all, there is something truly unromantic about being one of who-knows-how-many recipients of a computer-generated form letter.

Voice Mail

Normally when a woman responds to a man's personal she gives him her home phone, so he can contact her. If you want to avoid doing this, the best thing to do is simply run your own personal. In this way you only give out your phone number *after* you have screened the man by talking to him on the phone first, and then only if you two have decided to meet in person.

Another way for a woman to not initially give out her phone number is to use a voice mail number. It's the equivalent of having another phone number with an answering machine, and it's more personal than an answering service. It costs about $20 a month (see the *Yellow Pages* under Voice Mail), and some phone companies will supply it as an extra service (e.g. Pacific Bell in Los Angeles). If you do use voice mail, let the man know it - so he doesn't keep calling and hanging up trying to catch you at "home" in person.

Using Your Own Address

Some publications let you put a home mailing address in your personal ad. For women this is fine if you use a P.O. Box (just get one at your post office, or a post box rental outfit - they are inexpensive). While men sometimes use their home address in note and photo personals, it's a surprise to see women do it. There is no need for a woman to give out her home address or last name, until after she has at least talked with a man on the phone, or has met him in person.

2) 900 NUMBER PERSONAL ADS

PLACING A 900 NUMBER PERSONAL

The current national personals boom is driven by the extraordinary explosion in popularity of 900 number ads. They have literally made using the personals as quick and easy as picking up a telephone. The 900 number ad is user-friendly, both for the person placing the ad and the person responding. You can usually place a 900 number personal just days before its publication date, and then almost immediately start to hear from people.

This "instant gratification" contrasts with the note and photo personals in, for example, city-named magazines with long publishing lead times. With city-named magazines it can be several weeks before your ad appears, and several more weeks before you begin to receive your mail. As a respondent it can take a month (or more) to find out whether or not you're going to hear back from the person behind the ad. On the other hand, when you call in to respond to a 900 number ad, you will often hear back within a day or two.

Touch Tone Phone Required

You need a touch tone phone to use 900 number personals. You operate the system by making your choices using the touch tone keys. Anyone who has used an office voice mail system (or has called a company using a voice mail recording to route calls), will already be comfortable with the mechanics of the 900 number system. We will do a sample walk through a typical publication 900 number voice mail system later in this chapter.

Privacy

When you *run* a 900 number personal, the reader calls in and listens to the recorded message you leave with your ad. It contains information about yourself and what you are looking for in the other person. They then leave you recorded information about themselves in return, including their first name and phone number. You now have their first name and phone number, but to them you are just the information in your written ad and your recorded message. Women especially should note this information doesn't include your last name, home address, or phone number.

Blind Dating

In contrast to note and photo personals, 900 number ads are blind dates for both parties (although you will have talked on the phone first). 900 number personals are a more "casual" process than note and photo ads, because the time frame is much quicker, and it's not as formal as sending someone something in writing. Also, when you are an advertiser calling back someone who responded to your 900 number ad, there's less implied commitment by you upfront, because you have not seen a photo of the person first. This can help "loosen up" the whole dating process, allowing you to meet more people, and increasing your odds of success. For those unsure of their physical "marketability," 900 number personals also have the advantage of not initially leading with your looks.

Keep in mind that for blind dating to work effectively, you as an advertiser need to write an ad which attracts the right type of person, and screens out most of the inappropriate responses. We will cover this further in the next two chapters: How To Write An Ad That Really Works, Parts I and II.

Cost

Running a 900 number personal is often cheaper than a note and photo ad. Publications usually make most of their money from people calling the 900 number to respond to ads. The more ads publications have, the more phone traffic they create, and the more money they generate. Often publications will encourage people to place ads by giving low cost (or even free) specials. Additionally, many publications carry 900 number personals handled by national service companies, such as Microvoice in Minneapolis. These ads are often *free* to place using an 800 number call. However, there is then sometimes a charge for the advertiser to retrieve ad responses via a 900 number call at the same cost as people calling in to respond: $.99 to $2.00 per minute.

RICK: My three 900 number ads cost a total of $211 (the most expensive being my final one, at $91), but you can spend much less. On the other hand don't be too cheap. If the ad is free for the first 20 words, it's a major mistake to decide, "well I'll do it since it's free, and I don't have anything to lose - but I won't go a word over 20 and spend any of *my* money." A too-short ad that keeps down costs - but doesn't tell enough about you - will *not get you top results.* You can see numerous examples of these inexpensive too-short ads in any number of publications. My own final and most successful personal ad was 40 words. If what you want to say about yourself takes 30, 40, or 50 or more words, *spend the money.* As the saying goes, "if it's worth doing, it's worth doing right."

RESPONDING TO A 900 NUMBER PERSONAL
Taped Messages

It's a good idea is to read through the personals in a publication and find the ones which look like possibilities, and then call *only those ads.* This means you're calling only the ads with the most potential and you're keeping down the cost.

As mentioned, the person placing the written ad leaves a recorded message about themselves with their personal. When you call into the personal you'll listen to this recording. It's a big help in deciding whether you're still interested. Once you hear people talk it's funny how much your reaction can change, from what you thought when you first read their personal and said, "oh, this one sounds like a possibility." After listening, if you still want to respond, you leave them a taped voice mail message about yourself back, including your first name and phone number. They then decide whether they want to call you.

Scanning Random Personals

When you call in, if the publication's phone instructions offer you a chance to scan random advertiser recorded ad messages, pass! Scanning ads is a big moneymaker for the publication, but bad for you. For example, at this time *New York* magazine charges $1.50 per minute for your call. Suppose you are calling personal ads once a week, when the Sunday paper or a weekly publication comes out. Even at $10 to $30 a week, this adds an extra $40 to $120 to your monthly phone bill. It's money well spent if you first narrow down your calls ahead of time by reading *written* ads to find the ones which seem to have potential. It's *not* worth the money if you are scanning random phone ads, without being able to first read them and pre-screen for the person's age, interests, etc. Scanning quickly gets very expensive, and you will be slogging through all sorts of inappropriate people. You can have a large telephone bill at the end of the month, with nothing to show for it.

Thus responding to 900 number personals where you can't read written ads first is a bad idea. For example, *USA Today* runs national personals by area code, and gives a *sampling* of ads in writing listed by city. Unfortunately, you have to call and scan the rest of the ads by area code at a cost of $2 per minute. This is only a good idea if you live in an area short on local publications with personals.

Privacy
When you *respond* to a 900 number personal you have to leave your phone number. If you don't want to do this - or at least not at the beginning of trying the personals process - a way to get around it is to get a private voice mail number, as described earlier in the chapter. The other option is to run your *own* 900 number ad.

KATHY: However, I found giving out my home phone number when responding to 900 personals *not* to be a problem. I had a chance to hear what the guy sounded like in his recorded phone message before I did so, and I never had any bad experiences.

A 900 Number Option In Note And Photo Ads
New York, Los Angeles and many other city-named magazines offer a 900 number option with their note and photo personals. So do most singles publications. This means as an advertiser you can use your personal as a note and photo ad, a 900 number ad, or a combination of both.

However, if you choose a note and photo personals publication because you want to receive a *note* and a *photo,* then obviously if you instead allow your respondents to leave a phone message (and skip mailing you anything), you've short-circuited the process. Instead you can simply ignore the 900 number option in these publications, and use them for your purpose: getting a note and a photo.

Or, you can use the 900 number option, but not short-circuit the note and photo process. Leave the recorded phone message with your ad, and ask the respondent to leave you back a recorded "hello" with their name and phone number, but still request they send you a note with a photo, which you will wait for before contacting them. You can also use the message to describe a little bit more about yourself, and what you are looking for in the other person. This method gives both of you the advantage of hearing what the other sounds like upfront, as well as finding out more information about each other early in the process. If the respondent doesn't follow through with a letter, note, or card (and a number won't), you still have the option of calling them back anyway if they sounded interesting.

A Sample 900 Number System
To respond to a 900 number ad you simply call the number listed in the personals section of the publication. We will walk through a 900 number voice mail system using the *Los Angeles Times* as an example. Their phone number currently is 1-900-844-5566. You call it and hear the following recorded message:

"Welcome to Dateline, a service of the *Los Angeles Times*. This call is $1.39 per minute. The total cost depends on call length. You must be at least

18 and have a touch tone phone.   Hearing for this program begins three seconds after the tone. Hang up now to avoid being charged."

This is pretty much typical of what you will hear calling any personals publication: a disclosure of cost, that you have to be 18, and that up until now the call hasn't cost you anything. The recording goes on to say:

"Here is your main menu of choices.   You can return to this menu at any point during the program by pressing the pound key located in the lower right hand corner of your touch tone key pad.

Now, if you already know the box number of the advertiser you'd like to listen to, press "1" now. If you want to hear messages played at random from our different categories of advertisers, press "2" now.   Please make your selection."

You, of course, pass on the offer to scan "messages played at random." You now press "1" and the recording says:

"To hear an introduction from the advertiser you selected enter their four digit mailbox number now."

(Note: Publications which carry both 900 number and note and photo personals - like city-named magazines - will sometimes at this point remind you to look for a telephone symbol at the end of the personal in the magazine. If the ad doesn't have the little telephone symbol after it, the person has chosen to only permit responses by the note and photo method. If it does have a little telephone symbol, you can respond by phone).

With the *Los Angeles Times* system when you press the requested four digit code given at the end of the personal - let's say it's 4341 - you will hear:

**"The mailbox you selected is 4341.
If that number is correct press "1"."**

You press "1" and will now hear the advertiser's message about themselves.   At it's conclusion, you will again get a series of options: hearing the message again, leaving a message of your own responding to the personal, moving on to another personal ad (by pressing another four digit option), or returning to the main menu. With the *Los Angeles Times* system if you want to now leave a message you hit "2" and get some helpful hints on what type of information about yourself to leave, and then are told to record after the tone.

Once you leave your message for the person running the ad (covered in depth in Chapter 7, Create A Winning Phone Message), you will get another set of options: play back your message and listen to it, re-record it, or lock it in and move on (options "1," "2," and "3" on the *Times* system). If you chose to play back your message, after hearing it you will again get these same options, and at that point can re-record your message if you choose. It's a *very* good idea to play back and listen to your message once, for the simple reason you may discover you ran out of time and your phone number wasn't recorded. Or, that you forgot to leave it in the first place, and the person now has no way to contact you.

Once you have listened to your recorded message, and decide it is okay *don't just hang up. Be sure to wait and follow whatever instructions are given for "locking in" and saving your message.* If you just hang up your message will be erased. On the *Times* system you save your message by hitting "3". You then either listen to another advertiser's recorded message (by hitting their four digit ad code), return to the main menu, or simply hang up.

Fast Exits

If you immediately decide part way through hearing a person's recorded message that you no longer have any interest in responding, you can save money by exiting out of their message as soon as possible. Many systems offer an escape - sometimes just pressing any key on your phone (for example, Washington, D.C.'s city-named magazine, *Washingtonian*, has this feature). You go back to the main menu on the *Times* system by hitting the pound sign, then press another ad's code. With some practice you will learn how to dump out of recorded messages *quickly*, and save yourself money by hearing more recorded messages in less time. You will discover on many systems you can punch in the four digit ad code before they tell you to, and move more quickly through ad messages.

Retrieving Your Messages

A variation on the *Los Angeles Times* recorded instructions is a publication where the personals advertiser has to pay to retrieve his or her respondent's messages via a 900 number (for example, *Boston* magazine). Publications which do not charge people running personals for message retrieval, such as the *LA Weekly*, utilize a regular local number. Still others provide a free 800 number.

3) PHOTO PERSONALS

In addition to note and photo and 900 number personals, there is also another more rare type of ad: *photo personals*. These personals show a *photo* of the person who placed the ad (which can be either a 900 number and/or a note and photo personal). Photo ads appear in two glossy national singles publications: *The Bachelor Book* and *Single Gentlemen & Women*. *The Bachelor Book* is only for women to respond to, and features mostly black and white photos (along with bios) of men seeking a serious relationship. It's free for men to place an ad. Women contact men by writing them directly at the address they give in their personal (which can be a P.O. Box). At the back of the magazine are a few personals without photos called the Meet Market ($2 a word and open to both men and women with contact by-mail through the magazine). *The Bachelor Book* has about 50 photos and bios in an issue.

The Bachelor Book publisher, Mindi Rudan, a frequent talk show guest, is passionate about running a quality, ethical, above-board publication. She told us that men are first screened via phone interviews to ensure they are looking for a serious relationship. The men must be willing to give information about themselves to the magazine (like social security numbers). *The Bachelor Book* is available nationally and in Canada. Due to demand by women, Mindi is now also publishing *The Bachelorette Book* for *men* to respond to *female* personals.

Single Gentlemen & Women is for men *and* women, and features contact via a 900 number, or through the magazine by mail. About 85 people, appearing in color photos, advertise per issue. The magazine has also begun running some additional personals without photos. It is available in 37 states and Canada. The ads themselves are free to run, although there are some 900 number charges to retrieve messages, as well as letter forwarding fees.

You can check the National heading at the end of the

National Dating Directory for additional information on these publications.

While photo personals are fairly rare, some *local* magazines also carry them (e.g. *Single Connections* in Los Angeles). Photo ad publications are identified in the *National Dating Directory* with a "PHOTO" notation as part of the publication description.

4) COMPUTER BULLETIN BOARDS, ETC.

Personals can also be found on computer bulletin boards. If you're really into computers you may want to give it a try. It requires a computer, a modem, a telephone, and signing up with an online service like Prodigy. Using a bulletin board is much like using 900 number personals, except that you communicate by computer (until you decide to meet in person, or at least talk on the phone). If you participate in a bulletin board centered around a group interest, and then get together in person as a group, it's much like an organized singles activity. To get more information, we suggest you stop in and ask at your local computer store.

There are also TV infomercials popping up periodically with "personals" to respond to - usually featuring hunky guys and attractive women. We don't recommend any of the ones we've seen so far: 1) how bonafide they are is questionable, 2) they are often national ads (as opposed to much more useful local ads), 3) you can't read something about the person in advance to find out more about them first, 4) their charges can be higher then your typical local 900 number personal.

Now let's move on to How To Write An Ad That Really Works.

How To Write An Ad That Really Works: Hard Data 5

SECRETS FOR SUCCESS

Rule number one for writing a personal ad that really works - any type of personal ad - is be *specific*. You need to include specific *data* about yourself. This data functions as a series of *informational hooks*, which creates a recognition of potential *commonality* with the reader you're looking to meet. The more information the reader has to go on, the closer the resulting match can be, and the more *quality* responses you can generate.

Specific data also screens out *inappropriate* responses. While it's nice to get a lot of responses to your personal ad, they need to be the *right* responses. *An effective personal is one which gets potential matches to respond, not just a cross section of readers.* You're wasting valuable time and effort every time a poorly constructed ad results in respondents who are completely incompatible, yet are not screened out by your ad.

While your *primary* screening device is the personal ad itself, if it's a 900 number ad, the taped phone message you leave for respondents to hear is equally important. That message can be both a further description of yourself, as well as information about what you are looking for in the other person.

Too Many Responses
It may be hard to believe, but having *too many* responses to a personal ad can actually be a problem. With 900 number phone technology, and a personal running in a high volume publication, you can actually be swamped by responses. This is much more likely to occur if you're a woman, since women have been estimated to receive up to three times as many responses to their ads as men.

Remember those two women mentioned earlier who were featured on local TV news in Los Angeles? The ones who received 130, and 200 responses to their 900 number personals? Frankly, good as this sounds, *there is virtually no way to handle that many responses.* Retrieving recorded phone messages from that many people - and trying to respond to them - is just too time consuming. All you can realistically do is deal with maybe the first 50, and ignore the rest. However, suppose number 120 is Mister Right, and you never get to him because you are wading through also-rans: inappropriate respondents who weren't pre-screened from responding by your ad's data content, and by your recorded phone message.

Note And Photo Personals
One advantage of *note and photo personals* is that it's much easier to deal with a lot of responses. You usually have more information about each person with which to make a decision than a taped hello (e.g. a letter and often a photo). You can also consider your responses more leisurely, since note and photo respondents don't generally expect an immediate reply, while people answering by phone expect to hear back promptly. Additionally, it's easier to work from a stack of 60 letters - coming back a couple times to re-read the ones that appear to have potential - than trying to wade through 60 phone calls backed up from your 900 number ad.

Inspiration

Remember when you run a personal ad you're *marketing* yourself. In a sense you're competing for attention with the other personals in a publication, and you need to give it your best shot. Before writing your personal, for inspiration take a look through some of the personals in your publication of choice. Read them closely and mark the ones that grab your attention because of something they said, or the way they structured their ad. While you shouldn't blatantly copy them word for word, it's smart to incorporate something that works into your own personal - if it applies to you.

Style And Tone

The writing style of your personal needs to be tailored to the magazine or newspaper you are using. For example, some singles publications (e.g. the *National Singles Register*) tend to have longer, more wordy ads. The style we will use in this book is tighter, more concise and is typical of most newspapers, magazines, and alternative publications (and also many singles magazines). Regardless of style or publication, the *information* appearing in a personal ad stays the same.

The tone of your ad should be upbeat, positive and confident. *This is important.* Your personal should make people feel like they *want to meet you.* Not like one woman who began her ad: "Are you home alone 2?" What's wrong with this approach? She's forcing the reader to admit a negative - that he's "stuck at home" alone too. It's too downbeat an approach. So is the ad from a woman in *Indianapolis* magazine who suggested, "Together we'll end the loneliness." The word "lonely" in any form should always be avoided in personals.

HARD DATA & SOFT DATA

Now let's take a closer look at the type of specific data to include in your personal, and how to incorporate it into a successful ad. The specific data in your personal can be divided into two types:

1) Hard Data: your age, height, general physical description, marital status, etc.

2) Soft Data: your interests, the type of relationship you are looking for, what makes you uniquely you, etc.

In the rest of this chapter we will cover the Hard Data, and in the next one the more creative and unique Soft Data.

HARD DATA

At it's most streamlined, basic (and least expensive) Hard Data in a personal can be as simple as: **SWF, 32, 5' 4", 115 lbs, no children, pretty, in shape, blue eyes, friendly smile, ...** People often mistakenly leave out parts of this basic Hard Data from their ads. For example, *New York* magazine has some of the most expensive personals in the country (often written by very bright people), but a surprising number of these costly ads omit basic Hard Data.

Height

One personal in *New York* magazine described a "very pretty blonde, forty-two, divorced female advertising executive, Jewish, no kids." She has left out a very important piece of Hard Data - her *height*. Suppose a man is 5' 7", will he go to the trouble of sending her a note and a photo, when she could be - for all he knows - 5' 11"? Some men will, but some won't. In fact she may actually be 5' 3", or 5' 5", but she has cost herself responses, and worse yet invited *inappropriate* ones from men she may consider too short (the same problem Barbara had with Joe #1 back in Chapter 3).

Height is a piece of information which should be in *every* personal, men and women's. When your height is in the reader's range it's an immediate *qualifier*. It encourages the reader to proceed to the next piece of information in your ad, and look for more *commonality*. If your height is *not* given in your personal, the reader may simply skip on to the next ad.

Status

You need to tell the reader who you are. People usually use initials such as "SWF," instead of "single white female," because most publications charge by the word. SWF counts as only one word instead of three. Put in your ad SWM (single white male), SBF (single black female), DJF (divorced Jewish female), SAM (single Asian male), etc. This sets up who you are, and clues people into responding. Check the *Personals Glossary of Terms* at the very end of the *National Dating Directory* for standard personals abbreviations. Many publications also give their own glossary of terms listed at the beginning of their personal ads.

Age

Give at least an idea of your age, even if you're a woman who prefers to say "thirtysomething." The goal of your ad, after all, is to draw appropriate readers to you by giving them information for making an intelligent decision, as well as screening out inappropriate respondents with your specific data. What good is not giving your age and getting responses from people who are too old or too young? Be aware also that if you do say "thirtysomething," the assumption may be you are 38 (or

39), when actually you are 33.

In Shape?

It's good to give some indication of your *weight*. Since not being overweight is a *plus* to most people, capitalize on it by saying so in your personal. Don't assume the reader will assume you aren't fat! If you leave out your weight, you may encourage speculation that you could be overweight, and lose responses. As with height, it's just as easy for people to skip an ad that omits weight, and move on to the next one that gives it.

So, reassure them. Both men and women can say something like "trim," "lean," "slim," "fit," "in shape," "work out," "weight proportional to height," or just give your weight in pounds next to your height. If you're a little overweight (e.g. 10-15 pounds) don't feel compelled to disclose it in your ad.

If You Are Overweight

If you *are* substantially overweight, it's better to disclose it upfront. If you're a woman you can say "zaftig," "full-figured," "queen size," "Rubenesque," "large woman," "larger sized," or even "overweight." You're going to avoid embarrassing situations by being honest about it. More to the point, the responses you get will be from men interested in you *exactly the way you are*. Some overweight women make their ad sexier by accenting the positive: "Rubenesque, *voluptuous* SWF..." Or "SWF, *buxom*, full figured..." Or they use an upbeat, active word like "vibrant" to introduce themselves, as in "*vibrant*, Rubenesque DWF..."

If a man has a serious weight problem plenty of women want to know. The simplest way to deal with it is to give your height and weight - but also emphasize positives about your personality, career, being a homeowner, etc., and let the chips fall where they may. If you don't mention it in your ad, at minimum be sure to do so in your first phone conversation.

Hair/Eyes
Some people put hair and eye color in their personal, often to accent a special feature. They're a "strawberry blonde," or have "pretty blue eyes." You can put this information in your ad, or you can save it for the taped phone message you'll be leaving for callers to hear if you're using a 900 number personal.

Looks
A suggestion: even if you *are* handsome or beautiful (or think you are), don't use either term in your ad! Some publications are replete with "handsome" men and "beautiful" women. Humility (and accuracy) are often nonexistent. While a woman who calls herself "beautiful," or a man who says he is "handsome," may increase their response total, they: 1) need to live up to the description in person, 2) risk losing good respondents who may be turned off by someone who chooses to describe themselves that way, or who may feel intimidated because they're not sure they themselves are attractive enough.

Women
Instead of calling herself "beautiful," a woman can say she's "pretty," or "cute," or even "striking" (or possibly "very pretty"). She can also describe the specific features which make her physically appealing: "great smile" (or "warm smile," or "friendly smile," or "enchanting smile"); or "striking redhead," "cute blonde," "great legs" (or "sexy legs"), etc. This is a way to still flirt with appearance to help get results. *Frankly it's a good idea for a women to address looks in some manner in her per-*

sonal ad, and positive terms about physical appearance will get her more responses. She can still balance the physical with an emphasis on other, non-physical qualities in the Soft Data part of her personal.

Women And Sex

If a woman calls herself a "hot looking" female, she will very likely get more responses than if she doesn't. But if the tone of the ad is too sexual, she sets herself up for the wrong kind of responses. For example, one woman's ad in *Los Angeles* magazine read, "petite (yet well-endowed) SWF..." We think "well-endowed" is a bit too anatomically specific - at least for someone seeking a serious relationship - because it invites a sex-on-the-brain response. There are more subtle ways for a woman to flirt with her figure, including "shapely," "statuesque," "well proportioned," "curvaceous," etc. She can also simply emphasize being fit and in shape.

A good example of a flirtatious personal is another one from *Los Angeles* magazine: "Pretty, petite, curvy brunette SJF, successful professional with a warm heart, great smile, full lips..." She flirts with her appearance - and also slips in that she has brains by including "successful professional." Similarly, another woman in the same magazine addressed the whole package with this classy lead-in to her personal: "TRES MAGNIFIQUE. Tall, striking, happy brunette professional." Two ads by women in *Washingtonian* magazine combined looks with assertiveness and independence. One woman said she was "sexy and strong," and another called herself "attractive and outspoken."

Men

A man looking for quality responses and/or a serious relationship should avoid anything of an overtly sexual nature in his personal. It will simply turn off most women ("well endowed SWM?" we think not!). The man in *The Village Voice* who said: "Ex-male Model seeking Buxom woman for Exiting time. Age, race unimportant," is probably not on his way to a serious relationship anytime soon.

For men, putting something about physical attractiveness in their ad can be more easily ignored. That being said a man can still say he's "nice looking," "fit," "tall," "athletic," etc. The fact of the matter is women have to bear the "looks" cross more than men. Men, on the other hand, have to worry more about how their financial and career success comes across in their personal. While the sexism in these double standards is both obvious and unfortunate, it still exists.

Geographically Undesirable
What you say about where you live depends on the type and scope of the publication. People advertising in the *Los Angeles Times*, for example, use location abbreviations at the bottom of personals to identify where they live (e.g. "WS" for West Side). Since some people aren't ready to travel more than 45 minutes to meet someone, where you live is important. On the other hand, a regional or national publication is more likely to have an inherently wider definition among it's readers as to what constitutes "too long" and "too far" to travel.

If you're going to be judged "GU" (geographically undesirable), you can get it out of the way early. You can mention where you live in your personal, or in the phone message you leave with a 900 number ad, in order to screen out people for whom it is a problem. You may *not* want to do it if you are the one *answering* an ad, however. Suppose you are willing to drive an hour, or even two, to meet someone if their ad sounds terrific. They, on the other hand, might balk at the distance separating the two of you, and pass on calling you back when you first respond to their personal. If they don't find out how far away you live until *after* they talk to you, and if they like you, they're more likely to expand their *own* GU definition, and meet you anyway.

Unencumbered

If you don't have children, write "unencumbered," or "no dependents," or "no children." It's almost always a plus, because many people think twice about responding to an ad by a single parent, or one where the issue of children isn't addressed at all. If you describe yourself in your personal as divorced, there is then especially the question of whether you have children.

If You *Are* A Single Parent

On the other hand, if you are a single parent, things are a bit trickier. However, the rule of commonality once again applies. If you're upfront about having children, you'll get people responding for whom this isn't a problem. They may even be single parents themselves, which means you'll have respondents with whom you have life experience - as well as current circumstances - in common. If you *don't* disclose single parenthood in your ad, or your recorded 900 number message, or at least at some point in the initial phone conversation, you're taking a risk. You may go on to meet a man or woman in person only to find out they are vehemently opposed to getting involved with a single parent. The same applies to disclosing it yourself when answering someone else's personal.

Men Seeking Parenthood

If fatherhood is important to you, particularly if you're a man dating women in their mid-thirties (often with biological clocks ticking), either bring it up in your personal (e.g. "seeks relationship leading to marriage and children"), or respond in the affirmative when women bring up the subject of children on the phone, or when you meet in person.

Since single mothers generally have a tougher time dating, the man who led off his personal with "Single Mom Wanted!" likely found himself inundated with responses. On the other hand, don't do what one overeager guy did, announcing in bold letters: **"I WANT TO BE A DADDY!"**

No Kids, Please
If you're a man who does *not* want to have children, you should be upfront about it on the phone, or the first time you meet a woman in person. There are a lot of women who don't want children these days either, or at least who aren't in a hurry. For example, this ad: **"BIOLOGICAL CLOCK ON SNOOZE ALARM!** Southern classic beauty. 30. Intelligent, creative, looking for a good date/ relationship - not a husband!" Or the 31-year-old woman who sees marriage in her future, but notes "however children aren't."

Women And Marriage
If you are a woman seeking your future husband, you probably don't want to bother with a man who's using the personals only as a dating service, and/or is commitment phobic. You can make it clear in your ad that you're seeking a "serious relationship," or one "leading to marriage." However, the woman who began her personal with "Let's Get Married" might have been a little *too* direct. While the woman in *New York* magazine who led off her ad calling herself, "More or less marriage minded" found a more subtle way to separate marriage minded men from mere "daters."

Women Seeking Parenthood

If you're a woman who wants to find a husband *and* the
future father of your children, you might want to soft
pedal the issue of children a bit initially. But if having
children *soon* is important to you, at minimum find out
on the phone, or over your first cup of coffee together,
whether the guy is at least not *opposed* to having children.
If he is, forget it - you're in all likelihood not going to change
him. However, if he is genuinely open to the possibility
"with the right woman," you probably want to proceed.
But you first might want to find out a little more about
exactly what his time frame "with the right woman" is.

One woman in *Chicago Life* magazine neatly put marriage and children this way as part of what she was looking for overall: "Seeking masculine but nurturing, emotionally available, mature, sincere, honest, financially stable
S/DM for serious (and fun) relationship ultimately leading to marriage, and hopefully a family." ("S/DM" meaning single or divorced male).

MONEY/JOB
Financially Secure Men

A lot of women look for a man who is "financially secure," and in some publications men typically mention if
they are a "homeowner." If you're a man who *is* financially secure, it's worth getting this information across -
ideally a bit subtly - in your personal. You're marketing
yourself, after all, and this is a sales point. However,
avoid overkill and the risk of being obnoxious, or attracting the wrong kind of woman by overly stressing money.
For example, there are men who say they are "wealthy"
("affluent" is a slightly more subtle choice, "successful"
even better). Take the 43-year-old guy who said in his
ad in *Los Angeles* magazine he was "wealthy" (and "handsome" too). His ad went on: "seeks SLIM beauty, 20's,

with legs." (Ah, true love, it's a wonderful thing).

If you have a job that could be considered a plus, you probably want to mention it in your ad (and while this applies more to men than to women, a woman having a good career is a plus to many men). This can be as simple as writing "successful business executive." Dentists, doctors, journalists, etc., often include their profession in their personals. A lot of attorneys mention it too, and as one woman noted in her personal: "**J'Adore** attorneys."

Now let's move on to the Soft Data portion of your personal ad.

How To Write An Ad That Really Works: Soft Data

6

Your Interests And Values

What are your interests? What are your values? What kind of a relationship are you looking for? *What makes you uniquely you?* This is the Soft Data, and it's where you get an opportunity to be inventive and creative in your personal. Put something in your ad about what you like to do, even if it's simply going to movies and restaurants. Throw in hiking, or riding horses, or bicycling, or cooking, or reading, or attending musicals; and maybe that you are a dog lover, or a cat lover, whatever describes *you*. You're providing information about yourself that creates commonality with readers who share your passions.

A simple way to do this is to list things you enjoy, like a woman in the *Chicago Reader* who listed: "cycling, theater, WNUA concerts, movie Ravinia, good food, wine, travel..." Or a woman in the *Denver Westword* who listed: "hiking, biking, camping, skiing, country music dancing, theater, art, music..." Or a woman from another alternative publication, the *Maine Times*, who gave: "tennis, walking, biking, skiing, theater, dancing, movies, music, dining in/out..."

This works for men as well, like this personal from Wisconsin's *SingleLife*: "I enjoy travel, weekend getaways, good friends, tennis, the outdoors, dining out, an occasional trip to the theater, and quiet, intimate evenings at home." By being sure to give your interests, you will have people responding with whom you share things in common - things the two of you can do together.

Seeks...

What kind of relationship (if any) are you looking for? If you're a man who is looking for that "special person" - not just more fodder for the dating mill - this is especially important to say in your ad. Women who are looking for a serious relationship want to know you're not playing games. So if you can honestly write, "seeks lasting relationship," you will do yourself a world of good. If you aren't sure that you're ready for a serious relationship, you don't have to address the issue one way or another.

If you're placing a 900 number ad, you can use the printed personal to describe yourself, and then give specifics about what you're looking for in the other person in your recorded phone message. If you're running a note and photo personal *without* a recorded message, and want to describe what you're looking for in another person, it needs to be done in the personal itself.

Looking For Perfection

Some people set such high demands in their personals as to what they expect in the other person - making it their fantasy perfect match - they scare off most respondents. A 33-year-old woman in Chicago wrote she was seeking, "a very successful, educated, extremely attractive, classy SWM heartthrob." By insisting on "*extremely* attractive" and a "*heartthrob*," she no doubt intimidated some men, and turned off others, costing her quality men she likely would have enjoyed meeting.

Avoid Too-Cute Personals

"MOTHERS LOVE ME, YOU WILL TOO!!!" began a personal in *Los Angeles* magazine. This woman may think she's being "cute," but with this approach she no doubt just sent most men running for the hills. *Why* would a man's mother love her? If it's because she's "warm, fun, smart and supportive," then *that's* what she should say in her ad. Too often women write ads *they* think are cute, and other *women* may find cute. Some (female) writers of dating books and advice columns suggest doing cute ads. For example, if a woman sells real estate, she can use real estate terms to describe herself in her personal. But a woman isn't writing her ad to appeal to other women. She wants to reach *men*. Men respond to direct and simple. If it's a cute ad, it needs to be *smart* cute - like the examples we give under the Taglines heading later in this chapter.

Cliches

Try to avoid the major cliches of personals. Among the worst offenders are: looking for your "soulmate," taking "long walks on the beach," enjoying "romantic dinners," and most anything to do with "sunrises/sunsets." You can still talk about these in your personal ad, but try to be more inventive in doing so. For example, looking for your "soulmate" - in addition to being cliche - is very vague. Since it means looking for a true partner, instead discuss your *values* and the *specifics* of what you seek in the other person (the very things that would make them your "soulmate").

Positive Terms

A man needs to be sure he doesn't come off as a lech (in his ad, on the phone, or in person), and a woman doesn't want to invite unwanted or lewd responses. That being said, however, if a man regards himself as a passionate guy, there is a subtle way he can flirt with it in his ad. It's "sensuous" (or "sensual"). Women can also use it (or "passionate") as a way to flirt in their personal.

If you're a male, three other words might get you even better results than using sensuous. Try *"affectionate,"* *"communicative,"* and *"supportive."* If they don't describe you, don't use them - but they are three things you should be working on! If they *do* fit you, definitely use them. Some other positive terms for describing yourself include: "easy to talk to," "good listener," "warm," "friendly," "out-going," "emotionally available," "good sense of humor," and "romantic." All these work for women too.

One man who said in his ad he was "not afraid of inti-macy or commitment" - music to the ears of many women - was likely deluged with responses. But again, be sure to find positive descriptive terms that *accurately* describe *you.* Otherwise you are setting yourself up for a fall when, in person, you don't live up to your advance billing.

It's The 90's

The woman who called herself "petite (yet well-en-dowed)," in the last chapter, went on to say in her ad that she was in her early 30's, and then announced she had herpes. While it takes courage and honesty to make this revelation, it also pays off by effectively pre-screening responses and attracting: 1) people who accept her *with* herpes, and 2) respondents who *also* have herpes - and who'll jump at the chance to meet someone with whom there is not going to have to be a tough in-bed discussion one night down the road. This also applies to AIDS, which commonly appears in gay personals - but also oc-casionally in "straight" ads - when individuals disclose they are "HIV positive," or simply "HIV."

PERSONAL PREFERENCES
Smoking

If you're a non-smoker and want to only date non-smokers, write "N/S" (nonsmoker), or simply "nonsmoker," in your ad. This will discourage smokers from responding. If you don't, you may wind up in a 45 minute telephone conversation with someone who sounds terrific, until you discover you're talking to a chainsmoker. The same applies if you smoke; write "smoker" in your ad (or be sure to mention it *early* in your phone conversation). A smoker might also check out *Smoking Singles* magazine, a national smokers personals publication listed in the National section at the end of the *National Dating Directory*.

Drugs

Some people put "N/D" (no drugs) in their ad. If dating someone who smokes pot once in a while would be okay with you, *don't* write N/D. If that's definitely *not* okay, then write N/D. Keep in mind that "N/D" might paint you (perhaps unfairly) as conservative on a lot of other issues. But if you *are* conservative, it will create *commonality* with like-minded readers.

Religion

As with addressing drugs, this is optional. Usually it is only important to include for a person who has strong feelings about religion one way or another. If you're a born again Christian, you may want to at least put "Christian" in your ad to attract compatible respondents. Similarly, if you're *not* religious, you may want to put *that* in, with something like "non-religious" to discourage devout churchgoers. Some people also mention their denomination (e.g. Catholic) if they're looking to meet like-minded people. If you're Jewish, usually people include that as part of their status (e.g. DJF, "Divorced Jewish female").

Politics

This is another optional area. Unless you're very politically active, or your politics are fairly extreme one way or the other, you can leave politics out of your personal. However, sometimes people on the liberal side of things do mention, "left of center," or "liberal," or "politically progressive" in their ad. Presumably they don't want a Rush Limbaugh fan to answer their personal (conversely, a devoted Limbaugh fan might also mention their own more conservative politics in *their* ad). While including political leanings *is* a way to pre-screen people, why not just instead wait until you're on the phone to get into it? Sometimes people with differing views than your own make interesting and challenging dates and partners.

DEFINING THE REAL YOU

Now that you're past the basic Hard and Soft Data, you should exercise creative freedom in doing the remaining Soft Data. Beyond the physical stats, religious and smoking preferences, economic status, and your interests, try to define and describe yourself in additional terms that give the essence of who you are: the "real you."

Don't be afraid to turn off some readers with your description of yourself (and what you are looking for in another person), but turn them off for the *right reasons*. Remember your personal ad (and your taped phone message in a 900 number ad) is your way of pre-screening respondents before talking to them by phone. You *want* some people to say you don't sound like their type, and not respond. The ones that do respond will know more about who you are, and are more likely to be compatible with you. For every person you turn off, you are just as likely to pick up someone new.

The Tagline Or Hook

A descriptive tagline in your personal ad helps to sharply define you. It can be as simple as the guy in *New York* magazine who described himself as an "Englishman in New York." Or the woman in the *Chicago Tribune* who painted an instant picture of herself with "sexy & sarcastic" (or the woman in the *Chicago Reader* who took things a step further with: "sarcastic, voluptuous, casual, occasional bitch on wheels..."!). A woman in the *Sacramento News & Review* summed herself up as a "goodlooking, fun-loving, country girl." Another woman in *Los Angeles* magazine lead off her ad with the provocative tag: "EXEC BY DAY, SULTRESS BY NIGHT," which manages to be in equal parts smart and sexy.

Beginning your ad with a sharp opening line can be a very effective gambit in a personal. A man began his ad in *Indianapolis* magazine with, "Welcome To Our Future" - and continued in a warm, sensitive, intelligent vein. A woman in *Boston* magazine led off, "Sensuous, slim, sassy, smart, SJF." In *Washingtonian*, a woman tried a much different approach: "Anyone can send me flowers; I need to be challenged, not worshipped."

Your Values

Ideally get some of your *values* into your personal. Values can be covered in a fairly straightforward manner. One man put it this way: "Honesty, integrity, loyalty and sensitivity are qualities I value." A friend of ours who feels he is non-materialistic looked for a "non-materialistic" woman in his ad. In *Chicago* magazine a woman wanted to find a man "who values mutual trust and communication."

KATHY: You can also combine values with a tagline. Rick came up with a tagline in his final and most successful personal that touched on his values and caught *this* reader's eye: **"Former Sixties Rebel, Now Corporate But Iconoclastic."** It was a very effective screening device. It says in the past he was not a straight arrow (a "Former Sixties Rebel"), which discourages responses from women for whom that would be a problem. It also says that today he is solvent and responsible ("Now Corporate"), but that while he works in corporate America, he thinks for himself and exercises some independence ("iconoclastic").

A good tagline - values laden or not - imparts information in just a few words. It establishes commonality with readers who relate to it, and discourages those who don't from responding. It also gives *individuality* and *uniqueness* to your personal, differentiating you from the rest of the pack.

Don't Be Afraid To Be Different

If you are a woman who sees herself as an "exotic, sensuous, occasionally angst-ridden, non-religious, sultry, art crowd fellow traveller," don't be afraid to say so. Or how about the guy in the *LA Weekly* who said in his ad: "A male from the dark side. Coffee, caviar, film noir - I take 'em black." While he's definitely not every woman's cup of tea, this distinctive description should connect strongly with certain women. To emphasize their uniqueness, both the "angst ridden" woman and "male from the dark side" could place their Soft Data descriptions at the *beginning* of their personals (the Hard Data should still be there, but can come later in the ad).

If You Are More Traditional

If you don't relate to a "Former Sixties Rebel," or an "Art crowd fellow traveler," or "A male from the dark side," don't be afraid to sound mainstream in your ad. Even in large cities there are many people who put in their ads they believe in "traditional values." Or, if you're female and can relate to the woman in *Los Angeles* magazine who said she was "looking for my hero," don't be afraid to sound "unhip." It's more important to be yourself and to get responses from people *you* will be comfortable with.

My Final Personal Ad

RICK: You need to write an ad that describes you in an interesting, positive, appealing way. As an example, here is my own final personal (a 900 number ad). For me and the publication I was using, it was just right. Your ad should fit your *own* personality and the publication you are using.

> "Network TV Professional, former Sixties rebel now corporate but iconoclastic, SWM, 43 (look younger), 5' 8", trim, N/S, no dependents, affectionate, sensual, easy to talk to, strong, understanding, dry sense of humor. Enjoys intelligent conversation, books, movies, nature. Seeks lasting relationship."

The Taped Phone Message

A good personal ad will get compatible people to respond. If it's a note and photo ad, they'll write. In the case of a 900 number ad they'll now call in and hear your taped phone message. That all-important taped message you leave with your personal ad is the subject of our next chapter. We will also cover the important message you leave when you're the one calling to *respond* to a 900 number ad. In both cases you want to leave a message that gets you a response back.

Create A Winning
Phone Message

7

Introduction

Leaving a recorded telephone message is an intrinsic part of the 900 number personals process. First we'll focus primarily on the taped message you leave when you run a personal, and then on the one you leave when you call someone else's ad.

1) THE ADVERTISER'S 900 NUMBER
PHONE MESSAGE

An Extension Of Your Ad

When you run a 900 number personal, the taped phone message you leave with your ad is as important as the ad itself. You should think of it as an *extension* of your ad. It can make or break whether a caller decides to complete the process of answering your personal by leaving their name and phone number. A 900 number ad is usually a mutual blind date situation (unless it's a rare photo ad), and in your recorded message you need to make yourself sound appealing, interesting, and approachable. People will judge you by listening to your message, and if it doesn't connect with them, they'll move on to the next ad.

Done correctly, the advertiser's (and the respondent's) taped phone message is a potential *bonanza*. Because a 900 number ad *is* a mutual blind date situation, both messages are an opportunity to create a positive visual picture in people's minds. It is part of the personals marketing process, and an opportunity for even an "average looking" man or woman to shine.

A Well Done Message

Because your taped message should also do additional screening for you beyond that done by the ad itself, when someone calls your 900 number personal and hears a well done message, you can increase the odds that: 1) they will decide to leave their name and phone number, 2) that the *right type* of person will leave their name and phone number.

Be Friendly And Forthcoming

Just as important as the information you impart in your phone message - perhaps more so - is how you *sound* in your message. It's not just *what* you say, but *how* you say it. Men especially want to allay female concerns about dealing with a stranger by sounding *relaxed, forthcoming, conversational, upbeat* and *friendly*. A little "we're all in this thing together" humor doesn't hurt either. The idea is to sound easy to meet, like you have a brain in your head, and that you aren't some kind of "weirdo."

If a man's personal ad looks interesting, and a woman calls and listens to his message - but decides he sounds like a potential axe murderer, a rapist, lecherous, or even just *boring* - he's undone all the work he put into his ad. If a woman's ad looks interesting and a guy calls her message - only to discover she sounds curt, bossy, neurotic, or even just unfriendly and stand-offish - she has just undone *her* ad.

Common Taped Message Mistakes

Some of the most common mistakes people make in their taped messages are:

1) they repeat everything that's already in their ad,
2) they sound boring,
3) they leave too short a message,
4) they don't leave a taped message at all.

While you can choose not to leave a taped message with your 900 number ad, we don't recommend it. (If you don't leave a message, people calling in will usually hear a recording that your message has "not gone on line yet"). Since this is a blind date situation, many people will want to at least hear what you *sound* like, before they leave their name and number. Not leaving a message can cost you responses. The respondents you *do* get may be less compatible, because they are answering more blindly than if they'd heard what you have to say first. Only consider not leaving a taped message if you strongly suspect you're doing a really bad job of it (and have been getting very few responses). Normally a well done message is much preferable to leaving no message.

Recording Your Message
When you leave your taped phone message - either with your ad, or when calling someone else's personal - the publication's phone system will walk you through the procedure with simple directions. As discussed in Chapter 4, the standard voice mail setup allows you to record your message or response, and then play it back to review it. You can then re-record it if you're not happy with it. You may want to re-record your message, especially your first time using the personals. But don't obsess too much and insist on leaving the "perfect" message. Above all don't read from a prepared written version; it will sound unnatural. It is, however, a good idea to jot down a list ahead to time of things you want to say, whether you're running or responding to an ad.

New Data

If you realize that you left out some pertinent data from
your ad, your phone message is a good chance to put it
in. The phone message is also an opportunity to elabo-
rate on your personal rather than repeating what's *already* in your ad.

RICK: For example, I didn't say anything about how I
looked in my ads. But in my last and most successful
personal, I addressed looks head-on in my taped phone
message. Feeling that my appearance is not my strong
suit, I preempted the issue by saying I was "more average looking than handsome," and even that I had lost a
lot of hair (!).

Self-Deprecating - But With Confidence!

If you do choose to be self-deprecating, you should do it
in a charming and *self-confident* manner. You don't want
to undersell yourself, after all. For women, it is good to
remember we live in a sexist society, and downplaying
your appearance is not a particularly good idea. However, as in their ads, both men and women should also
avoid overly building up expectations about their looks
that they can't meet in person.

Leave A Long Message

Be sure to use most of the time allotted for the message,
or at minimum about 45 seconds. With many publications, both the person placing the ad and the person calling in can record up to a 60 second message. Unfortunately, a lot of people write a good personal, and then
leave a taped message which simply says "Hi, I'm Karen.
Leave your name and number." It is both too short to
encourage some on-the-fence callers to respond, while
not helping to screen out the wrong ones with new specific data about herself, and perhaps what she is looking

for in another person.

What *Are* You Looking For?

RICK: Initially, I was reluctant to describe what I was looking for in a woman - both in my personal ad, and in the recorded message accompanying a 900 number ad. I was afraid it would discourage some respondents - and I wanted as many as I could get. When I did finally give it a shot, I expected to cut my responses in half. The actual result? The personal was a two week ad that - because of a special offer - had an additional two weeks free. The overall response total was 46, with about 30 in the first two weeks. While that was a little lower than responses to my previous two week ad, the women were *much more compatible*. The reason? When you get specific about what you are looking for in another person it triggers responses from people fitting the description you give - the very people you want to hear from.

For example, your ad's taped message is a good place to say something about the age range of the person you are looking for. I was interested in marriage and having children. During my personals search I'd been dating many women my age and even older. In my last personal's taped message - with marriage and children in mind - I decided to say: "*ideally* you are in your mid-30's." I still left the door open for women who were older or younger than their mid-30's by only saying "ideally" - while still stating my preference. In fact, Kathy, at 32, was not in her mid-30's (but most respondents were).

Weight

If you are adverse to dating overweight people, in addition to describing yourself in your ad as "trim," "slim," etc., you can also figure out a way to tactfully cover the issue in your phone message. For example, as with your ad you can emphasize *fitness* by saying something like, "I like to stay in shape and watch my weight, and hopefully you do too."

Be Flexible

As with writing an ad that really works, when you're creating a winning phone message try to be *positive*. Say what you *want* in a person, not what you *don't* want. Try also not to be dogmatic about what you're looking for in the other person. Remember, flexibility is a plus.

KATHY: Rick gave his preferred height range for women in his taped ad message as, "*hopefully* you are between about 5' 2" and 5' 5". I ignored his self-imposed height limit and responded anyway, even though I'm 5' 6" (and I told him so in my taped message back). Rick decided to get past the fact that he'd *never* been involved with anyone taller than 5' 4" and met me in-person anyway.

Paint A Visual Picture

When leaving a taped message with your personal, paint a picture of who you are looking for on the physical level, and also make some comments on the *intangibles*. If you like *intelligent* women or men, say so. If you're a woman who wants a man who is communicative, say it. But also avoid giving such a laundry list of specifics that it results in coming off as obnoxious.

2) RESPONDING TO A 900 NUMBER PERSONAL

A Tip

When you are the one responding to *someone else's* 900 number personal ad, the taped voice mail phone message you leave when you call in is even *more* important than the advertiser's. Your phone message is the *only* thing people have to go on when making the decision whether to call you back.

RICK: The first few times I called other people's personals, my success rate in hearing back was only about one in four. Within a few months, however, if I called four personals I would hear back from at least three, and often all four. What accounted for this dramatic improvement? Two things: 1) projecting more *self-confidence* and *friendliness*, because I was more comfortable with the personals process, and 2) leaving substantially *longer* messages.

Leaving Your Message

When you call a personal the first priority is to get the advertiser to call you back. As mentioned, the biggest mistake people make is leaving too short a message. This is especially important for men calling women. Leave a fairly long, friendly, conversational message to set them at ease - remember you are a total stranger. Try to be open, confident, and not too demanding (e.g. avoid things like: "if you're really cute call me back"). After the person returns your call you can find out additional information, especially any data they left out of their personal.

Content

In your taped message tell the personals advertiser some of the same sort of information about yourself you would put in an ad of your own. Things like where you're from, what you do job-wise, some physical description, your age, and something you think you have in common or liked about their ad ("I really liked your ad because... " Or, "Your ad caught my eye because you said...").

Reciprocity

In social psychology there exists a phenomenon known as the Rule of Reciprocity. Saying positive things about a person's ad, or that you like how they sounded in their taped message, plus leaving a fairly long message, results in more of a sense of obligation for them to call you back. It differentiates you from the pack when they know more about you than the people who left short messages. When the advertiser is wading through a bunch of phone messages from a good ad in a high volume publication, the short "Hi I'm Joe/Jane - call me," is the one they are likely to skip calling back. Remember, like the person running the ad you're *also* marketing yourself - and you can't do that if you don't say something about who you are and why you're interested in them.

Re-Record Option

As noted in the 900 number voice mail walk-through in Chapter 4, there is an option to delete and then re-record when you call to respond to someone's ad.

RICK: One woman's humorous taped response message to me led off with a slightly frazzled sounding: "Personals ad response - take five!" Once again, it's not necessary to leave the perfect phone message. If you're tempted to re-record your message ad nauseam, remember you're paying for the time by the minute.

The Early Bird Gets...

When answering ads in a major city, respond as soon as the newspaper or magazine comes out - or at least within a few days of publication. You are more likely to hear back from someone if you are caller number 10 than if you are caller number *110*. It can be crucial to be early. This is especially true if you are a man calling a woman with an ad in a high volume response publication.

Almost *all* alternative publications come out mid-week (the *National Dating Directory* gives the day of the week for each one listed). The real flood of responses to the personals begins over the weekend. If you call the day the paper comes out the advertiser may not have left their message for you to hear yet (although you can still leave a message for them). On the other hand, if you call during the day on Friday, or that evening, their message is usually on line and you'll still be one of the early callers. You will have much better odds on hearing back by calling early.

Moving On
We will pick up where we left off with the personals in Part VI, Following Through For Success.   But first let's move on to sections on the other three date to win options: *organized singles activities, dating introduction services and matchmakers,* and *videodating.*

Organized Singles
Activities

Introducing Organized
Singles Activities

8

San Francisco, California: Jake and Linda
Linda pulls her Honda into a parking space at the BART
(Bay Area Rapid Transit) train station, in the Rockridge
district of Oakland, California. She's on her way into San
Francisco for a *Sierra Club Singles* eight mile "urban singles
hike." Usually when she goes on a hike, Linda carpools
with other *Sierra Club Singles* members. This morning,
however, because she parks her car and takes the train,
she will later look back and wonder if she was subcon-
sciously setting the stage for meeting a man on the hike -
one who could offer her a ride back across the Bay Bridge
to retrieve her automobile.

Originally from Los Angeles, and a single mother in her
late 30's, Linda has two sons ages 10 and 11. Her ex-
husband has custody of the boys once a week on either
Saturday or Sunday, and on that day Linda likes to attend
Oakland *Sierra Club Singles* functions. While she's never
tried videodating, or matchmakers and dating introduction services, or the personal ads, she's been going to
Sierra Club Singles activities for about 10 years.

Sierra Club Singles sponsors tennis, river rafting trips, literary nights with readings, singles dinners, bridge nights
and, of course, singles hikes. Linda refers to the club as
"the group," and it's an important part of her life. Between her job as a school teacher and raising her sons,

she spends most of her time surrounded by kids. *Sierra Club Singles* is a chance for her to be with adults.

Linda also likes the group's activities because, as she puts it, "it isn't overt pickup stuff, it has a more relaxed natural feel." At the beginning she didn't think of attending as a way to meet men. "Actually I enjoyed the company of the women!" she says with a laugh. Eventually, she did date some of the men she met through the group's activities, but as of today's trip into San Francisco, nothing serious has developed.

Jake
Like Linda, Jake also enjoys hiking. He's gone on a few Sierra Club hikes, where he heard about *Sierra Club Singles*, and this weekend's upcoming urban hike. The hike will begin at the San Francisco Ferry Building, proceed past Fisherman's Wharf, then across the Golden Gate Bridge to Sausalito. He decides it sounds like a terrific idea, signs up, and pays the $10 fee.

Jake is 40, never married, and like Linda also a school teacher living in Oakland. He's a bit cerebral and quirky, a tall intellectual Jewish guy, originally from Brooklyn, New York. He recently came out of a relationship which, although it didn't last, opened his eyes to what could happen if he met the "right woman." He resolved to take some action to find that special person. About that time he received a mailing from the videodating people at *Great Expectations*. However, after a visit he decided videodating was both too expensive and just didn't feel like the right option for him.

Next he tried a computer dating introduction service. For a fee of $200 they supplied him with 20 blind date matches. He met each one for lunch or coffee. Unfortunately, usually it wasn't even close to being a match. He felt he couldn't just "be himself" with the type of women he was meeting, and besides, the whole process seemed strange and "too slick."

The *Sierra Club Singles* hike appeals to Jake as a more natural way to meet women. Besides, even if nothing else happens, he'll have spent an enjoyable day getting some good exercise out of doors. On the day of the hike he drives over to San Francisco from Oakland, and parks near the Ferry Building. He spots about 15 men and 15 women gathering for the hike.

As they start off in the fresh July morning air, Jake talks with several of the women. Then he notices Linda and strikes up a conversation. Together they cross the Golden Gate Bridge, with its romantic windswept view out over the Pacific. Behind them the curved vista of San Francisco hugs the shoreline, while over on the other side of the Bay, the city of Oakland sits hazily in the distance.

Aside from their mutual enjoyment of hiking, as Jake and Linda talk they discover they have a lot in common, especially their experience as teachers. They also find some differences, such as the fact he's Jewish and she's Catholic. Jake is quickly smitten, while Linda thinks he's just a "nice guy."

The group troops into Sausalito at end of the hike and then takes the ferry back across the Bay to San Francisco. Once in the city, Jake offers Linda a ride back to Oakland. But so do three *other* guys. Jake wins the honor because he lives the nearest to where she's parked her car, and it makes the most sense. (Linda, however, later also goes on to see the three other guys!). After the drive back across the Bay Bridge to Oakland, they reach her car and Jake asks her for a date. She says "yes."

One date leads to another, and within a few months Jake and Linda move in together. On the first anniversary of their hike they become engaged. Seven months later they marry in a ceremony jointly officiated by a priest and a rabbi.

That was in 1990, and since then, just for old times' sake, occasionally they retrace their steps, and hike the eight miles from the San Francisco Ferry Building to Sausalito.

ORGANIZED SINGLES ACTIVITIES AND YOU
Organized singles activities have their own distinct advantages in relation to the other date to win options:

1) No Blind Dating
Unlike some of the other date to win options, with singles activities there is *no blind dating*. Regardless of our own earlier favorable comments on the pluses of blind dating, many people may prefer not to do it. At a singles activity you decide who you are interested in approaching based on seeing them in person, and who you'd like to date after talking to them face to face.

2) Bring A Friend
Organized singles activities are the only New Dating Option where you can easily bring a friend along. Together you can attend a singles dance, go on a ski trip, go to a singles dinner, take a singles tennis lesson, etc.

3) Pre-screening
You can pre-screen for *commonality* when deciding which singles activity is for you. If you're interested in hiking, nature and the environment, you'll meet like-minded people on a *Sierra Club Singles* hike. If you generally

enjoy other outdoor activities, there are groups offering singles bicycle clubs, tennis groups, snow skiing, white water rafting trips, and so on.   There are also movie-going singles groups, groups for restaurant junkies, book readers, *Single Republicans* and *A.C.L.U. Singles.*

4) A Plethora Of Choices

Instead of meeting one videodate, or one personals respondent, or one matchmaker or dating introduction service match at a time, you will have more people to chose from at a singles activity.   For example, at a singles dinner, there can be 20 or 30 members of the opposite sex attending, while at a singles dance there can be several *hundred.*   One friend of ours who enjoys singles dinners cites the larger number of people to select from as an important reason for choosing this option over the others.

5) Direct Access

Unlike some of the other New Dating Options, singles activities give you an opportunity to make *direct in person contact.*   There is no third party between you and anyone you might be interested in meeting, and no chance for a person to decline to meet you ahead of time - unlike with videodating and the personal ads.   You have the opportunity to directly approach anyone who's attending a singles activity and give it your best shot.

6) Time

Singles activities usually don't take up a lot of time.   For the busy person who complains they don't have enough time to run a personal ad, videodate, etc., singles activities can be the perfect antidote.   You can choose to engage in activities only as your schedule permits, and participation requires just a few hours a week.   Typically it takes three or four hours to attend a singles dinner, dance, or party, or to go on a short hike, play a volleyball game on the weekend, go to a movie with a singles film group, or attend a show with a singles theater group.

7) Cost

Many singles activities don't cost much, and virtually all of them compare very favorably with the more expensive date to win options, especially videodating, and matchmakers and dating introduction services. Just how expensive are singles activities? In Southern California, currently a typical *Young Executive Singles* (*Y.E.S.*) dance costs $15. In Phoenix, a singles dance given by *Singles Scene* magazine can run you $5. In Huntsville, Alabama, a large singles dance sponsored by *Connections Flyer* is $4. At the upper end of cost is a pricy overnight ski or white water rafting trip, which can cost up to several hundred dollars if it includes a hotel stay. A *Y.E.S.* Mexican weekend cruise tops out at $400 plus per person. Organizational membership fees vary, but can run as low as $10 per year for *Sierra Club Singles*.

SOME SAMPLE SINGLES ORGANIZATIONS
Y.E.S.

Young Executive Singles is in LA and San Diego. *Y.E.S.* gives up to 20 parties a month in Los Angeles, Orange County and the San Fernando Valley. Its members are in their 20's, 30's, and 40's, and cost is $10 for a six month membership, or $15 for one year. The group sponsors a variety of singles functions, including white water rafting, tennis parties, and cruises.

Several other groups are a part of *Y.E.S.* There is the *Jewish Association of Single Professionals* (*J.A.S.P.*), age range 21 through 49; *J.A.S.P. 40 Plus*, for women 35 and up, and men 40 and over; and the *LA Social Society* (age range 20's through 50's), which holds dressier functions at upscale locations, such as the Beverly Regent Hotel.

There is also *Club 40-Something* for women 35 and up, men 40 and up, as well as a *Fellowship of Christian Singles.*

California Singles
California Singles was founded by Jill Hankoff in 1991 as an off shoot of her *Westside Singles Cycling Club.* Based in West Los Angeles, its fast-burgeoning list of activities includes white water rafting trips, progressive singles dinners (dubbed Rotation Dinner Parties by Jill), day hikes, moonlight hikes, introductory mixers held in cafes and restaurants around town, etc. It costs $129 for a one year membership, but you can instead choose to pay a slightly higher (but still very reasonable) event fee each time you go.

The Athletic Singles Association
The *Athletic Singles Association* is a club for the seriously sports minded, with branches in Los Angeles, Orange County and San Diego. The club sponsors waterskiing, tennis, cycling, sky diving, paragliding, volleyball, rollerblading - you name it. Their excursions include kayaking trips and Baja camping weekends. They also feature instruction in their sports. Members are age 25 to 55, and the club boasts a 50:50 male to female ratio. The cost is more expensive than most singles groups, about $275 per year.

Parents Without Partners
Perhaps the biggest singles association in America is *Parents Without Partners, Inc.* It's for single parents, has over 500 chapters around the country, and costs $20-75 a year in dues (depending on the local chapter). This group is terrific if you're a single parent, because it functions as a support group in addition to a source for possible dates. For further information you can call 1-800-637-7974 for a brochure. If you live in California, call 1-800-969-4797. Local chapters in your area may be listed in your local telephone directory *White Pages.* The *Parents Without*

Partners national office phone number and address is:

>*Parents Without Partners, Inc.*
>(312) 644-6610
>401 North Michigan Avenue
>Chicago, Ill 60611-4267

While the organizations we have just looked at are located only in California (except for *Parents Without Partners*), singles organizations are located all over the country. We will cover how to find those in your own area in Chapter 10.

Choosing a Singles Activity 9

TYPES OF SINGLES ACTIVITIES
Your Dating And Relationship Goal

When making your choice of an organized singles activity, keep in mind your dating or relationship *goal*. If your goal is *casual dates*, then dances and parties can work out fine. If, however, you're looking for a *serious relationship*, you might want to chose activities which are more *contact-intensive* - where you tend to meet people both for *longer* periods of time, and in situations conducive to in-depth, one-on-one conversation. Such activities include singles dinners and virtually any regular, *ongoing* singles activity with a group of people. Let's take a closer look at some specific examples of popular singles activities you can consider participating in.

1) Singles Parties And Dances

Singles dances and singles parties have traditionally been the most popular singles activities. These events encourage mingling with the tried and true opening line, "hi, would you like to dance?" Parties and dances are usually inexpensive, often as noted in the last chapter in the $4 to $15 range. A dance put on by a church or synagogue might even be free. The following are some examples of singles parties and dances held around the country. All of them, along with contact phone numbers, can be found in the *National Dating Directory* listed by state, city, and under the heading **singles activities**.

In New England, Boston's *New England Singles Network* gives parties at hotels. *Singles Alternatives* puts on singles parties throughout the state of Connecticut. In the midwest, Gail Prince in Chicago throws singles parties, and in the Detroit area *Tri-County Singles & Entertainment, Inc.* puts on singles dances and parties at upscale locations, such as country clubs. *The Meeting Group*, operating out of St. Louis, gives large singles parties on a rotating basis in 26 major cities around the country (they advertise their upcoming parties in alternative publications in each city as the target date approaches, with ads in or near the personals section). In Pittsburgh, *The Network* sponsors large parties at quality hotels, and *Nancy's Sophisticated Singles* has singles dances every weekend. In California, the *Professional Guild* gives singles parties in the San Francisco Bay Area, plus Sacramento, Stockton and Modesto. Also in the Bay Area, *Young Unattached Professionals* (*Y.U.P.S.*), located in Walnut Creek, puts on parties at nicer hotels for single people age 25 to 45. In Southern California, Dianne Bennett hosts Personal Introduction Parties costing as little as $12 (plus a cash bar), at upscale Beverly Hills locations.

Some of the videodating outlets and dating introduction services we will cover in the next two sections of the book also sponsor singles dances and parties. For example, in Tampa-St. Petersburg, Florida, *Gulf Coast Singles* and the *Bay Area Winners Circle Videodating Club* allow you to participate in social singles activities without having to enroll in their videodating programs. There's also the *Post Club* in Boston, which puts on 10 to 15 activities a month, as well as the functions at *The Dr. Kate Relationship Center* in Chicago, and those at the *Relationship Center* in St. Louis (no affiliation with Chicago). Many singles publications also hold dances and parties, and we will cover them in the next chapter.

2) Progressive Singles Dinners

The progressive singles dinner (or Rotation Dinner Party in the case of *California Singles*) is a favorite way for single people to meet. A progressive singles dinner is usually attended by an equal (or almost equal) number of men and women (e.g. 30 men and 30 women), each paying about $20 to $50, and meeting at a local restaurant. At a progressive singles dinner there's the usual singles dinner male-female-male-female seating, but with either the men or the women getting up and changing tables after each course (in practice it's usually the men).

This is a singles activity where you are *virtually guaranteed to meet people.* No one is left out, and singles dinners can be a more comfortable way to meet people than some other singles activities. For many people, making conversation in a dinner group is easier than approaching a stranger across a dance floor and risking immediate rejection. At a progressive singles dinner you simply show up and sit down between the first of several sets of two members of the opposite sex who are just as likely to initiate casual conversation with you, as you with them. If a good "facilitator" is running the show, he or she will create an open, friendly atmosphere and will also help introduce people to each other.

Singles dinners are contact-intensive activities, where you will have an opportunity to talk to people for a fairly substantial amount of time, and then decide if you're interested in pursuing things further. At the end of dinner, usually everyone socializes for a while longer, and sometimes there is a cash bar to aid further mingling. This is a good time to go back to someone you found interesting (or speak to someone you missed), and exchange phone numbers. Since singles dinners tend to be especially popular with women, men are smart to seek them out. After all, to meet single women you need to go where they can be found.

Single Gourmet

The singles dinner option includes organizations such as *Single Gourmet* in Los Angeles and *Say Gourmet* in Houston. *Single Gourmet* is a singles organization costing $99 to join for one year, plus about $35-$60 per dinner. Group members meet weekly at very nice, upscale restaurants. The quality of the locations and the people is high. The group reports about 1,500 members, and sponsors other activities aside from dinners. At Houston's *Say Gourmet* the idea is the same, but the cost is $75 for one year. If you don't live in Los Angeles or Houston, keep your eyes open for similar activities in your own city. We will give you tips on how to locate them in the next chapter.

3) Singles Lectures, Seminars And Workshops

Listings for singles lectures, seminars and workshops regularly appear in newspapers, alternative publications, and singles magazines. For example, a look at a typical issue of *COSI* magazine in Los Angeles reveals advertisements and listings for several singles seminars, including a Relationship Development Seminar and All the Good Ones Aren't Taken. Seminars are a way to learn more about available singles activities in your area, and an opportunity to meet other single people attending.

4) Outdoor Sports

Perhaps, like Jake and Linda, you are attracted to the idea of engaging in an activity which is both healthy, and where you can meet people to date. While *Sierra Club Singles* is largely limited to the West Coast, you can sometimes find local singles hiking groups in your own area. Sports singles clubs, and other organizations which sponsor athletic activities, are also a good way to get involved with sports as a singles activity. Portland, Oregon, has *Sports*

Link, and Atlanta, Georgia, singles can participate in *Singles Outdoor Adventures* (*S.O.A.*). Southern California has the previously mentioned *Athletic Singles Association, Westside Singles Cycling Club*, etc.

5) Take A Class?
One book on dating gives the advice, "classes are a great way to meet singles." The author is referring to night school courses such as a photography class, art appreciation, or most anything where you can meet members of the opposite sex. Is this sound advice? In a word: *no.* Taking a class to meet people isn't all that different from hitting on a stranger at the supermarket, or a bar, or a club, or a party. A class does offer you the opportunity to get to know people better before asking them out (or hoping they take the initiative with you), however: 1) some of the people you meet in a class will be single, and some won't; 2) even the ones who *are* single may not be there to look for a date, much less a relationship. They may simply want to learn the subject at hand.

The bottom line? Taking a class in order to meet someone of the opposite sex ignores a cardinal rule of dating to win: *you want to be sure the people you're going to meet are single, and are participating in an activity primarily because they want to meet members of the opposite sex.* You won't get this as a given at a bar, club, party, the supermarket, the bank line, the bus, the subway, a coffee shop, on the beach, or at a *class.* You *will* get this as a given at an organized singles activity.

If you want to take a class, try to make it a class for singles. For example, you can find singles classes in all sorts of sports activities. If you always wanted to learn golf, you can. Or roller blading. Or sail boarding. Or bungie jumping. Or white water rafting. Or skiing. Or square dancing for that matter. But do it with other single people! You can check for singles classes in the singles activities resources we will give in the next chapter.

Finding Local Singles Activities 10

The National Picture

Beyond your dating and relationship goal, your choice of singles activities is determined by what's available in your area. Usually, the greatest variety of organized singles activities are in cities and their suburbs. If you live in or near a large city you likely will have a variety of choices at your disposal. If you commute into a Boston, Baltimore, Philadelphia, New York, Chicago, San Francisco, etc., you can stay in town after work and attend singles activities. If you live within driving distance of a large city, you can also come in for weekend singles functions. We will cover how to utilize the nearest city for any or all of the New Dating Options in Chapter 17, Dating to Win in Oshkosh.

While organized singles activities are available across the country, in many smaller towns your choice may be limited to the most common activity: local religious sponsored functions, such as dances. If you find you are in an area which lacks a variety of singles activities - and are far from the nearest city - frankly you may want to consider using another date to win option.

The National Dating Directory

To find singles activities in your area, you will need to do a little research. The *National Dating Directory* at the back of the book is a good place to start. The *Directory* lists sample singles activities for major cities, such as New York, Los Angeles, Atlanta, Chicago, Boston, and San Francisco. More importantly, it gives local resource material for further checking, such as singles magazines which carry calendars of singles events. The *National Dating Directory* also lists activities in some smaller cities and towns. While church sponsored singles activities are not included (there are far too many to list), they can easily be found in local newspaper and magazine singles activity listings.

INFORMATION RESOURCES: MAGAZINES
AND NEWSPAPERS
If you didn't already read Chapter 4, How to Use the Personal Ads, you might want to go back and take a look, because the best source for singles activities information in your area are listings and advertisements in the same newspapers and magazines which carry personal ads. Let's take a look at these publications with singles events instead of personal ads in mind. You can consider subscribing to these newspapers and magazines if you live outside their immediate distribution area.

1) Singles Publications
Due to the plethora of personal ads available in other types of publications, singles magazines have lost their once nearly exclusive hold in the personals arena. But they still have the most complete listings for singles activities and singles organizations. The *National Dating Directory* notes whether each singles magazine listed publishes a roster of singles organizations and/or a calendar of singles events. For example, Boston's *Singles Scene* runs an extensive singles events calendar. So do *Atlanta Singles, Jewish Singles News* in New York City, *Quality Singles Lifestyles* in Pittsburgh, *Metrolina Singles* in North Carolina, and so on.

In Los Angeles the *National Singles Register* carries an ongoing list of Southern California singles organizations. *Single Connections Magazine* features an Events & Activities section listing singles functions. As noted earlier, *COSI* magazine is a also a good source for singles activities information.

Phoenix, Arizona, has *Singles Scene*, which carries a terrific calendar of activities. For example, on one weekend you can find listings for a singles party at a hotel, singles happy hours at several restaurants/bars, a singles tennis night at a resort hotel, a free golf clinic sponsored by *Singles Together*, a dance by the *Young Single Parents* branch of *Parents Without Partners*, and a dinner and a movie sponsored by *West Valley Singles*. The same publication also features a Phoenix Singles Club Directory listing about 80 singles organizations in the Phoenix area, and also gives some for nearby Tucson.

A number of singles magazines also sponsor their *own* singles activities, such as parties, dances, and even cruises. These include *SingleLife* in Milwaukee; *Dateline New England* out of Portsmouth, New Hampshire; *Ohio's Finest Singles* in Cleveland; *Trellis* magazine in San Francisco; *Singles Scene* in Phoenix; and *Connections Flyer* in northern Alabama.

2) Alternative Publications

Alternative publications are another good source for singles activities listings. The *LA Weekly* carries a weekly Bulletin Board section, with listings for singles events ranging from *California Singles* to the *Christian Singles Network*. A number of alternative publications have taken to sponsoring their own cross-promotional personals parties for single people to attend and find out more about running a personal ad. The publications hope that when potential personals advertisers see and meet the other people who are considering running ads, they will decide to sign up. However, you can also attend these parties purely as singles events.

Some alternative publications also sponsor singles events without the personals tie-in. One of the most active publications in this regard is the *Riverfront Times* in St. Louis, which routinely co-sponsors singles parties around town. The *Houston Press* regularly sponsors singles events they've dubbed "singles mingles." Other alternative publications sponsoring singles events and personals parties include the *Las Vegas New Times*, the *City Paper* in Philadelphia, the *Dallas Observer*, and the *City Paper* in Baltimore. Watch for ads in or near the personals section of the alternative publication in your area, both for their own singles events and for events sponsored by other groups.

3) Newspapers
Newspapers routinely feature a calendar which lists singles functions. In the *Los Angeles Times*, for example, there is a Singles subheading in the Calendar of Events, which currently appears in the Sunday and Thursday editions of the paper. A sampling of activities listed in the *Times* includes parties given by the *Jewish Association of Professional Singles (J.A.S.P.)* and by *Y.E.S.*. You can check your own local newspaper for singles activity listings.

4) City-Named Magazines
While city-named magazines are a more limited resource for singles events, you can check for classified ad listings next to their personal ads. Some city-named publications, such as *Baltimore* and *New York* magazines, sponsor their *own* singles parties and events. Look for announcements in their personals sections, or call them for

information.

The Yellow Pages
Singles event information can also be found in the *Yellow Pages,* listed under Dating Service. The *Yellow Pages* are also a *major* resource for locating videodating, and matchmakers and dating introduction services in your area. A caution, however, that in some localities, *Yellow Pages* listings may include adult "escort services" (which are clearly identified as such). In a very few cities, the *Yellow Pages* listings are primarily adult escort services. But in most areas this will *not* be the case. Local suburban *Yellow Pages* directories are especially good sources for *legitimate* singles activities, videodating, matchmakers and dating introduction services, and often a surprisingly large number and variety of them.

Other Information
Keep your eyes open for recorded singles information telephone lines given in any of the sources we have discussed. For example, there is a 24-hour *Singles Dance Line* serving central Massachusetts (listed in the *National Dating Directory* under Worchester, Mass.). There is a *Singles Event Info Line* in San Diego, and in San Francisco an alternative paper, the *Bay Guardian,* has a 900 number singles events line. St. Louis offers the *Heart to Heart* line, with recorded singles event information.

Major cities also have Jewish organizations which sometimes operate free recorded singles events lines, including the *JASSLINE* in Los Angeles, and the *Jewish Association Serving Singles* in Pittsburgh. New York has a *Jewish Singles Party Line* giving information on large parties at major hotels, and in San Diego there is a *Jewish Singles Club Hotline.* All the information phone lines we have mentioned can be found in the *National Dating Direc-*

tory under their city and the heading **singles activities**.

Good Luck

Remember that you can do singles activities and other date to win options *simultaneously*, in order to maximize your chances for success. For example, you can do singles activities during (or in between) running personal ads, or in addition to using a dating introduction service or match-maker. Once you have located a singles activity in your area that you're interested in, all you need to do is show up and be *open and friendly*.

Matchmakers And Dating
Introduction Services

IV

Introducing Matchmakers 11

New York City: Lisa and Edward

Lisa works as an executive recruiter in New York City. A 49-year-old divorced mother of two (a son out of college, a daughter still a student), she was married for 20 years, and now wants to remarry. Lisa is self-confident, and in her own words thinks of herself as still "looking good." She isn't desperate, and she won't just settle for anyone. She wants to "hear bells"; she wants "true love."

Not long ago she ran a personal ad in *New York* magazine, and was pleasantly surprised at the quality of the men who responded. In fact, she actually got engaged, but then changed her mind and broke it off. Recently she signed up with matchmaker Denise Winston, who's ad she'd spotted in the personals section of *New York* magazine. The ad featured a photo of Denise and copy which read in part:

> "The traditional ways of meeting someone are gone. Today, quality people prefer to meet through introductions. My clients are extremely attractive, educated, accomplished people. In the most dignified manner, allow me to introduce you to each other. I make meaningful introductions that can lead to long-lasting relationships."

Lisa called the phone number given in the ad and made

an appointment to meet with Denise. The two hit it off immediately, and Lisa decided Denise's substantial fee was worth it. After all, her kids were out of the house now, and it was time to spoil herself a bit. As an executive recruiter, she saw the logic in having someone *else* look for the right person for her. So she told Denise she was looking for a nice Jewish man with education and taste. She then met several matches set up by Denise, but not that special someone.

Now after work on a June night, Lisa is on her way to a midtown Manhattan bistro to meet her newest matchmaker date. They've already talked on the phone. It was not the be-all-and-end-all of phone calls, but it was pleasant enough. His name is Edward, he's British, he's in the computer field, and he's a WASP. So much for her nice Jewish "mensch"! But as an executive recruiter she knows that sometimes she herself finds people for the job who don't match the original employer profile. She then has to go to bat for the person, to convince the client they're the right one for the position. So, she's willing to give Denise the benefit of the doubt.

Lisa arrives at the restaurant wearing black slacks and a red Lilli Chou jacket. She waits outside for her date. Meanwhile inside Edward sips a drink. He's 51-years-old and like Lisa also divorced, but with three children instead of two. One night not too long ago Edward had been out for the evening and wound up seated next to an attractive blonde at a party. They talked, and she was quite to the point and outgoing. She told him her name was Denise Winston, and she was a matchmaker. Would he like to meet women to date in his search for a relationship? Well, yes he would.

The woman he is meeting tonight will be his fourth matchmaker date. The others had all been interesting, but not anyone he could see himself in a relationship with. After each date Denise talked with him about how it went, and how each date did or did not meet his expectations. Then later she would call him with the next match. She'd describe the date-to-be (but not show him a photo), and he could say no to meeting her if he wanted to, but he never did. It was just an evening after all, and he wanted to cooperate and meet women. Besides, each new match was a little closer to what he was looking for.

Now peering out the restaurant window, he spots an appealing looking woman standing out in front. He goes outside. "Lisa?" he queries. "Edward?" she responds. Together they go inside for dinner. Edward immediately impresses Lisa as being "sweet, charming, and witty, with a twinkle in his eye." Both will later remember immediately feeling "surprisingly comfortable" with each other.

After dinner they go to a movie, and then out for a cappuccino and more conversation. Eventually they say their goodnights with plans to see each other again. They both give Denise glowing reports of their meeting. When they talk on the phone again, Lisa invites Edward to visit her at her Long Island home to watch Fourth of July fireworks. Despite how well their first date went, Lisa confesses she felt, in her own words, "sheer terror" going into their fireworks date. What were they going to do for a whole day together? She needn't have worried. They have a terrific time, and start dating steadily. The following April they are married.

THE OLDEST DATE TO WIN OPTION
Matchmakers are probably the original New Dating Option. Matchmakers used to arrange marriages, and in parts of the world they still do.   Here in the U.S. they

usually only arrange dates, but almost always with the hope of the dates leading to relationships or marriage. Matchmaking is a thriving date to win option, and this section of the book includes information about some of the top matchmakers in the country, as well as the many dating introduction services. The first two chapters in this section are devoted chiefly to matchmakers, and the third chapter will focus on dating introduction services. All the matchmakers and dating introduction services discussed are included in the *National Dating Directory* under their state, city, and the heading **matchmakers/ introduction services**.

Matchmakers

When discussing matchmakers, we will usually be referring to the Denise Winstons of the field. They are the Cadillacs of dating to win, and their usual fee is $1,000 to $5,000. What if you can't afford a matchmaker? There is more variety and flexibility than you might expect in their rates, with some room for negotiation.   There are also less expensive matchmakers, such as Dr. Bonny Bull in Los Angeles, who charges $500 for an open-ended search. Or Marvin Roth of *Greater Pittsburgh Matchmaking Associates*, who reports that the cost to his clients is, "in the hundreds."   There is also a generally less expensive alternative - some of the dating introduction services we will discuss shortly.

Pluses To Using A Matchmaker

Why should you use a matchmaker? First, because you can afford one! Like Lisa in our success story, you can have someone *else* do the work of putting you together with dates, and hopefully a relationship. Top matchmakers stress the upscale nature of their clientele - something many people find appealing. Trish McDermot, the head of marketing for a major upscale matchmaker, the *Patricia*

Moore Group, Ltd. in California, notes that client appeal also lies in the element of *confidentiality.* For example, a CEO of a major corporation is not likely to go out and use videodating, where anyone of his employees could stumble upon his tape. He (or she) also isn't as likely to use personal ads or go to an organized singles activity. For people concerned with privacy, matchmakers can be a more discreet and less public way to date to win.

Another plus of matchmakers and dating introduction services is, 1) you are *virtually guaranteed to meet people and go on dates,* and 2) *rejection is initially largely absent* from this date to win option. In order to cooperate with the matchmaker's efforts, people usually don't turn down meeting the person the matchmaker, or a dating introduction service, proposes for them. Also, since people are being put together by a third party, they don't have to put themselves on the line by asking a stranger to go out with them - unlike, for example, with personal ads and videodating. And people don't have to take as much responsibility for the date's success (or lack of it), because a third party is setting it up. Additionally, the phone call before a date is usually a friendly "hello," not the screening session of a 900 number personal ad call.

Photos
Matchmakers almost always require that you blind date. Although a few matchmakers do allow a photo preview option, most don't. Matchmaker Debra Winkler of Los Angeles, who like most matchmakers doesn't use photos or videos, puts it simply: "pictures lie." She explains, "normally people pick people (for dating) from their *unconscious.* Let me, an *objective* person, do some picking of a suitable mate." Her criteria for doing so include "values, goals, and lifestyles." She asks clients questions like, "do you want to have children?" and "what are your

religious beliefs?"

For those people who feel seeing a photo first is *crucial*, there are some dating introduction services which offer you the opportunity to self-select your dates by photo. To avoid blind dating you also, of course, can consider using note and photo personals, videodating, or organized singles activities.

Personal Safety

For women, using a matchmaker or dating introduction service can provide a greater sense of personal security than meeting men through personal ads or at organized singles activities. Men who use a matchmaker or join a dating service, not only usually pay a fairly substantial sum of money, but are also on file - name, address, and often social security number. Since the dating is done through a third party, there is someone who knows the two of you are out together, and may indeed have set up the actual date.

A Contact-Intensive Option

Matchmakers and dating introduction services are a contact-intensive option. When you meet someone, it's for a set amount of time, anywhere from at least half-an-hour to several hours (if it's an evening date). It's a one-on-one, just-the-two-of-you situation, where you can really concentrate on each other, without the competition and distractions from other interested parties which there might be, for example, at a singles activity. It's an opportunity to get past initial first impressions and shine as a person, and to get to know your date on a more substantial level.

How To Find A Matchmaker

Top matchmakers advertise. A favorite place are city-named magazines, such as *New York, Los Angeles, Bos-*

ton, and so on. As noted, premier New York City matchmaker Denise Winston, the go-between for Lisa and Edward, currently runs a weekly ad featuring a photo of
herself in the personals section of *New York* magazine.
In Chicago, matchmaker ads can be found in *Chicago*
magazine in the classifieds, next to the personal ads.
Chicago magazine carries, for example, ads for matchmaker Page Greytok's *Selective Search, Inc.*, and Dr. Kate
Wachs' *Relationship Center.*

The *National Dating Directory* includes matchmakers in
major urban areas. You can also find them in smaller
cities and suburban areas by checking the *Yellow Pages*
under Dating Service.

How To Make Matchmaking Work For You
Every New Dating Option is a potential catalyst for change
in your life. As with all the options it's important to go
into matchmaking with an open mind, and in this case a
willingness to put yourself into someone else's hands.
As noted, Lisa found it easy to relate to this concept because she worked as an executive recruiter. She could
see the value of someone else doing the search.

Lisa's husband Edward thinks it really helped that he was
in his 50's. He knew what he wanted in a woman. For
example, he considered his ex-wife back in England too
"cold and unemotional." He felt one of his first matches
from Denise Winston was also too emotionally cold for
his taste. So, he expressed to Denise that he wanted
someone warmer and more outgoing. Lisa fit the bill. It's
also good to know when to be flexible. Lisa originally
wanted a nice Jewish man. But when Denise told her
about Edward - and that she should definitely meet him,
even though he wasn't Jewish - Lisa went ahead and did so.

Choose Carefully

While using a matchmaker involves letting go and trusting someone else, it should only be after you've carefully considered the matchmaker first. A matchmaker needs to be someone you have confidence in. Your initial phone conversation and in person interview with a prospective matchmaker is very important. Selecting a matchmaker is like choosing the right attorney, doctor, real estate agent, accountant, or anyone else you hire to work for you. And they do work *for* you. Don't be railroaded into using a matchmaker you aren't comfortable with.

Since the amounts of money involved in using a matchmaker (and some dating introduction services) can be substantial, we suggest following these steps before you spend it:

1) On the phone find out if the initial interview is free, and what is the total cost of their service.

2) Ask if they are a member of the Better Business Bureau, and call your local Better Business Bureau and inquire about whether they have received complaints about them.

3) If you find out anything negative about them from the Better Business Bureau (and maybe even if you don't), call the state's Attorney General office to check further.

4) Find out how long they have been in business. This is important, since many matchmakers and dating introduction services can come and go in six months. Your money can go with them.

5) Pin down your matchmaker on what their service is.

Exactly how many people will you meet? Is there a partial refund if the search is unsuccessful, and so forth. All this can be included in the contract most will use.

6) Find out what constitutes the matchmaker's definition of "success" for clients. It's usually two people starting to date - *not* getting married. Make sure you and the matchmaker or dating service are operating on the same wavelength on this question.

It helps to find matchmakers who have been in business for a while in the same city (e.g. Denise Winston seven years; Patricia Moore in Los Angeles for more than 10 years).

Matchmakers U.S.A. **12**

Introduction
In this chapter we will survey a sampling of matchmakers across the country.

LOS ANGELES
Debra Winkler
Back in the 1980's, Debra Winkler co-founded *Young Executive Singles* (*Y.E.S.*), which we covered under organized singles activities. She has since founded *Personal Search* in Los Angeles, which is a one-on-one matchmaking service with offices in Orange County, Los Angeles, and San Diego. Her fees range from $1,000 to $5,000. That's for up to two years of her services, with five to 15 introductions a year. Most of her clients are in their 30's and 40's, but she says she also has people from 20 to 60. She reports 700 active clients, plus access to several *thousand* other single people as potential matches, due to her extensive experience in the singles business (she says she knows "more quality single people than anyone in Los Angeles," and reports she's been the go-between for 224 marriages).

Debra, a social worker by training, begins the matchmaking process with an introductory interview. If the client signs up for her services, there is then a much longer second interview. She says she delves into what the client is looking for in terms of "appearance, person-

ality, age, ethnic background, values, sophistication, emo-
tions, habits, career, style, interests and life goals."

Her fee (like that of many other matchmakers) varies according to what she feels she will have to do to be successful in finding someone a match. (Costs can commonly include running ads in magazines and traveling to
meet potential matches). Before there is to be a date, she
discusses the two people with each other, and then the
man calls the woman. Next the two meet, often for dinner. Debra re-interviews her clients after each date to find
out how it went, and if it didn't work out, why it didn't.

Patricia Moore, Ltd.

Trish McDermot is head of marketing for *Patricia Moore,
Ltd.*, a successful matchmaker with both San Francisco
and Los Angeles offices. *Patricia Moore, Ltd.* has been in
business for over 10 years, and their fee is $4,500 for
about eight to 12 introductions. Trish McDermot stresses
the service will not engage in hard sell when you call,
and reports they turn down hard-to-place clients rather
than take their money, because they want to avoid hard-
to-match situations and subsequent unhappy clients. A
number of matchmakers report they won't take smokers,
or even a wealthy men if he's crude.

Patricia Moore, Ltd. has an impressive package of literature they will mail to you upon request. It stresses the
quality of their clients: 98% have an undergraduate degree, and 60% of men and 54% of female clients have a
"Masters level degree." These matchmakers present themselves as "your consultant in locating an appropriate life
partner," and have several hundred clients all over the state
of California and the rest of the West Coast. Some clients
own their own planes and fly into San Francisco for their
initial interviews, and later for their dates. The man com-

monly calls the woman, and then they meet. Afterwards the client fills out a questionnaire on the compatibility of the person just dated. The matchmakers use the questionnaire to aid them in successfully working on the next match.

Dianne Bennett

Based in Los Angeles, Dianne was a journalist for many years, and she feels her interviewing skills serve her well in identifying what people are really looking for in a match. Dianne's initial fee is $500 for three dates, and $500 for the next three. The frequency of dates is about one a month, and her service also includes attending premieres, dinners and parties to meet people. Dianne thinks of herself as a "personal manager" for her clients. She says she is very picky about taking on new people, and reports she has been doing matchmaking for 25 years.

Bonnie Bull, Ph.D.

Dr. Bonnie Bull is a much more low-key, less expensive, matchmaker than many of the ones we have covered so far. A psychologist, she's located in Pasadena, just to the northeast of downtown Los Angeles. Her matchmaking grew out of her therapy sessions with patients. She charges $500 for an open-ended membership. She gets to know her clients by giving them a personality test and by interviewing them. She says her matchmaking clients tend to be professionals, such as attorneys and accountants. They are people who are ready, she says, to concede that when it comes to relationships, they've "botched the job themselves," and are looking for some help.

NEW YORK
Denise Winston

Denise thinks of herself as a "love coach." This confident matchmaker and former travel agent isn't shy about her success (she reports that in 1992 she introduced 22

couples, resulting in 10 marriages). She says she (and
the Better Business Bureau) don't get complaints from
unhappy clients, and she volunteered success story couples
for us to talk to (including Lisa and Edward). She's also one
of four matchmakers (Patricia Moore was another) recommended in a June, 1991 *Cosmopolitan* article.

Denise says she does a thorough background check on
potential clients. Like several of the matchmakers interviewed, she has clients sign contracts which state that if
they misrepresent themselves to her (e.g. if a married
man signs up claiming to be single), she is entitled to
keep the fee and drop them. That fee is over $5,000 for
two years. She is willing to return half the fee should she
fail after one year.

CHICAGO
Selective Search, Inc.
Page Greytok is the woman behind *Selective Search, Inc.*,
and her ad caught our eye in *Chicago* magazine. Page is
highpowered and impressive, a former executive headhunter who sees matchmaking as similar to her old profession and she relies on her skills from that job. Her
matchmaking search costs $3,000 plus expenses, but she
also has a lower $900 annual fee to join her dating pool
of several hundred people (dating pool clients get less
intensely serviced matchmaking). More of her
matchmaking clients are men, and more of her dating
pool signees are women.

As with the other matchmakers, Page stresses that she
turns down clients for matchmaking if she feels she won't
be able to successfully match them. This can be, for
example, because they are overweight, chain smokers,
or not sufficiently well educated. Even if a man is rich
but "lacks class," she says she will pass on representing
him. She notes that she is currently doing matchmaking

searches for about 30 people, with about two or three joining per month. Her searches take her abroad, including running ads in London and Prague.

Kate Wachs, Ph.D.

Dr. Kate Wachs is the effervescent woman with seemingly boundless energy behind *The Dr. Kate Relationship Center* in Chicago. We mentioned her back in the organized singles activities section for her singles events, but she's also a matchmaker. She has two main matchmaking programs. The first is IntiMate Introductions, which currently costs $1,875 for two years, or $1,575 for one year (both payable over five installments). This service provides nine introductions a year, and unlike most matchmakers, viewing *photos* of prospective matches first *is* an option (but she notes most clients decline).

The second service Dr. Wachs offers is a special matchmaking service she's dubbed Ultimate. It's for difficult matchmaking searches and costs clients extra. For example, she charged one woman $1,200 extra, while another time (the most expensive ever) it cost the client $10,000. Dr. Wachs has been in business 10 years, and says that as a psychologist she screens people to eliminate "psychos and gameplayers," and tends to attract clients who like the fact they are getting coaching and counseling from a therapist.

She also is very active in the American Psychological Association, and has made many media appearances, including *Oprah* and *Donahue*. Dr. Wachs dubs her center "the country's first and only full-service introduction and relationship center." As mentioned it includes singles functions, and even helps people write personal ads. The center also does marital and sexual dysfunction therapy.

Other Matchmakers

There are numerous other matchmakers available around the country: *Mandy's Matchmaking* in New Jersey; Ann Wood and *Leora Hoffman Associates* in the Washington, D.C., area; Abby Hirsch and Kathryn Hason in New York City, etc. To find them check the *National Dating Directory* or your *Yellow Pages* under Dating Service, or look for ads in publications in your area.

If matchmakers sound like the right choice for you - and you can afford them - go for it. If you like the general concept (but not the prices!) read on to find out more about dating introduction services.

Succeeding With Dating Introduction Services

13

Types Of Dating Introduction Services

Dating introduction services run the gamut from inexpensive computer dating services to the ever more popular (and more expensive) urban lunchtime matchmaking services; and from local independent dating services to outlets for large national chains. Cost can vary greatly. The Los Angeles based computer dating service, *Selectra Date*, currently charges $35 for a minimum of five matches, while lunchtime dating services commonly run in the $400 to $700 range. A typical membership in *MatchMaker International*, a national dating service chain reporting over 90 branches around the country with over 100,000 members, typically costs from about $1,000 to $1,500.

The list of suggested routine checks - the Better Business Bureau, length of time in business, etc. - appearing at the end of Chapter 11 applies here too. While the amounts of money involved are often smaller, a $1,000 membership with *MatchMaker International* is nothing to sneeze at, and you want to make sure your local outlet has a good reputation. You also want to consider how many members a service has, especially in your age range. Additionally, chain services are to some extent only as good as the person running each local outlet, and this can vary from city to city. Dating services also probably won't provide quite the same one-on-one service as a matchmaker.

Now let's examine in detail examples of the different kinds of dating introduction services to choose from.

1) National Dating Service Chains
In addition to costing less than upscale matchmakers, dating introduction services are available nationally, including many in smaller cities. *MatchMaker International*, which started in Buffalo, New York, has branches in many mid-size cities, plus in suburban areas such as Fort Lee, New Jersey, and also larger cities like Philadelphia, where they have four outlets.

The chief rival for *MatchMaker International* in the national dating service business, *Together Dating Service*, also advertises over 100,000 members and 90 outlets around the country. They're in cities like Memphis and Knoxville, Tennessee; Charleston, South Carolina; Greensboro, North Carolina; Providence, Rhode Island; and they have three outlets in the Philadelphia area.

We interviewed *MatchMaker International* Marketing Director, Jim Lallemand, about how *MatchMaker* works. He told us applicants fill out a personality profile covering such areas as "religious attitudes and conformability." Clients are also interviewed to discuss relationships and what they're looking for in another person.

After joining, each person is given the name of one potential match at a time. Both parties are notified simultaneously, and both agree to meet before they are given each other's phone numbers. No photos are used, so it's a blind date. *MatchMaker International* recommends their matches keep their first meeting simple (e.g. a cup of coffee), to see how it goes. After the initial meeting, both report back to the agency on how it went before they are set up with someone else.

The base cost is $1,000, on up to a special individualized VIP membership for $5,000. But the average is about $1,500 for a one-and-a-half to two year membership. There's a minimum of 18 matches with a two year membership. Jim concedes there is flexibility in cost, with *room for negotiating*. People *MatchMaker* finds desirable (usually because they are in short supply on their membership rolls, for example women under 30 and men over 45), can try to negotiate a better deal for *under* $1,000.

Getting The Best Deal

With any dating introduction service (or matchmaker) you should always try for the best deal you can get. Two key rules to follow are: 1) get in for the *least money* possible, and 2) sign up for the *shortest period of time* they will let you. If you can get it, shoot for a six month, or eight month membership. You can always extend your membership later. The idea is to protect yourself by putting the least money at risk. Only spend what you have to, in case the service goes out of business (as mentioned there is a very high turnover in the dating business). One factor in considering the two major chains is that *MatchMaker International* and *Together Dating Service* outlets are probably more likely to still be around in a year or two.

MatchMaker's Jim Lallemand considers videodating (e.g. *Great Expectations*) his major competition as a dating service. Indeed, both *MatchMaker* and *Together* don't have outlets in California, home of *Great Expectations*. But Jim feels *MatchMaker* has some advantages over videodating. He says there is more emphasis on compatibility. The selection process is done *for* people, and is more "objective," he feels, than people doing their own selecting; and, unlike videodating, *there is virtually no upfront rejection* of potential dates.

2) Local Dating Services

There are also local dating services which compete with *Together* and *MatchMaker*, and they are sometimes located where the national chains aren't. To give you an idea of what's available, the following are some local examples from around the country. In Philadelphia, *Connections* uses a psychologist to aid in matchmaking, costs $700 for six months and $1,200 for a year, and reports that the average client gets one match per month. *Connections* also provides the option of using photos if you insist, and notes they've been in business 19 years. In Cleveland, Ohio, *Encounters By Karen* is a dating service costing just $95 for two months, with 15 introductions. Karen says she has 400 members and has been in business 20 years. *Date Mate* in Tampa-St. Petersburg, Florida, allows *you* to do the matching, using photos and profile information sheets. It's $125 for 10 introductions, and they report 1,000 members.

A Sample City

Now let's take a look at a sample mid-sized city - Rochester, New York - to see what options are available there. Rochester has several local dating services and demonstrates the range of choices you may have in your own area. Current Rochester options include *Better Beginnings*, costing $150 for a four month membership. There's also *Heart to Heart* at $100 for six months, plus $15 for each selection you meet. Like most dating services *Better Beginnings* does the choosing for you, while *Heart to Heart* uses profile fact sheets and photos, and *you* do the selecting. Also in Rochester, *Date Mate* gives you a choice of using photos or not using photos. They do the initial selecting, but you make the final choice of who to meet. The cost is $195 for three months and six introductions or, if you don't use photos, $185 for six months.

Under the Hartford, Connecticut, listing in the *National Dating Directory*, both the *Jewish Dating Service* and its sister organization, the *New England Dating Service*, were impressive when we talked with them. They seem to avoid customer hard sell, and were very forthcoming with information. Fees run $400-$800 for six months to two years, with a minimum of one match per month. They serve New York and New Jersey in addition to Connecticut.

3) Computer Dating

Computer dating is usually the least expensive type of dating introduction service. *Selectra Dates* ($35 for five matches), reports they've been in business for 25 years. When computer dating with *Selectra Date*, both the man and woman receive each other's name and phone number, and then talk by phone and decide if they want to go out. It's more of a you-are-on-your-own option, especially when compared with a dating service like *Together.* Candidly, we suspect there may be less serious compatibility testing with computer dating. On the other hand, if the price is right, it's still worth it, if only as a way to get out and meet people with the advantage of a third party paving the way by introducing you.

Comp-U-Match in Las Vegas combines computer dating and videodating, with memberships costing from $399 to $2,000. Some of the other dating services we've mentioned earlier also use computers to aid in matching.

4) Lunchtime Matchmaking

Currently very popular in major cities is the lunchtime dating service. Generally you are interviewed, sign up, and then meet people over lunch. A big difference among these services is that with some services you and your match set up the lunch, while with others the service does it for you. Some examples of lunch date introduction services available around the country include the following:

Los Angeles: *Lunch Dates* - $495 for one year and 24 introductions. Matches talk on the phone and set up lunch themselves.

San Francisco: *How About Lunch* - $400 for one year and six introductions. The service sets up the lunch, you both pay dutch.

Chicago: *It's Just Lunch!* - $500 for six lunches. They set up lunch, you meet and go dutch.

Philadelphia: *Let's Go Dutch!* - $400 for six months and six dates, they set up lunch, and there's no contact between matches ahead of time.

New York: *Lunch Dates* - $495 for one year and 18 introductions. This is the New York branch of LA's *Lunch Dates*. New York also has a branch of Chicago's *It's Just Lunch*.

Boston: *LunchDates* - $850 for 20 introductions, and they set up lunch, with no advance contact between matches. They have a number of branches in the Boston area. Boston also has *Lunch Couples*: $275 for five introductions, and matches talk and decide how to meet each other.

Boston shows the main lunch date choices: 1) advance contact or no advance contact between the matches, and 2) the service sets up lunch, or the matches set it up. *LunchDates* operates with no advance contact, and they point out the advantage for women who may be concerned about privacy and safety. The man doesn't even have her phone number, and the arrangement allows her to give him her number only *after* she meets him, *if* she decides to. On the other hand, there's more flexibility with *Lunch Couples*, since you can easily re-schedule lunch if you need to, and you can know more about meeting each other since you've talked directly first.

How To Find Dating Introduction Services

The *National Dating Directory* lists more than 80 outlets for *MatchMaker International* and *Together Dating Service*, along with dozens of other services around the country. As with matchmakers, the local *Yellow Pages* are an excellent source for information which can be found under Dating Service. There are also ads in alternative publications, city-named magazines (in both cases near the personals section), and singles publications.

Now lets move on to the final New Dating Option, videodating.

Videodating   V

Introducing Videodating ⸻ 14

Los Angeles: Ann and David

Ann is in the *Great Expectations* Los Angeles/Encino office, waiting for her turn to do her video. Nervous about coming across as too serious and unapproachable on her tape, she's brought along her fun, high energy friend Jennifer to help keep the mood light. As Ann waits for her on-camera interview, Jennifer keeps her smiling and laughing.

Ann goes in to do her video, and emerges a little while later confident she came across as friendly and approachable. Bringing Jennifer along was a smart move, but then Ann is a smart woman. She's a successful professional, and holds a Masters Degree in her field. Ann's co-workers sometimes find her a bit dour and career-driven, and she herself admits she's a bit "impenetrable." With her offbeat good looks and lean figure, she knows many men find her appealing, but she just can't seem to meet the right "type" of guy. She wants to have children, and her biological clock is ticking.

Ann comes from a warm and loving family, and always assumed one day she would get married. After all, her parents had been happily married for almost 40 years. So, it was with some dismay that Ann went into her 30's still single, and with no real prospects for a serious relationship on the horizon. She was increasingly frustrated by the lack of balance in her life - her professional success versus what she had begun to perceive as failure in her personal life.

Finally, at age 36, she decided to do something she never in a million years thought she'd ever seriously consider. She paid a visit to *Great Expectations* to find out about videodating. Always a goal-directed achiever type, she allowed herself be talked into a full three year membership for an amount of money she isn't comfortable talking about.

Now Ann wonders what her future holds. Will she meet the husband-to-be she's looking for? Or, will joining *Great Expectations* turn out to be a waste of time and money?

David

David, 34-years-old and successful in a technical manufacturing career, has also never been married, and has also decided to try videodating. Somewhat less serious and more affable than Ann, he received a mailer from *Great Expectations*, and decided to go down and find out more about it. He visits the same suburban Encino *G/E* location Ann does. In David's case he limits his membership to one year, but it still costs him a healthy $1,200. After signing up he does his video.

Once a week Ann makes herself go down to *G/E* to look through the three ringed binders filled with photos and profile information fact sheets. The profiles contain information such as height, weight, religion, whether a person smokes, do they want children, and most helpful of all, they include snapshot photos. She selects the most promising men and then screens their videos. On each visit to *G/E* she makes herself pick at least one guy to request a date with. Meanwhile she turns down the first guy who picks her, because there was just *no* potential with him.

David also comes in to look through the three ringed binders filled with profiles and photos. He spots a couple of women who look interesting, including Ann, screens their videos, and fills out the request form to meet them. Ann gets his request and takes a look at his video. He seems like a nice guy, doesn't look bad, so she decides to take a chance with him.

Meanwhile, David is a little annoyed that one of other woman he's picked is taking her sweet time about going through with their date - despite saying "yes" to his request, and agreeing to meet him when they talked on the phone. Then he gets back the positive response from Ann, along with her phone number, and gives her a call. The conversation goes well, and they go out on a date and hit it off immediately. They are in fact each other's *first* videodates. Because of this, they are understandably skeptical of the serious relationship which quickly follows. Meanwhile, Ann's friends at work marvel at the change in her. She's more outgoing, more "fun," and obviously enjoying her life more. Ann is falling in love.

After dating for several months Ann and David move in together. Soon they are engaged, their skepticism about their good fortune meeting each other so quickly having long since disappeared. Ann pays off her credit card *Great Expectations* bill, and feels it was well worth the cost, although she wishes she had signed up for a shorter (and less expensive!) period of time. In the spring of 1994, Ann and David are married in a large church wedding. They decide to start working on having a baby on their honeymoon.

PRE-SCREENING BY VIDEO

Why do people choose videodating as their New Dating Option? No doubt an important reason for many people is that like organized singles activities, videodating *eliminates blind dating.* Videodating allows people to *thoroughly pre-screen* potential dates - including how they look - *before* meeting them in person.

With videodating you have information about people available from their profile fact sheet, plus what they say about themselves on their tape. Do they have kids? Do they want kids? Have they been married? Are they a smoker? Do they stay in shape? What is their occupation? What are their religious beliefs? What are their interests? All this can be found out *before* you ask them out (or say "yes" to their own dating request). It can be found out before you even talk to them.

It's true that some of the other date to win options also allow you to pre-screen people before you meet in person. With 900 number personals you pre-screen by phone, but without knowing what they look like. With matchmakers and dating introduction services you usually have to trust a third party to screen *for* you. With organized singles activities, you can see what someone *looks* like, but you have to talk to them without first knowing anything else about them. The only other date to win options that offer the same advantage as videodating are note and photo personal ads, and those dating introduction services and matchmakers which use photos. And in both those cases you can't find out as much about potential dates before talking to them as you can with videodating.

Videodating And Women's Safety

Like matchmakers and dating introduction services,

videodating can provide women with a sense of personal security that's missing from the personal ads and organized single activities. As with men who join matchmaking and dating introduction services, the men who sign up with *Great Expectations*, and many other videodating services, have not only usually paid a substantial sum of money for the privilege, but are on file with their name, address, photo, and video. Dating is done through the videodating outlet in writing, and every pairing leaves a paper trail. A third party knows that you two are meeting.

Cost
Videodating is one of the most expensive date to win options. Many videodating services will try to sell you a lifetime membership, or one good for several years. For *Great Expectations* a three year membership can cost you about $2,000. A shorter one year membership costs about $1,200. However, *G/E* will *not* reveal these figures to you over the phone; rather you will have to come and get them as part of a sales pitch. While *G/E* fees are *not* usually negotiable, fees at non-*G/E* videodating services often are. Videodating services will commonly let you pay on an installment plan, but if you pay upfront instead (such as by check or credit card), you can sometimes negotiate a better deal.

As with dating introduction services, you have more leverage in negotiating a less expensive membership if you're considered "desirable." That means a woman in her 20's, for example, or a man in his 40's. Videodating outlets, like dating introduction services, usually have too many men in their 20's, and too many women over 40. They want younger women (who can be asked out by both men their own age and by older men), and older men who can be potential videodates for both women their own age and younger. (Videodating in this competitive environment can be tough for women over 40, and they should keep this in mind when deciding which date to win option is the right one for them).

Passive Memberships

Some videodating outlets (although not *G/E*) offer "passive memberships," which allow you to do a video and be on file to be selected, but not choose people yourself. A passive membership is substantially cheaper than a full membership, and tends to be used much more by women than men. A passive membership, however, negates the opportunity presented by dating to win for a woman to take the initiative and do her *own* selecting of the men she'd like to go out with. Passive memberships are not usually a good idea for men, unless they are convinced that they have so much to offer a lot of women will choose them.

How To Find Videodating Outlets

The *National Dating Directory* lists many videodating options around the country, including all the current *Great Expectations* branches. Another good idea is to check your local *Yellow Pages* under Dating Service. If there's a *Great Expectations* outlet available, they will be listed, and likely will also have a hard-to-miss ad. You can also check for videodating ads near the personal ads in alternative publications, singles magazines, and city-named magazines such as *Los Angeles, Philadelphia, Boston, New York, Washingtonian*, etc. Outside of major cities and their suburbs, it's hard to find videodating outlets; videodating is the most limited date to win option in terms of complete national availability.

THE GREAT EXPECTATIONS STORY

Great Expectations opened its first videodating location in Los Angeles in 1976. Today there are more than 40 outlets in cities around the country, including Baltimore, Boston, Chicago, Cleveland, Columbus, Dallas, Denver, Detroit, Houston, Los Angeles, Miami, Milwaukee, Minneapolis-St. Paul, Nashville, Philadelphia, Phoenix, Pittsburgh, San Diego, San Francisco, Seattle, and St. Louis. There are also many independent local non-*Great Expectations* videodating services around the country, some of them quite good, and we will explore them shortly. But it's *Great Expectations* which has been around the longest, has the most members to choose from, and has become synonymous with videodating. Your local *Great Expectations* outlet is also more likely than the competition to still be around and in business six months after you sign up. (In fact, over the years *G/E* has bought out a number of it's less successful competitors).

Great Expectations was founded by Jeffrey Ullman. He is considered quite a character, and in a recent 1994 *Los Angeles Times* profile he was dubbed "the love God from Hell" for his drive and his antics (like firing his own sister from the company). However, he has put together a topnotch, very well organized operation which boasts over 100,000 members. Unlike the dating introduction service business equal-footed rivalry between *MatchMaker International* and *Together Dating Service*, no other videodating company even remotely approaches the size and success of *Great Expectations*.

G/E is the leader and innovator in the videodating field. Recently, for example, *G/E* in Los Angeles has started offering videodating using computers to call up members by height, age, etc., and see their photo on the screen, plus the information on their member profile sheets (after that you still screen their video). The membership fee for this particular service is a little more expensive than a regular one, about $2,300 for a year.

When you join *G/E*, they present you with an 86 page handbook entitled *How To Be A Great Success At Great Expectations*. The booklet is quite helpful, and the advice is usually solid. It encourages being flexible in the standards you set for choosing your videodates, and being open to accepting dating requests from other members without insisting on absolute perfection. There are exercises to help you focus on what you are looking for in another person, and the handbook includes a First Impressions Member Review sheet to take notes on people as you peruse the member profile sheets and videos. Also included are basic tips for making your video.

G/E Versus The Competition
As noted, there are also other videodating possibilities aside from *Great Expectations*. Some may be better (more consumer-friendly, cheaper, have more local members), and some are located in areas where there is no *G/E* outlet available. Let's look at a sampling of other videodating opportunities around the country, including their cost.

San Francisco Bay Area
Video Introductions is the East Bay alternative to *Great Expectations* (there are four *G/E* outlets in the Bay Area), and is located in Concord. As opposed to *Great Expectations*, they *will* give you a price quote over the phone, are *very* consumer-friendly, and do not use hard sell. They have been in business since 1977, which is an unusually long time. Their fee is $1,495 for three years, with an unlimited number of selections allowed. They also have a terrific passive plan which is very popular with women, and costs just $50 (you do a video, keep it on file, and can be selected, but cannot make selections yourself). While some other videodating services around the country have a passive plan option, nowhere did we find it even close to being this inexpensive.

Boston

In Boston two alternatives to *Great Expectations* are the *Post Club* and the *Mazel Dating Service*. The *Post Club* is a member-controlled social club with a onetime $1,000 membership fee, plus dues of about $25 a month. It features many social activities, including progressive singles dinners, along with videodating (with 50 to 60 selections allowed per year).

The *Mazel Dating Service* is run by Allison Sherman. She promises no hard sell, has been in business more than 10 years, and charges $900 for a one year membership, with an unlimited number of selections. Incidentally, Allison (who also teaches a course on how to be married in a year) successfully used the *Boston* magazine personals to find her husband.

Milwaukee

In addition to *Great Expectations*, in Milwaukee there is *Single Attractions, Inc.* Founder Barbara Zaugg says they are the oldest videodating service in the city, have been in business for 10 years, and are responsible for about 500 marriages. They currently have about 1,000 members, and the minimum cost to join is $495 for one year. For that you make your video and come in once a month and can select up to three people to meet. You can also pay a higher fee (in the $700 to $800 range) for more visits and a more liberal selection policy. Either way there is no limit on how many people can choose you. Barbara says she also does some introduction work, recommending people to each other who are in the videodating program and who she thinks will be a match.

Tampa-St. Petersburg

Less expensive than the local Tampa-St. Pete *Great Ex-*

pectations outlet are the *Bay Area Winners Circle Video Dating Club* and *Gulf Coast Singles*. We mentioned them earlier under organized singles activities. Both clubs put on social activities you can attend before joining to get an idea if they're for you. With memberships available in the $300 to $400 dollar range, if you live in the area you might want to find out more about them. In both cases they have 400 plus members. This is still a fairly limited number for videodating, so be sure to check how many of the members appear to be men/women, and in your age range. You may also want to compare this with the local *Great Expectations* outlet, which although more expensive may have a larger membership.

Nebraska, New Hampshire, Ohio, Etc.

Many other local videodating services are available across the country. For example, in Omaha, Nebraska, *New Beginnings Video* has been in business for 14 years, and costs about $1,000 for an open-ended membership. *Videodates* in Nashua, New Hampshire, has over 1,000 members, and has been in business five years. This service costs $700 plus for six months and has a lower fee available for a passive membership.

Visual Choice International in Columbus, Ohio, reports 3,000 members, and a $795 until-you-are-married membership. *Single Station* in Tulsa, Oklahoma, says they have almost 3,000 members and have been in business 14 years, but they don't give price quotes over the phone. *Times Remembered* in Providence, Rhode Island, also won't give a price quote over the phone but reports that cost is in "the low hundreds." *VIA Video Dating Service* in Austin, Texas, costs $500 for one year, with 50 selections allowed. They are very forthcoming, low key and friendly on the phone.

The Videodating Experience

15

RICK: MY OWN VIDEODATING EXPERIENCE

Before I used the personal ads, I tried videodating. The videodating service I used shall remain anonymous, but it wasn't *Great Expectations*. Let's simply call it *LA Videodating*. I don't remember how I first heard about them, but they probably mailed me a flyer. I called and tried to get an indication over the phone of what it would cost. A woman told me nicely but firmly, "I'm sorry, we don't give price quotes over the phone." Leaving little room for argument, she continued, "first we screen applicants with an interview before deciding if they are suitable for membership, and then we discuss the cost of the different plans to join."

My Appointment

I went in for my screening appointment. *LA Videodating* was located in a modern office in a nice part of town. I walked into a large room which looked like a cross between an office reception area and a library. The woman at the counter gave me a fact sheet about myself to fill out, and I sat down on a couch and went to work.

In between writing, I looked around the spacious room. Soft rock music was piped in, and there were a number of tables with people at them, as well as rows of videocassettes on shelves along the wall. There were also rows of three ringed black binders below the videos -

binders which I soon found out were filled with alpha-
betized profile fact sheets (like the one I was filling out),
along with photos of each member. The main room was
very quiet, with little conversation between people. I
noticed the women were using several tables, and the
men were at separate ones. The main social interaction
was occurring behind the reception counter among the
employees, which included several attractive women and
good looking men.

I went back to filling out the information sheet, which
included facts about myself, such as an (optional) income
level classification (e.g. $20,000 and under, $20,000 -
$35,000, $35,000 -$50,00; $50,000 - $75,000, over $75,000);
my education level; where I lived; and my occupation. It
also asked for information about what kind of person I
was looking for, including age range, smoker/non-smoker,
how far away they could live, their race, religion, their
interests, if they had children, etc.

When I was finished, a guy came over to give me a tour.
We walked past a long row of about a dozen video screening cubicles. Each cubicle had a small TV monitor with a
built-in VCR. In some cubicles a man or woman sat with
headphones on, watching five minute video interviews
of other members.

The Sales Pitch
My tour guide then introduced me to a pretty, blonde
thirtysomething saleswoman. She took me into a room,
looked over my information sheet, and asked me what I
was looking to get out of videodating. "A lasting relationship," I replied. She told me videodating was the
right way for me to achieve my goal, and stressed "it just
takes one person" to make the whole thing worthwhile.

She encouraged me to look through a couple of the binders filled with female members' profile fact sheets. They were organized by first name in alphabetical order, and each one included at least one photo. To protect privacy no last names were used, and no phone numbers or addresses were included. A sufficient number of the women appeared to be appealing, and I was ready to go on to the next step.

A Lifetime Membership?

She pitched me on a "lifetime membership" for $2,500. When I blanched, she came down quickly to a one year membership at $1,850. When I made it obvious I was about to leave, she came down below $1,000, to $800 for a "special six month membership." I told her it still was too expensive. She asked me to wait a minute, while she talked with her boss to see what she could do for me.

A few minutes later she came back with another offer. Was I prepared to pay in advance (in other words not on an installment plan)? Well, yes, I planned on using my credit card. How about $675 for six months? Well, that sounded pretty good (especially after the figures she'd been talking about). So I said, "I'd like to think about it overnight and then decide."

"I'm very sorry, that's not an option," she replied. "The offer is only good today." Hmmm. I was not happy to be put into a corner. "Tell you what," she said, "we'll make it eight months instead of six, and remember, if you meet somebody and want to go inactive for a couple months, that doesn't count against your eight months." Well, after all, I had decided to do something about my dating and relationship search, so I said, "sign me up." I did get the best deal I ever heard of anyone receiving (a couple of women I videodated both paid about $1,000 for a one year membership).

A Photo
She gave me the option of bringing in my own photos or having *LA Videodating* take a couple Polaroids for free to include with my information profile sheet. I elected to let them take the photos, and was now ready to make my video.

The Video
A room was set up with a camera on a tripod. The interviewer was a pleasant woman in her 20's, who talked to me first for a few minutes before we started. She told me I could redo the video for free anytime, if I was unhappy with it. Then, standing off-camera, she asked me questions about myself. We did about a five minute video on who I was, where I was from, and what kind of woman I was looking for. When I screened the tape afterwards, I was pleasantly surprised. I thought I came off as relaxed, approachable, and as appealing as could reasonably be expected.

Screening Videos
Weekend mornings were a good time to come in to look for potential matches. The place wasn't too crowded, and the screening cubicles - which tended to sometimes all be in use - were available. First, I perused the binders and the profile fact sheets and photos. I found it was surprisingly tough to pick women to request dates with. It was easy to find something "wrong" with most of them. Often, it was simply how they looked in their photo. They didn't fit my picture of who I could see having a relationship with (fuzzy as that picture was). Sometimes it appeared from their profile sheet that we probably just didn't have a whole lot in common.

After an hour or more of reading profile sheets and looking at photos, I would have a few member videocassette numbers and some scribbled names and notes on the women who looked interesting (i.e. physically appealing and reasonably intelligent). Then I'd screen the videos that appeared to be worthwhile. Each individual cassette had four or five women on it, and I would fast-forward down and find the right one according to the counter numbers listed on the cassette.

Women On Tape

It was even tougher to pick women once I saw their video. There was almost always something "wrong" with them as potential candidates for my desired serious relationship. Over a period of five months, picking one or two a weekend, I did eventually find 19 women I wanted to date. Of these, several were "out of my league" - very attractive "wish list" choices. But the rest were not any more physically good looking than other women I'd dated.

Asking For A Date

The procedure for dating was to ask the person out by writing down their first name and member number, and turning in the slip at the front desk. A woman I'd selected would be informed via computer printout the next time she checked in that I was interested in meeting her. She could go look at my profile fact sheet and photo, and then - if she felt I was a potential "yes" - my video. I would come back and retrieve my own computer printout at the front desk to see her response. In addition, any woman who had asked to date *me* would also appear on the printout, and in that case, I would go check out *her* fact sheet, photos, and video.

Only two of the 19 women I picked in my time with LA Videodating said "yes" to going out. Coming in and getting my computer printout became a bit of an exercise in frustration. Because each choice - and their subsequent negative response - was added to, and remained on, the computer printout, each time I picked up a new printout I was greeted by an ever-growing list of women's first names, with their member number, and a "no" after them. I felt that if I only had a chance to meet in person the women I was trying to date, I'd have a shot with them; but I wasn't getting the opportunity.

Is It My Video?

I went back and took a look at my video several times to see what was wrong with it. The answer? Nothing. Well, nothing that couldn't be cured by me being better looking, or a little more glib. Actually, I was pleased at how relaxed and friendly I came across. I thought I'd done a pretty good job! I would decide each time not to take advantage of the standing offer to redo my video.

The Ones Who Picked Me

Three women asked to go out with me. One of these was a no-go because she was *extremely* overweight. The other two I was more open to meeting (and because of my own experience being rejected, I would have said yes to *anyone* who wanted to meet me who was at *all* a dating possibility). I met one of the two women (an attorney) for brunch, and met the other woman for a drink. Both were nice enough, and the attorney and I dated once again for a movie. I also met the two women *I'd* picked - but nothing developed with either one.

That was my videodating experience. Was my lack of success due to something intrinsic about videodating, or was it somehow my own fault? After all, my experience obviously is not true for everyone - Ann and David can attest to that - and *Great Expectations* reports that nationally they are responsible for five marriages a week.

So, what was my problem? Did I pick women based too much on their looks, and not enough on potential compatibility? Did I come across much more poorly than I realized on my tape? Was I just the victim of an unlucky streak, and should have picked 19 *more* women before giving up? There's probably some truth to *all* of these reasons. Looking back on it, I very likely was picking potential dates based too heavily on their looks. I also should have stuck with videodating longer, and selected more women before throwing in the towel.

Unfortunately, when a person tries videodating (or *any* date to win option) they may be at a point where they need a dating confidence *booster* (I did). After all, you aren't always dating to win at a time when you feel great about yourself and your love life. In fact, you may feel shaky and insecure, and a bad videodating experience can quickly exacerbate that. Sticking with it can be difficult.

In the next chapter we will examine videodating more closely, including the mistakes I made. You can avoid these mistakes, know more about videodating, and hopefully be more successful than I was if you choose this date to win option.

Videodating: Pitfalls And Tips

16

RICK: THE NATURE OF VIDEODATING

There are qualities intrinsic to videodating which are unique among the New Dating Options. Sometimes they can be a negative, and you need to be ready to overcome them if you want to successfully use this date to win option (and avoid making the same mistakes I realized later that I made).

1) No Direct Contact

With videodating, despite your best efforts you can have trouble being able to talk directly to people, much less meet them in person. You can be rejected without any opportunity to "sell" yourself in person (or even on the phone). The video itself isn't the same as real contact in person (you can be nervous on your tape, it's not a two-way conversation, etc.).

2) Rejection

Rejection is a built-in part of videodating. Buried in the middle of the *Great Expectations* handbook is the following: "*Our statistics indicate that Members are accepted on average once for every four selections.*" Because of this, *G/E* recommends you pick *five* people a week to average *one* date, since you will be shot down three times on average for every one person who says "yes."

I selected 19 people over five months. By *G/E*'s law of

averages I should have had about five "yes" responses, but with a little bad luck, it was easy to get *two.* *You should try to pick the five people a week G/E recommends, regardless of which videodating service you use.*

3) Looks And Too Much Data

There is a risk in videodating of making decisions about people based too heavily on looks, since you have so much *visual* information about them, rather than selecting by real potential compatibility. Additionally, the profile fact sheet, snapshots, and video can actually provide you with *too much data,* and make it *harder* to make a dating decision. With all this data there can simply be *too many reasons to reject someone, and for them to reject you.* In my own case I found myself going back to re-screen a video a second and even a third time trying to decide whether to choose someone, or respond to their request with a "yes."

The video alone supplies a tremendous amount of information, as you examine it with a critical eye. Do they talk with a grating New Jersey accent? Do they try to tell a joke and aren't funny? Do they sound smart, or do they sound stupid? Are they relaxed and appealing, or nervous and uptight? Do they smile, don't they smile? How are they dressed? Would your parents approve of them? Would you be proud to introduce them to your friends? *Could you see them as your husband or your wife?*

4) The Perfect Date Syndrome

Videodating can provide too many reasons to reject all but the "perfect" potential date/mate. Moreover, videodating itself predisposes you to evaluate candidates with a critical eye. You're spending a lot of money, after all, and you are more likely using videodating if you're looking for a serious relationship/husband/wife. You're probably less likely to use videodating for casual dates than someone using personal ads or organized singles activities. So why go out with someone you aren't sure is a major candidate to be that very important person in your life?

As noted earlier, the name of this book is *Date to Win*, and if you subject every potential videodate to the scrutiny of "could I see this person as my serious relationship/husband/wife," instead of thinking of them only as a *casual date* at this point, you may end up not choosing anyone - and rejecting the ones who select you.

5) The Control Thing

Videodating appeals to the *"control freak"* in all of us. We often don't want to risk an uncomfortable situation by going out with someone we aren't sure about. We can be tempted to avoid anything short of what appears to be a potential guaranteed successful date. But many happy couples who met through the other New Dating Options, *never* would have met had they done videodating - they never would have considered the other person as a "prospect" for dating. Kathy says she would have turned me down if she'd seen a video or a photo first. Linda - who met Jake on that *Sierra Singles* hike - also says she would have turned *him* down if she'd seen a video first.

6) Too Much Commitment

Saying "yes" to dating someone when videodating can imply more commitment and interest than with the other New Dating Options, because you do have all that profile sheet information about them, plus you've seen a photo and a video. This can freeze you into inaction if you are on the fence about selecting someone or responding back with a "yes" to their request to meet you.

Your Photo

I also made a couple of *my own* basic mistakes when videodating - mistakes which you can avoid. The photo (or photos) you include with your profile sheet can be *crucial* to your videodating success. Many people will not bother looking at your *video* when deciding whether to say "yes" to your dating request; they will simply look at your *photo* included with the profile sheet. Allowing a polaroid (generally not the best quality photo to begin with) taken by the videodating service to make or break your videodating experience is a *major* error, and one I made. As with note and photo personals, either use a *very flattering* snapshot or go to an inexpensive photography studio and get a good headshot of yourself. The goal is to successfully self-market yourself, in order to get people to proceed to the next step in the process - taking a look at your video.

What Are You Looking For?

I was also unclear as to what I was looking for in a woman, beyond some sort of physical attraction. This was, I suspect as much a problem as the photo I used. The more clear you are on what you are looking for in a person in terms of *values* and potential *genuine compatibility*, the better your chances of connecting with someone. The more you simply rely on looks in choosing people, the less successful you are likely to be.

To the preceding let's also add some handy rules to keep in mind when shopping for and signing up with a videodating service.

TIPS WHEN SHOPPING FOR A VIDEODATING SERVICE

Rule number one: *Do comparison shopping* if there's a

choice of videodating services in your area. Since *Great Expectations* will try to hard sell you on the spot (and may succeed), you probably want to visit the competition first. Call a *G/E* competitor and tell them you're looking around at videodating options, but that you haven't visited *Great Expectations* yet. If you like how the competitor sounds on the phone, go in and visit. Since they know you're also going to probably visit *G/E*, they will tell you why you should go with them instead, and they are more likely to offer you the best deal they can. But don't sign up just yet (even if *they* try hard sell); go visit *G/E*. Now tell *G/E* you've already been to the other videodating outlet, and let *G/E* try to convince you why you should go with them instead. If they have negotiating flexibility, you are more likely to then get the best deal from *G/E* you can. If you decide they are the best option in town, you sign up.

Rule number two: *Negotiate tough.* Your videodating experience may begin with high pressure sales, but remember, it is *you* the customer who really holds all the cards in this kind of negotiation! The only power the salesperson has is if you hand it over because you want their service too much. Appear to be ready to reject their offer and leave - even if you are bluffing, and particularly if you are someone they want - a woman in her 20's, or a man over 40 (especially with a solid professional career). They say they won't make the same offer (or almost the same) on another day? Not likely.

Rule number three: *Find out how many active members the videodating outlet has.* Look around at the number of videos, and do your own rough count. After I'd already joined *LA Videodating*, I realized that after excluding the half of the cassettes who were men, there weren't really that many female members available. This is especially true once you eliminate the people who are too old, too young, too tall, or too short, or appear to have little in common with you.

Rule number four: *Join for the shortest period of time possible*, just like with dating introduction services. Try to get a six month membership if possible. You can always extend your membership, and very likely for more favorable terms than you were offered when you first joined (because they want to continue to maintain the size of their client base). Remember also the number videodating services which go out of business every year is high. By investing less money you minimize your chances of getting burned. If videodating doesn't work out for you from a dating/relationship standpoint, you have also minimized your cost.

Rule number five: *Check with your local Better Business Bureau.* Is the videodating outlet a member? Do they have a history of complaints? Have they tried to make amends with refunds for some unhappy clients?

Rule number six: *How long have they been in business?* In the *National Dating Directory* we often provide this information. Ideally try to find a videodating company which has been in business for at least five years.

In Closing

In summary, when videodating remember to pick more than one or two people a week. Try to avoid decisions based too much on looks and not enough on potential compatibility. Use the best photo you can for the profile sheet, dress well for your video, and try to be relaxed and friendly on tape. If the videodating service also holds in person social activities for members, attend (I didn't).

There you can approach *anyone* you are interested in *directly*. If you are having an unsuccessful videodating experience, be sure to talk to the people running the service about the problem (again I didn't). They may point out mistakes you are making, or even help connect you with people who might be good matches.

If you still have less than spectacular videodating results, evaluate your strengths and weaknesses and take a look at the other New Dating Options. For example, I had *much* more success using the personal ads. Maybe the women using the *LA Weekly* personals (or personal ads in general) were more compatible as a group for me than the type of women using videodating. The personals also played more to my strengths - being good on the phone and doing better with women the better they got to know me - first by phone, and then in person.

Perseverance is as important in videodating as in any other New Dating Option. Remember in our videodate success story David was annoyed by a woman who agreed to meet him, and then didn't follow through? Just by coincidence we happen to know her. While she was ambivalent about meeting David - and so she didn't follow through with their date - she has stayed with videodating for *two years* now. When last we talked she had just met a man she thinks has real relationship potential.

While my own experience with videodating was negative, there is no doubting the success Ann and David and many others have had with it. Ann - once chagrined at spending a lot of money on the process - now feels it was completely worth the money. A female acquaintance of ours has recently started videodating with *Great Expectations*. She is in her late 30's, is generally considered "cute," has never been married, has a sister engaged to a man she met through *G/E,* and her one year membership cost her a little over $1,200. Ten men asked her out the very first two days she was an active member. Because she points out she would - in her own words - "*never* try the personal ads," videodating is likely the right date to win option for her. It may also be the right date to win option for you.

Following Through For Success

VI

Introduction

This section covers implementing the previous information in the book to achieve a successful date to win experience. Chapter 17, Dating to Win in Oshkosh, examines dating to win in smaller cities and towns, including those without New Dating Options, or with limited option availability. Chapter 18, Meeting on the Phone, discusses how to follow through and successfully contact people. Chapter 19, Women, Men, Singles and Safety, provides dating to win safety tips for women. Men should read this chapter too, because it will help them create a positive date to win experience for both themselves and the women they meet. This chapter also gives helpful suggestions on meeting in person the first time. Chapter 20, Troubleshooting the Date to Win Process, gives corrective steps to take if dating to win isn't working out to your satisfaction.

Dating To Win In Oshkosh   17

New Dating Options In Smaller Cities And Towns
Oshkosh, Wisconsin is a small city of about 50,000 people
located approximately 75 miles north of Milwaukee, and
160 miles northwest of Chicago. We selected Oshkosh as
an example of how to date to win in a town far removed
from the plethora of New Dating Options available in a
major city like Los Angeles.

We called the local Oshkosh paper, the *Northwestern*, to
check whether they carried the most commonly available
New Dating Option, personal ads. A very nice lady in
the classifieds department cheerily informed us, "Oh sure
we have personals!" It is indicative of just how popular
personals have become that you can "even" find them in
Oshkosh. And not just in Oshkosh, we found personals
a few miles to the north in nearby Appleton, and to the
south in Fond du Lac.

Suppose *you*, however, live in a small city or town which
doesn't have New Dating Options available, even personal ads, or where those opportunities are limited. What
choices are open to you for dating to win?

OPTION #1: USE THE NEAREST MAJOR CITY
First of all, you can look for a nearby place which *does*
have New Dating Options, especially the nearest major
city. For example, for someone living in Oshkosh who

feels their local opportunities are limited, Milwaukee can be explored. Milwaukee is home to *SingleLife*, a quality singles lifestyle magazine with personals covering the entire state of Wisconsin. For additional ads, Milwaukee also offers a major newspaper, the *Journal & Sentinel*, an alternative paper, the *Shepherd Express*, and another singles publication, *Singles Choice*, which has over 300 personals.

SingleLife magazine also sponsors *singles parties*. The Milwaukee area has several *videodating* outlets, including *Single Attractions* (profiled in our earlier section on videodating), and also a *Great Expectations*. Additionally, Milwaukee has *dating introduction services* available (e.g. a *Together Dating Service* branch), plus local *matchmakers*. A person living in Oshkosh could make the drive into Milwaukee to use any of these options.

Chicago

Someone living in Oshkosh can also use the New Dating Options available in Chicago, about 160 miles away. They could consider placing (and responding to) personal ads in publications like *Chicago Life* and *Chicago* magazines, the *Chicago Reader*, or the Chicago *Singles Choice*. Indeed, in one issue of *Chicago* magazine there appeared a long personal from a "NEAT, NICE GUY, THREE HOURS AWAY," in Michigan.

Being some distance away - with the extra work that entails - means usually it's a good idea to exchange photos first, even when using a 900 number ad. How to effectively meet the most people over a packed, whirlwind, weekend of coffees, lunches and drinks will be covered in our upcoming Women, Men, Singles and Safety chapter.

Since using New Dating Options long distance does take extra work, they are best used by people looking for a *lasting* relationship. And if things work out and become serious one of the two people will likely want to relocate. If you live some distance from a city and expect to stay where you are, with no plans to relocate, be very clear about this in your personal ad, video, interview with a dating service or matchmaker, or conversations with people you meet at a singles activity. Be sure to seek someone who is willing to relocate to where *you* are. If you *are* willing to relocate to a city, if the right relationship comes along, make *that* clear.

If you live within a couple hundred miles of virtually any major city you can consider dating to win long distance. For example, with personals, if you live in the northeast, try *New York* magazine (we once noticed a personal from a guy in Vermont), plus other city-named magazines, such as *Boston, Philadelphia,* and *Pittsburgh.* Similarly, metropolitan areas such as Atlanta, Houston, Denver, Dallas-Ft. Worth, Seattle, and San Francisco can serve as excellent New Dating Options resources for anyone living within hailing distance of them.

City-named publications usually have note and photo personals, and are especially good for dating to win long distance - since you need to pre-screen respondents with notes and photos (and longer than normal phone calls) to make the extra effort and travel worthwhile. In the case of long distance note and photo ads, if there's a 900 number option available, you can use it to explain in your recorded message extra details about yourself and your own specific situation. If you're willing to relocate, again be sure to mention it in order to further motivate people to go to the extra effort of contacting you.

You can also *respond* to other people's personals long distance, and explain where you live in your letter or phone message. Some of the advertisers may be willing to come out and meet you, but you also need to be ready to go and meet *them*. However, for many people you will simply be geographically undesirable. Running your *own* personal in a major city personals publication is likely to be more successful than responding to ads, in order to find those people interested enough to pursue a possible long distance relationship. Using the other New Dating Options long distance is also possible.

To research your nearest major city's New Dating Options, check the *National Dating Directory* to find the nearest big city publication you can use for personals, or look at the *Directory* listings for dating services and match-makers, videodating outlets, and organized singles activities. When using personals you will need to subscribe to the publication, so you can take a look at their personals and track your own ad's appearance. Subscribing can also be a good source of information about the other New Dating Options in a city. Before you subscribe, most publications will provide you with a sample issue for a few dollars, if you call and request one. Another excellent way to find out about opportunities available in a nearby city is to get hold of the city's *Yellow Pages*, and check under Dating Service (if you don't have the city phone book look at your local library).

OPTION #2: REGIONAL AND NATIONAL PERSONALS PUBLICATIONS

If you live in a smaller city or town like Oshkosh, you can also give *regional* and *national* publications a try, both for running and responding to personal ads. While using national and regional ads isn't normally the most productive and efficient personals method, it can be worthwhile when you live in an area lacking local personals opportunities, or if those choices are limited.   To find some potential publications, see the special National heading at the end of the *National Dating Directory*.   In Chapter 3 we discussed three glossy national singles publications, the *Bachelor Book, Bachelorette Book* and *Single Gentlemen & Women*.   Also mentioned earlier were two more erudite national choices: *The Nation* magazine (a friend of ours knows a man who met his wife through their personals) and the nationally distributed *New York Review of Books*.

Another important option for people in non-metropolitan areas to consider are singles publications.   A large number are *regional* in coverage.   The *Dating Page* out of Boston covers most of New England.   *Sincere Singles* and *Singles Network* serve wide areas of Michigan.   *Solo RFD*, based in Sioux Falls, South Dakota, reaches Iowa, Nebraska, North Dakota, Minnesota and Illinois.   Check through the *National Dating Directory* carefully for a singles publication which looks like it serves your area. Call them to get a sample issue for a few dollars, and then decide if you want to subscribe.   Additionally, these publications will provide you with an excellent New Dating Options information resource, especially for finding out about singles activities in your area.

There is also a special "national personal ad" available in singles publications.   Some of the magazines we just mentioned (e.g. *Solo RFD*) participate in running your personal ad simultaneously in each of 15 singles publications around the country.   The cost is currently $175 dollars for a 50 word personal.   Obviously, using this method can necessitate some serious travelling to meet people, which will probably be the man's responsibility.

OPTION #3: A CREATIVE LOCAL PERSONAL
If you are a resident of a town *without* personals, you can also consider trying to get the local paper to sell you ad space for a stand-alone personal, in the form of a regular advertisement: your own regular little 2" x 2", 4" x 4", or whatever, ad. It could be anywhere in the paper, ideally where it will be especially noticed by the opposite sex (although the paper may insist it appear as a regular ad in the classifieds section).

You could use a separate phone number and an answering machine for your ad (or use a P.O. Box and do a note and photo personal). Set up the phone just as you would with a 900 number, including leaving a message about yourself and what you are looking for in a person, and have them leave their name and number. If it's a stand-alone advertisement, since this somewhat novel approach will likely raise some eyebrows at the newspaper, you should be willingly to meet with them in person to assure them you aren't some sort of "weirdo."

OPTION #4: MORE DATING TO WIN LOCALLY
Since Oshkosh *does* have personals, there is also the option of running (and responding to) regular local personal ads. If you also live in a small city or town *with* personals, using local personal ads will be an option available to you. Since many smaller cities and towns are not listed in the *National Dating Directory*, you should do a little of your own research and take a look at your local newspaper. You can also check your *Yellow Pages* under Dating Service for local dating introduction services and matchmakers, or videodating listings. You also may find some listings for a nearby city or town.

Running A Local Small City Personal Ad
KATHY: A few years ago a cousin of Rick's living in

Redding, in northern California (population about 120,000), ran a personal ad. Susan was divorced, thirty-ish, and a single mother of a little girl. She decided to run a note and photo ad in the local paper, the *Redding Searchlight*. The paper didn't have the option of a 900 number personal at the time, although it does now. Susan began her ad: **"WHERE ARE ALL THE NICE GUYS?,"** followed by a Hard Data description of herself, including being a single mother. She asked for a note and a photo, and had the men correspond to her via a P.O. Box at the newspaper.

Susan received 38 responses, which stacks up very favorably against personals results in a much larger city. However, a big difference between running an ad in a small city versus a large one is that Susan already knew a number of the men who responded. But they, of course, didn't know she was the one behind the ad, since it was a note and photo by-mail personal, and one without a recorded message from her.

Susan divided her respondents into three piles: 1) definite callbacks, 2) maybe's, and 3) no way's. In a thoughtful gesture she sent thank you notes to the respondents she decided not to call (without giving them her last name or home address). While this was easy to do in her case, it isn't always so in other note and photo situations, where you don't have the respondent's home address, because a publication has been the mailing address go-between.

RICK: Aside from just being "nice," there is another reason for writing thank you's (or calling and talking with someone, or leaving a thank you message on their answering machine). It allows you, if need be, to return to that respondent at a later time. For example, what if you start seriously dating someone before you have an opportunity to complete the process of talking to and meeting all your other respondents? Then suppose your apparently burgeoning relationship goes belly-up in three, four, or six months? It's tough at that point to call someone who answered your ad months earlier, and who hasn't heard back from you. On the other hand, if you laid the groundwork with an earlier thank you contact, it's much easier.

When Kathy and I were beginning to get involved, I left thank you messages on the answering machines of a few of the most interesting respondents to my ad (and I also talked with a couple on the phone directly). In our earlier personals success story, Barbara did the same thing after she began dating Joe. Luckily, I never had to go back to follow up on anyone else (and neither did Barbara), but it was an opportunity available if things hadn't worked out so happily.

Results
We wish we could report that Susan found her husband through the personals, but she didn't. She did, however, call, meet, and date a number of the men. In addition to the Redding paper, she also responded to some personals from men in the nearby *Chico News & Review*, an alternative paper. Overall Susan says she had a *very* positive experience with the personal ads, and *highly* recommends them to people. Shortly after using the personals, she did meet and marry a local man. And who's to say that her positive get-out-and-take-charge-of-her-love-life-via-the-personals attitude didn't lay the groundwork for her success?

Meeting On The Phone 18

Phone Tips

When you call the person at the other end of your New Dating Option, don't be insulted to find out they answered five personal ads aside from yours, or picked several other videodates, and can't remember which one you are. So introduce yourself first, and mention the name of the publication you ran your personal in, or the videodating outlet, or the dating service, matchmaker, or singles activity where you met. If it's a personals call, you might throw in a catchphrase from your ad to refresh their memory.

While first names should suffice initially, a man should be ready to be forthcoming with his last name, where he works, and other information about himself, in order to relax a woman's concerns about safety. He is, after all, still a virtual stranger to her. Besides, openness on the phone by a man can help pave the way for a successful in person encounter.

How much *time* you spend on the phone is determined both by which date to win option you are using, as well as how many people you need to call (if you're busy meeting a lot of personal ad respondents, you need to keep your calls to a reasonable length of time, in order to get back to everyone). When you make your initial telephone call, usually a 20 minute or half-hour conversation should suffice. By going on and on for a couple hours in what is, after all, often a *blind date* situation (even with a note and photo personal ad, the phone call is still a blind date for one side of the call), two people may set up expectations which can be dashed instantly upon meeting each other in person.

Different Options, Different Calls
The initial phone call you make is different with each New Dating Option. For example, in the case of videodating, after examining each other's videos and profile sheets, generally you have both *already* decided you want to meet in person, *before* talking on the phone. Videodating is a somewhat unique New Dating Option since you already know so much about each other, and a longer phone call (and higher expectations of where it all may lead) makes sense. On the other hand, when using personal ads, both of you will probably rely on the phone call to decide whether to meet in person.

With dating introduction services and matchmakers, most of the time you have agreed to let a third party put you two together. Thus, you are usually doing less screening of each other on the phone and are more likely to quickly set up a date to say "hello" in person. If you both strongly trust the matchmaker, your phone call can feel like being introduced to each other by a mutual friend, which can make for a more comfortable (and longer) call. Finally, with organized singles activities, a phone conversation is usually a follow up to having *already* met in person. Hopefully mutual interest has been sparked. The more uncertain you are about the other person the more this situation is similar to a personals call, as you decide whether to proceed with another in person meeting.

Answering Machines
If you leave a message on an answering machine, leave information about yourself and a good time to reach you. If you're a man calling a woman, you should also indicate you will try phoning her again. This gives her the option of calling you, or waiting for you to phone her back. Be sure to call her back when you said you would, it shows you are reliable. If you're calling someone who responded to your personal, also mention the box number of your ad. This gives them an opportunity to go back and refresh their memory about your personal before you call again or before they phone you.

Try To Keep It Light
It's a good idea to keep the tone of the first phone call light, while still being sure to find out the information about the other person that's important to you. If you don't know their height, their age, whether they have children, if they're a smoker - and if these questions are important to you - find out the answers as early in the conversation as possible.

Don't Tell All
We recommend you don't spill your guts and tell someone your complete personal history in the first phone call. Do they really need to know you are currently in therapy? Why your marriage or last relationship crashed and burned? Instead, be open about the fact you were married once, but spare the details of any hostility to your ex, at least until you know the person better. It's more exciting, and ultimately more rewarding, to make sharing your complete personal history conditional upon it meaning that you have developed a bond of trust with the person you are dating (or at least being smart enough to make it appear so!).

Additionally, telling a virtual stranger your complete life history over the phone (or the first time you meet in person), can make you appear awfully self-involved, and can also result in you monopolizing the conversation. Conversational skills are better put towards keeping things moving if the other person is initially uncomfortable. Being a good listener is a real plus, and you'll find out more about the other person the more *they* do the talking.

The No-Go Phone Call

Ending the phone call when you have decided not to pursue an in person meeting can be difficult. Ideally the other person agrees with your decision. Just say something like, "Well, I really enjoyed talking, but I think you'll agree we don't seem to have that much in common. Good luck." Hopefully they don't argue the point, and even if they do, be firm. Don't let someone "guilt trip" you into meeting them if you two don't seem to share any common ground. Even if you were the one who called someone else's personal, don't be reluctant to take control of the situation, and gracefully but firmly end the call yourself.

Waiting Too Long

Try to return calls as soon as possible, although waiting a day or two (playing it a bit "cool") before calling back your 900 number personals respondents can't hurt. Keep in mind, however, that responses to your 900 number ad can back up *very* quickly, especially over the weekend. Even 10 or 15 calls can be hard to keep on top of if you let them pile up, since it generally takes at least 20 minutes per return call.

Waiting too long to respond to people is a problem with *all* the date to win options. You're insulting a person by taking your time to phone them, and the longer you wait, the less likely you are to follow through and actually call. The more people you talk to on the phone (and later meet in person), the more dates you will have and the more chances for success. Don't make excuses, make phone calls!

CHOOSING WHO TO CALL
There is, unfortunately, no sure-fire formula for choosing which people who select you through the New Dating Options to call back in the first place. If you are using a 900 number personal ad, obviously the way someone sounds and what they say in their taped message is the basis for your decision. If you run a note and photo personal, what respondents say in their letters, and what they look like in their photos will determine your decision.

RICK: I found myself calling back about three-quarters of the women who left 900 number messages, and about one-third of my note and photo respondents, feeling that only by talking with them directly could I make a decision about meeting in person.

Videodating is similar to deciding on whether to answer a note and photo respondent - but you are armed with a lot more information from the video and the profile information sheet. A dating service or matchmaker usually requires clients to at least talk on the phone to selections and meet most of them in person (unless there's just *no* connection when you talk on the phone).

Note And Photo Personals
Judging letters and photos is in some ways a tougher process than evaluating phone calls, since you *do* know what the person looks like, and it's easy to be too picky. There can also be a tendency to sit around with your little pile of notes and photos, taking your time and ago-

nizing forever over your decision about who to call (or gloat, drunk with delusions of power and adorability, over all your would-be dates and suitors!). Then, when you *finally* call people, you promptly discover the one you thought was so appealing in his or her *photo* is much less interesting when you actually talk. The one you almost didn't call because the photo wasn't so great now seems to have a lot of potential.

RICK: SO-WHAT-IF-THEY-DIDN'T-SEND-A-PHOTO

We encourage flexibility and a willingness to put yourself out there and talk to people on the phone, and then *meet as many as you can in person.* This includes being willing to do the blind dating required by some of the New Dating Options. In addition to our own blind date success story, as I mentioned briefly earlier, I had another lesson in the pluses of blind dating.

In response to a note and photo personal of mine, one woman sent me a little card and no photo. She wrote: "Hi there. You're not getting a picture! This is the note. We appreciate the same things. I'm bright and cute. Call soon." She gave her first name and phone number. Initially I put it aside, mildly annoyed that: 1) she didn't send a photo, and 2) she said next to nothing about herself. I had, however, noticed from her phone prefix she must live near me. One night a few days later I said what the heck, and gave her a call.

The conversation went better than average. She was indeed smart and was doing some work in my job field, which gave us something in common. We also discovered we had a mutual acquaintance, who was one of her best friends. She did live near me, and we decided to meet for a cup of coffee at the Beachwood Cafe at the foot of the Hollywood Hills. I got there first and awaited her arrival. When she walked in, it was hard to miss the fact my blind date had a terrific figure and was exceptionally attractive. I already knew she was very intelligent.

The Blind Date Advantage

When we first laid eyes on each other, I was *quite* happy, but her eyes betrayed disappointment. Her prince charming I was not! I took it as a challenge, and proceeded to be as charming as I could be. After about half-an-hour I tried to break off the encounter, figuring she was ready to move on (and having decided, as they say, she was "out of my league"). To my surprise she didn't take the hint, and she proceeded to prolong our get-together for another half-hour.

Here was someone I'm sure would not have normally considered me as a dating prospect, now enjoying herself, and apparently reconsidering her initial reaction to me. This is an example of our earlier point that *personal ads, and blind dating in general, "forces" people who normally wouldn't consider each other "dating material" to meet in a dating context.* This is a *big* help for those of us who are not incredibly physically attractive in person, and that's *most* of us. It gives us more of a chance to "sell" ourselves as *people,* beyond superficial appearances. It also provides an opportunity to get out of our *own* biased reactions to what we consider 1) our type, and 2) good looking enough for us to date.

Postscript

So what happened after our coffee at the Beachwood Cafe? A few days later I invited her to meet me at my office for lunch. She accepted. In person she was once again very intelligent and attractive, but I hesitated to pursue things further. In addition to her being "out of my league," I wasn't sure I could just "be myself" around her. Since I was looking for a relationship, not a "trophy date," I needed to find someone I could be more relaxed and open with.

The moral of the story? My blind date from the too-short-no-photo note was the classiest, most attractive, and overall most appealing woman I met through that particular personal ad. So, don't let the lack of a photo, or receiving a too-short note, stop you from at least *calling* your respondents to find out more about them. Try to be open to blind dating, including through dating introduction services and matchmakers. Err on the side of meeting *too many* people (at least on the phone, if not in person), not too few.

Women, Men, Singles And Safety

19

Introduction: Not For Women Only

To some women the advice in this chapter will seem a little uptight, and they may be right. But it's also harder to go wrong if you follow it. Men should read this chapter too. It will sensitize you to safety and privacy issues many women will have when dating to win, and can help you create a more positive dating experience for both you and your date. Also included in this chapter are tips for successfully meeting in person which apply to *both* sexes.

Meeting In Person

You are talking on the phone with a member of the opposite sex. You responded to their personal ad, or they responded to yours. You picked them for a videodate, or they picked you. You were put together by a matchmaker, or a dating introduction service. Maybe you met at a singles function and exchanged phone numbers, and this is the follow up call. After about 20 minutes on the phone, one of you broaches the question of getting together. You both agree it's a good idea. What's the best way to meet in person?

There are three basic common sense safety rules for a woman to follow when meeting a man for the first time:

1) Meet during the *day*, for breakfast, brunch, or coffee on the weekend, or lunch during the week. A less desirable alternative is a drink after work.

2) Meet at a *public* location, ideally a restaurant, bar, or cafe you are familiar with. Don't hesitate to suggest one of your own choosing.

3) Always have your *own transportation*, which in a city can include public transit or a taxi. *Don't* have him pick you up at your place. There's no reason he has to know exactly where you live until after you've met in person and have decided you are interested in seeing him again.

Why A Brief In Person Introduction?
Coffee, brunch or lunch are for short periods of time, about a half-hour to an hour-and-a-half. For women they don't present the potential problems of a traditional evening date, where the date is open-ended, and it can be a problem getting out of a sticky situation. The open-ended evening date is also less preferable if only because what if from the very beginning it's obvious this date is not going anywhere fast? The two of you can be stuck with each other for *hours*. Coffee, brunch or lunch avoids this problem, and is also a more low-key, casual way to meet, without the same pressures and possible miscon-strued mutual interest of an evening date.

An exception to the no-evening-date-rule-of-thumb might occur when using matchmakers. There, hopefully, you have been put together with some forethought. Also, a matchmaker may feel you're not giving each other a proper chance without meeting for an evening date. Anytime there is a third party involved who at least knows you two are meeting (e.g. a matchmaker, videodating), you may want to play it on a case by case basis and sometimes go out for an evening date. You should still use your *own transportation* and meet your date at a *public place*, just like Lisa and Edward in our matchmaker success story, who met at a mid-town Manhattan restaurant.

Meeting For Coffee

Instead of an open-ended evening date, we highly recommend having coffee at a nice cappuccino spot for about an hour on Saturday or Sunday. Depending on what's available in your area, and your own personal style and preference, it could also be a meeting for coffee, tea, brunch, etc., at any local restaurant. It's both a good way to meet someone in person for the first time, or to follow up with someone you met at a singles function, if the two of you really didn't get to spend a lot of time getting to know each other initially.

If you are meeting a lot of people (for example through the personal ads), meeting for coffee is especially attractive as a way to easily meet more than one person a day. Frankly, if things are really humming along, you can actually schedule up to *three* or even *four* coffee get-togethers on Saturday, and again on Sunday (at, for example, 11:00, 1:00, 2:30, and 4:00). Don't be embarrassed about doing these "serial coffees." People you are meeting may be doing the same thing. Add a lunch date, or two or three during the week, and an occasional after work drink, and you can meet 10 to 12 people a week. This may sound a bit overwhelming (or maybe just like an active and fun social life!), but it *works*.

RICK: Serial coffees is exactly what I did in the middle of running a personal ad. While it's a bit hectic, it's a pace you normally only have to keep up for two or three weeks at a time, while you look to meet someone you really want to focus on.

Ending Weekend Encounters

To gracefully end weekend coffee dates (or weekend brunches), you can establish early on that you have somewhere to be afterwards, perhaps in an hour-and-a-half or so. The best way to do this is on the phone beforehand, so it doesn't appear that you're merely disappointed by seeing the other person, and are just trying to bail out. If things go well you can always "run late" for that place you have to be (a friend, a visit to relatives, whatever) and extend the encounter.

Lunch?

If one or both of you are commuters into a city, you're likely to want to focus on lunch, or an after work drink. Lunch offers the advantage that both of you are looking your best (if you have office jobs), and there is a *built-in time restriction*, which cuts your time investment if it's a "no-go" situation. Also, unlike an open-ended evening date, sex isn't as likely to be an immediate issue. For women, lunch during the week - using your own transportation - is the *safest* way to meet men. Finally, lunch dates *automatically* eliminate any ending-the-encounter hassles, since you both have to get back to work. On the other hand, lunch lacks the more relaxed feel of meeting on the weekend, where you can sit down together and get to know each other leisurely, rather than having to rush back to the office.

A Drink After Work

Sometimes getting together for a drink after work is necessary to be able to meet everyone you want to. Some people are busy on the weekend, or your schedules can make a lunch difficult to arrange. While an assertive women may feel she can easily end an evening drink encounter whenever she wants to, it can be easier if before a woman meets a guy for a drink she mentions in their phone call she has to catch a train or bus home (e.g. the 7:15 train to wherever). If she is driving a car, she can say she plans on leaving by a certain hour, since she's got a busy day at work the next day.

The idea is to set a limit on the length of the encounter *beforehand*, to prevent it from becoming an unwanted, "just one more drink" open-ended evening date. This is especially helpful if the personals respondent, videodate, or dating service or matchmaker introduction who seemed so potentially interesting when you talked on the phone (or even someone you met in person at a singles function) turns out to be a bust upon closer examination. Now you've got a built-in "out" to end the evening. Like getting together for coffee, if you decide you want to extend the encounter you always can.

Actually, a smart *man* will set this time limit *himself* during the initial phone call. It puts him in control of the situation by letting the woman know upfront he isn't going to come on to her like gangbusters at their first meeting. If it's a "no-go" situation from *his* point of view, he has also just given himself a graceful early exit. And he has helped relax a woman by taking away the pressure of ending the encounter, making for a more enjoyable meeting for *both* of them.

Valet Parking
KATHY: If you're driving to an encounter, it's also smart for a woman to choose a place to meet that has *valet parking*. This means the *goodbye is in front of the restaurant* - with the valet looking on standing there holding open your car door - instead of a goodbye around the corner, or in a parking lot in the dark. Rick and I met the first time for an evening drink, and the restaurant had valet parking.

Meeting The Most People

In summary, for *both* men and women, meeting for a weekend coffee, brunch, or breakfast is the best way to meet the *most* people in the *shortest* period of time, because:

1) Along with lunch during the week, for women it is the *safest* way to meet.

2) It *cuts your potential losses* by keeping the initial meeting short, which is especially valuable in blind date situations.

3) It allows you to *meet more people*, which increases your chances of successfully dating to win.

4) Meeting for coffee is the *least expensive* way to meet. This helps keep the meeting much more casual than a dinner date, and avoids any major "who pays" questions. It sidesteps a man feeling a woman is obliged to him because of an expensive evening date.

5) If you are a woman who wants to meet some men for an evening drink, take your own transportation, set a time limit on the meeting in advance, chose a place you are comfortable with, try to make it a place with valet parking, and don't meet anyone this way you are not comfortable with.

SOME MORE MEETING IN PERSON TIPS

Voice Mail

As discussed in Chapter 4, using voice mail is a way for a woman to preserve her privacy and avoid giving out her home phone number early in the date to win process. It gives her the equivalent of an answering machine without using her home number, and it's more personalized

than an answering service. Check the *Yellow Pages* under Voice Mail for availability in your area. The cost
should be about $20 per month.

Keeping Notes

Throughout the date to win process you should keep
notes on your potential videodates, matchmaker matches,
dating introduction service and personals respondents,
before you meet. With personals respondents, you can
write down their name and pertinent data when you first
get their message from the system, and then add to it
when you talk with them on the phone. Do the same
thing when you follow up note and photo responses with
a phone call (it's easy, just write on the envelope they
send). With videodating and dating introduction services,
take notes from profile information sheets, from screening videos, and from phone calls.

Then when you go to your in person meetings, you can
bring a little crib sheet made from your notes if you like.
This is especially important when doing a weekend of
"serial coffees." It will come in extremely handy when
you are about to meet John or Jane in person, and can't
for the life of you remember if they were the one into
Rolfing or surfing. With your notes in hand (or at least in
your purse or wallet), you know if it's 2PM Sunday, you're
meeting "Barbara/Bob, 5'6", a divorced redhead, into jog-
ging, Tai Chi, and Brahms." It's also very flattering to be
able to sound like you hung on to their every word when
you two talked on the phone, or when you watched the
person's video.

Keeping notes also gives you a nice organized system of
phone numbers, names, and general information about
people you may be meeting. You can leave yourself
reminders on the status of things along with each name

(e.g. "left message, will call back Tuesday," or "coffee Saturday, L'Express 2PM confirm Friday," etc.).

Use The Hostess

If it's a blind date, you can recognize each other by giving mutual descriptions over the phone, including what clothes you'll be wearing, or even putting on something special (e.g. a hat) just to be easy to spot. If there's a hostess at a coffee shop, or restaurant, you can also use her to point you out to each other ("I'm meeting someone named Andrea, who is going to be asking for James. Could you point us out to each other when she comes in.").

Check Etiquette

At the end of the encounter there is the matter of paying the check. The pendulum has swung back from women insisting on paying their own way, especially if it's only a $6 cappuccino or drink tab. But a man should still ask, "how do you want to handle this?" If he's smart he'll add, "I'll gladly pick up the check." Men have to at least *offer* to pay, but must respect a woman's decision to pay for herself. On the other hand, if you *don't* offer to pay, and assume the bill is being split 50-50, a man will look awfully cheap. For women, if you like the guy, it's a perfect opportunity to let him pick up the check, but say "I'll get it next time." Or pick it up yourself and say *he* can get it next time. Either way you slip in neatly that you'd like to see him again.

KATHY: I always paid for my half of the bill on a first date. I liked what it said about me. Also the "balance of power" remains equal: no one feels monetarily beholden (sexually or otherwise!).

Seeing Each Other Again
If the first encounter went well, now that you have met someone you are potentially interested in, don't let opportunity slip away. Don't be shy about following up about another date. A good rule of thumb is to be sure to leave the first in person meeting knowing - or at least being pretty sure of - whether the other person wants to see you again. This also applies to meeting someone for the first time at an organized singles activity.

If another date is a possibility - at least from your standpoint - you can try to make another date right then. But you might want to instead keep things more casual. The risk of trying to get a hard and fast next date commitment at the end of the first meeting is that the other person may just want to avoid an uncomfortable confrontation and will commit to a date they later will not keep. Or worse, they will shoot you down - ouch! - painfully on the spot.

Instead of dinner next Saturday, you might want to leave things at: "I really enjoyed meeting you - maybe we could get together again soon?" The reaction of the other person will help you get a feel for how interested in you they are. Either person can initiate this exchange. If the response to this gambit is positive, tell the person you will call in a few days to set something up. This way you end the initial encounter both with an idea of the interest level of the other person, and a plan of action to follow up. And then be sure to follow through and call them!

Women Taking The Initiative
Since one advantage of dating to win is women's dating liberation - that you as a woman can pick the men you want to date - *you* should follow through during the first in person meeting if you're interested. This is the 90's,

and you can feel free to initiate talk of seeing each other again, especially if you sense the guy is interested in you but about to drop the ball (he's shy, unsure of how to handle the situation, whatever).

Remember, regardless of the decade, rejection is tough. Paving the way for a guy to call you by having him know you want to see him again could make all the difference in his following through. If you're at a singles function, you should be sure to get *his* phone number too, just in case he flakes out, and you sense it isn't because he's not interested. Don't leave seeing each other again entirely in his court.

KATHY: When Rick and I met our first time, at one point we talked about music. So, when we said our goodnights, I loaned him a couple cassettes I had in my car. This was a low key way to show I wanted to see him again, and set up us seeing each other to return the tapes.

Not Seeing Each Other Again
On the other hand, if you're *not* going to see each other again, it really isn't necessary to address that question at all. Simply let the other person know you enjoyed meeting them, and part. It smacks of obnoxious power tripping to feel compelled to let the other person know they don't have a snowball's chance in hell of seeing you again when the subject hasn't even come up. Whatever you do, *don't* lie and say you'll call if you have no intention of doing so.

Troubleshooting The Date To Win Process   **20**

Something isn't working:

1) You tried videodating, but are unhappy with the results.

2) You had 20 dating service introductions, but only dated two of them so much as a second time.

3) You responded to a few personal ads, and met some truly less than impressive members of the opposite sex. You wonder what to do next.

4) You ran your own personal ad, received only six responses, and none of them developed into anything.

5) You got plenty of responses to your personal ad, 53 people to be exact. You called five of them, met three in person, and then decided *none* of the 53 was even *close* to being a match.

6) Your problems occur on the phone. You are losing people during that first phone call; they just don't seem to want to go on and meet you in person.

7) You do meet in person, and they never want to see you again. Frankly, you are on the verge of saying to hell with dating to win.

Mediocre Responses

The fact is that while there are a host of things that can go wrong on the road to successfully dating to win, most of them are correctable. For example, if you've been running personal ads and getting mediocre responses - either in terms of numbers, compatibility, or both - closely re-read the two How to Write An Ad That Really Works chapters plus Create A Winning Phone Message.

Make sure you are not making any basic mistakes. Did you ignore all that stuff about listing your Hard Data? Did you decide to keep the cost of your personal down by running a too-short ad, omitting basic information about yourself as well as what you're looking for in another person? Did you decide it was too nerve wracking to leave a taped message with your ad, so you just skipped it? Did you be sure and try another publication when it became apparent the first one was not producing results? If responding to other people's ads was unproductive, did you then run your *own* personal? Remember your personals experience is not complete unless you have run your *own* personal ad. Even if the results of responding to other people's personals are disappointing, this has little or no bearing on the success you will have running your own ad.

Phone Calls

Dating to win successfully requires following through and *calling* and *meeting* people. A *lot* of people. You need to respond back to people who choose you through videodating, personal ads, a matchmaker or a dating introduction service; or who try to get to know you at a singles activity. You also need to be sure to follow through and meet the people *you yourself* selected.

Too Picky

If you are getting a lot of responses via a personal ad, or a video, etc. - but are rejecting almost all the people as "unsuitable" - be sure you're not being unrealistically picky. Don't demand the other person be your ideal Mister or Ms. Everything, before you will even *consider* them. (For example, the person who only called five of 53 people responding to their personal ad is a major candidate for either being overly picky, or not following through with their phone calls). If you date to win with the caveat you will only actually call or meet people who are clearly so good you can't possibly lose by contacting them (sort of "no fault dating"), you have a problem. Dating to win is about taking some chances - not holding out for a sure thing.

If you are serious about finding the love of your life (or even just having a lot of dates), consider blind dating if you haven't already yet. Blind dating is a way to force yourself to get out there and meet more people, whether through the personals, dating introduction services or matchmakers.

If you *are* blind dating, and still find yourself not calling enough people, try making yourself meet a set percentage of your respondents, at least over the phone. For example, if the person with the 53 responses used a 900 number personal, they should call back at least a quarter of their respondents, rather than dismiss 48 of the 53 out of hand. If you're using a note and photo personal, and find yourself calling very few of them (based primarily on their photo), you can also make yourself call a percentage of them (e.g. once again a quarter), *regardless* of your initial reaction to their picture. You will very likely be pleasantly surprised at the results.

The same thing applies to videodating. Visit your videodating outlet regularly (once a week, twice a week, etc.), and never leave without selecting at least *one* person (or better yet two, three, four, or the *Great Expectations* recommendation of five). Try not to get hung up choosing only on the basis of their looks; instead consider their real potential *compatibility*. Otherwise, even if they say "yes" to dating, the possibility of a relationship developing is likely "no."

If you're a woman with mediocre videodating results, be sure to take control of the selection process. Don't just passively wait for men to choose you. The same applies to taking responsibility for meeting people at singles activities. If you're a woman, don't wait for the men to make the first move. Take the initiative, and choose activities (e.g. group sports functions, singles dinners) where this is easy to do.

With matchmakers and dating introduction services, both sexes need to make clear what they are looking for, and why people the service sends you aren't quite right (if they're not). A good matchmaker will interview you after each encounter to get feedback, and then tailor the next selections accordingly. One matchmaker (Dr. Kate Wachs in Chicago) sometimes asks hard-to-match clients to bring in photos of old girlfriends/boyfriends to get a better idea of the type of people they date. You might suggest this to your matchmaker.

PLAY TO YOUR STRENGTHS

Be sure throughout the date to win process that you play to your own strengths and recognize which New Dating Option is best for you. For example, if you have a suspicion you are not very good on the phone, and have been unsuccessfully running or responding to 900 number personals, you have several choices. If you're *running* a 900 number ad, try again *without* leaving a taped phone message for respondents. While this normally isn't recommended, in some cases it can be helpful. Then, rather than having to "sell" yourself in a brief 45-90 second taped phone message, you'll have a 20 minute or longer return phone call.

Since the same phone weakness can hurt you when you respond to *other* people's 900 number personals, consider instead answering by-mail note and photo ads. An even better idea is to *run* a note and photo personal (without using a 900 number option, if it's available). Finally, you could consider another option completely, such as a dating introduction service or matchmaker, where a third party is helping you out.

Average Looks
If your looks are not your strong suit, *responding* to note and photo personals with a photo may be troublesome (and videodating can also be tough). But if you *run* a note and photo ad, your looks are initially *irrelevant*.

RICK: My own results responding to note and photo personals were average. I did much better responding to 900 number phone ads. Similarly, I didn't exactly burn up the track videodating, where results can also be looks-dependent. If you have been *answering* note and photo ads and haven't been getting many phone calls back, try responding *without* sending them a photo with your note. You will now be a blind date with an opportunity to "sell" yourself on the phone first, and establish a bond of commonality *before* you meet in person. Another solution is to respond to 900 number blind date ads, where looks also don't come into play until after an introductory phone call. You can also *run* your own personal ad of either type.

Videodating

If you are videodating with so-so results, you can consider another New Dating Option. But first, take an objective look at your video to see how it stacks up. It is
common for videodating outlets to allow you a free re-
record option, if you feel the problem might be your
"performance" - you are stiff and appear unfriendly, for
example - try again. Think of it like re-recording your
phone message using the personals. Take a look also at
your profile sheet photos. If they don't make you look as
good as you've ever looked in a photo, replace them
(and get good studio-quality photos if necessary). The
same applies to dating introduction services which use
photos.

If things aren't going well at a videodating or dating introduction service outlet, you should ask advice from the
people running the service. If you still do poorly, then
be willing to try another date to win option. If one reason you are using videodating is to avoid blind dates,
consider running a note and photo personal where you'll
have photos from your respondents, but your own appearance won't come into play until later in the process.

Singles Activities

Maybe you find you are not comfortable approaching
people in person at a singles activity, or your attempts
are unsuccessful. Perhaps you are 43-years-old, and everyone else at the functions you have been attending is
22-34, and you want to meet people closer to your age.
Maybe you are a woman and not enough men approach
you. Or, you find you just don't like having to compete
with other people for someone's attention at a singles
function.

All these problems can be rectified by trying one of the other New Dating Options, and some can be corrected by trying other singles activities - ones with a different age range, or activities which almost "automatically" cause interaction between the sexes (without a long walk across a dance floor), such as singles dinners or group sports.

The Over 40 Woman
Singles activities (and videodating) can be tougher for the over 40 woman, because some of the over 40 men are likely to date women who are substantially younger. You should keep this in mind when considering which date to win option is for you. If things aren't going well, you also may want to consider another date to win option - one where it's easier to target men who will know your age and still are interested in you (e.g. personal ads or a matchmaker).

THE PROBLEM IS WHEN YOU MEET ON THE PHONE OR IN PERSON
If you are losing people the first time you talk on the phone, be sure you are not trying too hard to impress them and coming on too strong (guys especially). If after you meet in person they almost never want to see you again, you should also be aware of the impression you are making. Be sure you aren't coming on too strong (especially sexually).

Perhaps you just seem to be too full of yourself to other people. Are you always trying to top the other person's anecdote with one of your own? Are you boasting and bragging, and generally overcompensating for nerves and insecurity? Are you talking about former relationships, and how many people you've slept with? If you are monopolizing the conversation and being overbearing, a good rule of thumb is to be sure the other person does at least *half* the talking. Try also to relax, avoid "overselling" yourself, and don't feel compelled to "wow" the other person with how terrific you are.

Guys need to be careful not to come on like gangbusters and tell women things they *think* they want to hear, especially when they aren't true. Both women and men should avoid coming off as overly needy and desperate when they meet someone. A little self-confidence goes a long way. So does a little restraint.

Appearance
There is only so much you can do about your appearance, but do the most with what you have. When you meet someone in person, look as appealing as you can. If you have been meaning to lose a few pounds, taking control of your social life is a good time to take control of your weight. It's also a good time to update your wardrobe, get a new haircut, and generally spruce yourself up. These are confidence boosters, and especially apply to people re-entering the dating world after the breakup of a marriage or a long relationship.

Telling Your Problems
Don't tell someone all your problems when you first meet them, either on the phone or in person.

RICK: One 40-year-old woman I met for coffee brought along a pillow for her bad back. Then she *talked* about her bad back. All I could think about was that she was an *old* 40. Instead, she should have taken an aspirin ahead of time and left her pillow in the car - along with her medical history.

KATHY: I met several men who used our first meeting to complain about dating, or women in general, or their jobs. Talk about a turn off! Keep it positive. The first meeting is not a therapy session with coffee served!!

Remember to come off like you *enjoy your life*. Men especially should appear as if they enjoy their *jobs*. One of the most perceptive personals we ever saw was written by a woman who stressed she was looking for a man who "*loved his work*." While she runs the risk of spending less time with a man in love with his job, a man who *hates* his job is unhappy - so who wants to spend more time with him anyway?

Avoid Underselling Yourself
Be sure you are using all your positive attributes and not *underselling* yourself. For example, a man can give his profession - *when it's a plus* - on his profile sheet, in his video, or in his personal ad. A friend of ours who is a college professor once ran a personal ad calling himself "non-materialistic." That was fine. However, we had to talk him out of calling himself a "teacher," instead of a "college professor." His rationale was that because he wanted to attract a non-materialistic woman, he should downplay his job. But "college professor" is an occupation women will generally find more exciting, interesting, stimulating, and further up the ladder of success than a teacher. But it's still a career unlikely to attract a highly materialistic person responding.

If you're not sure about the marketability of your job (and frankly in our sexist society, judging a person by their profession or pocketbook is still applied more to men than to women), you might be a little vague about your profession in your personal. Or don't mention it at all. You want to have an opportunity to "sell" yourself on the phone, and you might not get that far giving your occupation in your personal ad, profile sheet, video, etc.

RICK: If you are a man you may want to have a woman already talking with you on the phone before knowing your occupation. If she likes you, she may very well decide to meet you anyway, whereas if she knew your job *in advance*, she may not respond in the first place. She shouldn't really be faulted for this: if your job status was critical to her, she wouldn't say "yes" to meeting you at all, even *after* talking with you.

People need a way to weed out who to respond to and who not to, and occupation is often a factor. What you do and don't say about your job (and everything else) in a personal, a video, etc., is *self-marketing*, after all. So, rather than mentioning a job you're not sure is a plus, concentrate on personal things about yourself, and use other indications of financial success or at least financial stability (e.g. mention you own a home).

Attitude: Being Recognized
One friend of ours was so mortified by the possibility that someone he knew might call in and recognize his voice that he wouldn't leave a taped phone message with his 900 number personal. He also "disguised" his personal, changing his height by several inches, and being circumspect about how he described his professional life. This feeling that using the New Dating Options is something to be embarrassed about is *not* conducive to having a successful date to win experience! Personal ads, videodating, matchmakers and dating introduction services, and organized singles activities are a *perfectly legitimate way to meet people*. Being public about it, especially with friends, is part of a *positive mental attitude* that allows you to plunge right in, and be open and friendly with the people you meet, instead of uptight.

RICK: My close friends knew I was videodating, and then

that I used the personals. While I didn't exactly advertise it around the office, I did let a couple of people know, and I was prepared to be *completely* open about it if the subject came up (for example if someone who knew me at work called my personal, recognized me, and word got around the office). In fact, when a woman I knew from business did actually call my 900 number personal, it was hardly an embarrassing experience.

KATHY: My best friend and I used to go through the personal ads together. I told a lot of people I answered personals and was positive about the benefits. Many friends were intrigued, some enough to try them too. My outlook changed a lot of negative attitudes about the personal ads.

Flirting
Some attorneys and executives have a bad habit of sounding like they're on a business call when calling a personal ad respondent, phoning their dating service selection, etc. Remember, this is a phone call to attract a *lover*, not a client. A good idea for both men and women is to make their date to win phone calls at home, not at the office. Avoid being in a business-like frame of mind, and instead try consciously to sound *warm, approachable*, and even *sexy*.

Speaking of "sexy," perhaps you are a woman who has been reluctant to flirt a bit in your personal ad - this could be limiting your responses. Play around with how you describe yourself. Did you say anything about your appearance beyond the basic Hard Data? Remember you can say something as simple as "sexy smile," or "sensuous" in your ad. Do the same thing in the phone message with your ad, or when you respond to a man's personal with a note, or a 900 number taped message. You can also work on your choice of language. Even using an evocative word in your personal can help (e.g. "SWF female *craves...*").

Persistence! Persistence! Persistence!
RICK: Once I told a woman about the personals and helped her write a 900 number ad. She ran the ad, got over 40 responses, called back some, and told me that was "fun." But then she came up with all sorts of excuses as to why she only went on to meet a couple of the men in person.

Another female friend attended one *Y.E.S.* singles dance with a girlfriend. They hung out together, decided they didn't see any men they were interested in, and went home. (Be aware that while you can go to a singles activity with a friend, alone you are more approachable. Above all, avoid hanging out with your friend for the duration of an activity talking about what a waste of time the whole thing is). My friend completely dropped out of the date to win process after the one dance. She attended our wedding, and said she's now considering using the personals, but she still hasn't done anything about it.

Another female acquaintance is a television vice president. She's smart, attractive, and hardly the "type" most people would expect to use the personals. Once she had a serious relationship with a man she met through a personal ad, but then stopped using them. She's well into fortysomething now and last I heard still single.

Finally, a male friend wound up in a heady relationship with an attractive woman with his very first personal ad. In fact, she was one of the very first respondents he met. The relationship lasted eight months, yet he has used the

New Dating Options inconsistently since then, and not the personal ads.

Failures?

To consider relationships resulting from New Dating Options "failures" because they end is a mistake. Au contraire! They show that dating to win works - it leads to dates and relationships. But you have to *keep at it*, even if your first relationship does do a "crash-and-burn."

More Than One New Dating Option

A common denominator in almost all the date to win success stories in this book are people who *try more than one New Dating Option* and who *stick with the date to win process*. In our personal ads success story, Barbara tried singles activities before she ran her personal ad. In our matchmaking story, Lisa tried the personals (and even got engaged) before signing up with matchmaker Denise Winston. In our singles activity success story, Jake had tried a dating service before he met Linda on the *Sierra Singles* hike.

RICK: In our own success story, of course, I tried videodating before the personal ads. *KATHY*: I tried a couple singles activities before answering personals.

RICK: Commitment - The Grass Is Always Greener?

When I began dating to win I met some women who had been doing *Y.E.S.* parties, personals, videodating, etc., for several *years*. As soon as I found out how well the personals worked, I understood this temptation to become sort of a "professional single" - running ad after ad, attending one singles activity after another, each new one holding the promise of endless new possibilities. Maybe *this* time I would find that "perfect" member of the opposite sex! This is a trap which appeals to commitment-phobic tendencies in all of us, as well as to those who are too picky about who qualifies as our potential partner, or even just a date.

In my own case, at first it was an adventure each time I ran a new personal ad. There was always the possibility of greener pastures with each new set of respondents. But for me successfully dating to win meant finding a lasting relationship, and then marriage. Anything from "trophy dating" to dead-end pseudo-relationships, was a waste of time. I wasn't in my 20's anymore (or even my 30's!), and merely using the personals as a perpetual dating service (even an excellent one) wasn't my goal.

The longer I dated to win without finding that special relationship, the more frustrating it got. First, I changed my choice of New Dating Options from videodating to personal ads. Then after running four personals, getting about 125 responses - but no lasting relationship - *I didn't give up*. I decided to try even *harder* to find that special person. When I called the *LA Weekly* to place what ended up being my last personal ad, I had actually *already* ordered an expensive personal in *Los Angeles* magazine. Between the two personal ads, damn it, I was going to find a relationship!

I totally immersed myself in the personals process for well over a month. I met six, even eight women a weekend for coffee or brunch - plus weekday lunches, after work drinks, and follow up dates on Friday and Saturday. *I made finding a relationship the number one priority in my life. And it worked.* I got almost 75 responses between the two final personal ads and found my special lasting relationship - and it changed my life.

It took *200* responses to find Kathy, but I stuck with the date to win process. Allow me to state the obvious: if I'd quit after my unsuccessful videodating experience, I would have regarded dating to win as a failure. If I'd stopped after any one of my first four personal ads, I would have said, "well, it's great for dating, but I don't know if you can find a lasting relationship." But instead I tried more than one New Dating Option and more than one personals publication, modified my ad several times, and ran it more than once. I talked with about 120 respondents on the phone, and met about 80 in person. Dating to win requires ongoing initiative on your part, but your efforts will be rewarded - whether it's getting the dates you want, or finding that special someone.

Let us know how it goes. Send us your comments, success stories (with your phone number - we may ask to use them in future editions of the book), complaints, corrections, and suggestions. The address is:

> Date to Win
> P.O. Box 110
> Hollywood, CA 90028

You can also order additional copies of *Date to Win* from this address. Just send your name, address and phone number (the phone number is in case there's a problem making out your name and address), along with a check or money order ($12 for each copy of the book plus $4 for postage, handling, and any applicable sales tax) made out to Date to Win.

Good luck!

The National Dating Directory

VII

THE NATIONAL DATING DIRECTORY

HOW TO USE THIS DIRECTORY

1) PERSONAL ADS:
All *Directory* listings which are not under a specific boldface heading (e.g. **videodating**) are publications carrying personal ads. These publications are abbreviated by type:

(A) alternative publication
(CN) city-named magazine
(N) newspaper
(S) singles magazine
(S/C) shoppers guide/classifieds publication

There are two kinds of personal ads. They are denoted by either *900#* (for voice mail phone ads), or *N&P* (for note and photo response by-mail ads). For a detailed explanation of the types of personal ads see Part II, Chapter Four.

Note: *National publications* carrying personal ads are at the end of the *Directory* listed under National.

2) SINGLES ACTIVITIES:
Organizations sponsoring organized singles activities are listed in the Directory under **singles activities**. For a detailed explanation of many of these activities see Part III of the book.

3) MATCHMAKERS/INTRODUCTION SERVICES:
The two major dating introduction services are *MatchMaker International* and *Together Dating Service*. They are described in detail in Part IV of the book. Many of their outlets are listed in the *Directory* under **matchmakers/introduction services**.

4) VIDEODATING:
Great Expectations outlets around the country are listed in the *Directory* under **videodating**, along with local competing companies. For more specifics on *Great Expectations* and videodating, see Part V of the book.

ALABAMA

BIRMINGHAM

Birmingham Post-Herald &
Birmingham News (205) 325-2246
(N) 900#/N&P Fri, Sun. About 150-
170 personals, under Heartlines in
the Sunday classifieds.

Fun & Stuff (205) 252-0200
(A) 900#/N&P free monthly. Major:
about 200 personals.

matchmakers/introduction services

MatchMaker International
(205) 985-0955
3075 Highway 150, Hoover.

videodating

Dating Your Choice (205) 879-DATE
201 Beacon Parkway West, Suite 206.
In business 10 years with 750
members. Cost: $149 to join (includes
cost of video).

HUNTSVILLE

The Huntsville Times-News
(205) 532-4000
(N) 900# Thur, Sun. Approximately
40 personals.

The Connections Flyer (205) 880-5804
(S) 900#/N&P free monthly publication. Major personals publisher for
northern Alabama/southern
Tennessee: about 300 personals per
month. Some PHOTO ads. Also
sponsors singles activities, including
large monthly singles dances. Lists
area singles organizations. Address:
The Connections Flyer, P.O. Box
16104, Huntsville, AL 35802.

videodating

Great Expectations (205) 882-3045
7529 South Memorial Parkway, Suite
C&D.

singles activities

See *The Connections Flyer* above for
singles activities listings.

MOBILE

Mobile Press Register (205) 433-1551
(N) 900#/N&P.

MONTGOMERY

Montgomery Advertiser
(205) 262-1611
(N) 900#/N&P Thur, Fri, Sun. Look
for personals under the Central
Alabama Meeting Place.

ALASKA

ANCHORAGE

Anchorage Daily News
(907) 257-4237
(N) 900# Sun. About 1 1/2 pages of
personals.

Penny Saver (907) 563-2800
(S/C) 900# free weekly (Thur). About
1 1/2 pages of personals.

Alaska Men (907) 522-1492
(S) N&P. Published approximately
every two weeks. Showcases Alaska
men to women willing to relocate.
Contains photos, bios and costs $8.95.
Address: 1013 E. Diamond Blvd., Suite
522, Anchorage, AK 99515.

FAIRBANKS

Fairbanks Daily News (907) 456-6661
(N) N&P Sun under Meet Your Match.

JUNEAU

Juneau Empire (907) 586-3740
(N) N&P six days a week.

ARIZONA

PHOENIX

Arizona Republic & Phoenix Gazette
(602) 271-8704
(N) 900#/N&P Fri, Sun (in Arts Section).
Major: 200-300 personals a week.

New Times (602) 258-1073
(A) 900#/N&P free weekly (Wed).
Major: 300-500 personals per issue.
Also lists singles events.

Single Scene (602) 990-2669 Scottsdale
(S) 900#/N&P. Monthly publication
costing 75 cents at newspaper boxes
outside post offices. Major: 250
personals covering the Phoenix area.
Excellent source for singles activities
and singles group listings. Address:
Single Scene, Box 10159, Scottsdale,
AZ 85271.

Phoenix Jewish News (602) 870-9470
(N) 900#/N&P weekly paper (Fri).
About a dozen personals per issue.

Penny Saver (602) 839-5700 Tempe
(S/C) 900# free weekly (Wed). About
100 personals per week covering
Phoenix/Tempe.

**matchmakers/introduction
services**
MatchMaker International
(602) 956-6500
2701 East Camelback Rd.

Together Dating Service
(602) 970-8422
6330 E. Thomas Rd., Suite 228.

videodating
Great Expectations (602) 941-0500
5635 N. Scottsdale Rd., Suite 190,
Scottsdale.

singles activities
Chevra (602) 967-7563
Jewish singles age 21-33.

Sierra Singles
Join the Sierra Club (602) 253-8633 for
$35 and check their newsletter for
Sierra Singles information/phone
numbers.

West Valley Singles (602) 867-1814
(event information line).

Note: For additional singles activities
listings see the Phoenix Singles Club
Directory and Arizona Singles
Calendar in *Single Scene* magazine
(listed above under Phoenix).

TUSCON
Tuscon Weekly (602) 792-3630
(A) 900# free weekly (Wed). Major:
300 personals per week.
(Since they use a local phone exchange
technically it's not a "900#" system).

Tuscon Star Citizen (602) 573-4343
(N) 900#. About 100 personals a week
in the Meeting Place.

YUMA
Yuma Sun (602) 783-4433
(N) N&P. About 20 personals.

ARKANSAS

LITTLE ROCK
Arkansas Democrat-Gazette
(501) 378-3452
(N) 900#/N&P. Major: 1 1/2 pages.

**matchmakers/introduction
services**
Together Dating Service
(800) 753-2896
One Financial Center, 650 Shackleford Rd.

CALIFORNIA

BAKERSFIELD
Bakersfield Californian
(805) 322-7355
(N) 900# Wed, Fri, Sun.

Bakersfield News-Observer
(805) 324-9466
(N) 900# weekly paper (Wed).

CHICO
Chico News & Review (916) 894-2300
(A) 900#/N&P free weekly (Thur).
About 100 personals per week.

FAIRFIELD
Fairfield Daily Republic
(707) 425-4646
(N) 900#/N&P. The same personals
appear in the *Travis Times* serving
Travis airforce base, plus a shopper's
guide, the *Express Line*.

FRESNO

Fresno Bee (209) 441-6111
(N) 900# Fri, Sat, Sun. Major: 2 1/2
pages of personals.

Fresno Bulletin Board (209) 486-5600
(S/C) 900#/N&P. Weekly classifieds
publication.

**LOS ANGELES and surrounding
cities**

Los Angeles Times (213) 237-5000
(N) 900#. Fri Life & Style section, Sun
classifieds. In Orange County look for
local personals Thursday. Major: 1,500
personals (more than any other
newspaper in America). Also lists
singles events under Singles in
Sunday Calendar of Events.

LA Weekly (213) 667-2620
(A) 900#/N&P free weekly (Thur).
Major: 600+ personals per week. Also
sponsors some singles events. Excellent
source for personals (the authors of this
book met through them).

Los Angeles Magazine (310) 557-7592
(CN) N&P/900#. This glossy upscale
city-named magazine is an excellent
source for personals. About 100 per
month.

Daily News (818) 713-3711 San
Fernando Valley
(N) 900# Tue, Thur, Fri, Sun in the
classifieds Meeting Place. About 200
San Fernando Valley personals.

Jewish Journal (213) 738-7778
(N) 900#/N&P. Weekly newspaper
with about 50-80 personals.

Southern Sierran (213) 387-4287
(N) N&P. The publication of the Sierra
Club and a good source for personals.
About 20 ecology minded ads per
issue. You get it free when you're a
local Sierra Club member.

Whole Life Times (310) 317-4200
(A) 900#. Personal ads for New Agers
in this monthly free magazine based

in Malibu (include your "sign" in your
ad!). Look for it in bookstores. Major:
200 personals.

Gateway Magazine (310) 450-0018
(A) free magazine published every
two months in Venice. Another New
Age publication (in the personals
there's an ad for a "Mystic Channeler
& Finder of True Love"). About 75
personals. Look for it in bookstores.

The Recycler (818) 501-6700
San Fernando Valley edition,
(213) 660-8900 Los Angeles edition
(S/C) 900#/N&P. Weekly classifieds
publication (Thur) with LA and San
Fernando Valley editions. Check
newsstands. Major: 300 personals,
plus several hundred *international*
personals.

LA Reader (213) 933-0161
(A) 900#/N&P free weekly (Thur).
100+ personals tending toward the
uninhibited. *LA Weekly* is the better
alternative publication for serious
relationship personals.

Single Connections Magazine
(714) 628-4940
(S) 900#/N&P at newsstands monthly
($1.00). Major: 300 plus personals
with many PHOTO personal ads. Also
a source for singles activities. Address:
Sunset Communications, P.O. Box
5020, Diamond Bar, CA 91765.

National Singles Register
(310) 864-2741
(S) N&P/900#. At newsstands every
other week ($1.25). Major: 300+
personals (heavily Orange County)
per issue. Also separate 900# national
section with 200 more personals.
Traditional singles magazine audience.
Good listings of singles organizations.
Address: *National Singles Register*,
P.O. Box 509, Norwalk, CA 90650.

COSI Community of Singles
(213) 962-3890
(S) 900#. Free monthly in supermar-
kets and other locations from Ventura
to the South Bay. General interest
singles oriented publication. About
100 personals. Good source for
singles activities. Address: *COSI*, 1923
Tamarind Ave. #9, LA, CA 90068.

Southern California Social Guide
(213) 656-6611, (213) 650-7100
(S) 900#/N&P. This is the publication
of *Young Executive Singles* (*Y.E.S.*).
Lists singles events, and also has 100+
personals. Cost is $1.00. The first
phone number above is their
recorded information line. Address:
Y.E.S. Network, 270 N. Canon Dr.,
Suite 1430, Beverly Hills, CA 90210.

Senior World (310) 820-1125
(N) 900#/N&P. Free monthly
newspaper for seniors in Los Angeles
County. About 25 personals.

Santa Monica Outlook (310) 540-5511
(N) 900# Mon, Wed, Fri. Major: 300
personals per week.
The same personals also appear in the
San Pedro News Pilot, and the
Torrance Daily Breeze, and a dozen
free home delivered publications from
Malibu to San Pedro, including the
*Beverly Hills Independent, Brentwood
Press, Culver City Independent,
Manchester-Ladera Reader, West LA
Independent, Westwood Press.*

Pennysaver (310) 793-4200
East Westchester
(S/C) 900# (Wed). 250+ personals.

Orange Coast Magazine
(714) 545-1900 Costa Mesa
(CN) 900#/N&P. This is Orange County's
glossy upscale version of *Los Angeles*
magazine. About 30 personals monthly.

Pennysaver (714) 642-0811
Costa Mesa
(S/C) 900#.

Easy Reader (310) 372-4611
Hermosa Beach
(A) 900# free weekly (Thur). About 30
personals.

Irvine News (714) 261-2401 Irvine
(N) 900# weekly paper (Thur).

Long Beach Press Telegram
(310) 432-5977 Long Beach
(N) 900# Fri. Half page of ads under
Heart to Heart.

Inland Daily Bulletin (909) 987-6397
Ontario
(N) 900#. Same personals also in
Pomona's *Progress Bulletin.*

Pasadena Weekly (818) 584-1500
Pasadena
(A) 900#/N&P free weekly (Thur).

Riverside Press-Enterprise
(909) 684-1200 Riverside
(N) 900#.

Orange County Register
(714) 835-1234 Santa Ana
(N) 900#. Major: 400+ personals under
Orange County Connections.

Random Lengths (310) 519-1016
San Pedro
(A) 900# free every other Thursday.

Coast Weekly (408) 394-5858 Seaside
(A) 900#/N&P free weekly (Thur).
About 50 personals.

Torrance Daily Breeze (310) 540-5511
Torrance
(See the listing above for *Santa
Monica Outlook*).

San Gabriel Valley Tribune
(818) 962-8811 West Covina
(N) 900#.

singles activities

Advanced Degrees, Ltd.
(818) 348-1747
P.O. Box 455, Woodland Hills, CA 91365. Parties for those with Masters degree and above but in reality also allow college grads. Low event fees.

Athletic Singles Association
(310) 827-5680 (event line),
(310) 827-0382 office. 4637 Admiralty Way, Marina Del Rey. Orange County: (714) 855-3010, 25255 Cabot #211, Laguna Hills. Athletic activities (and parties) for the seriously sports-minded age 25- 50. About $275 per year. Waterskiing, tennis, paragliding, etc.

California Singles (310) 364-3343
P.O. Box 88251, LA 90009. Singles dinners, outdoor activities, etc. One year membership $129. Monthly activities newsletter. Events open to non-members for slightly higher event fees.

Dianne Bennett introduction parties
(213) 859-6929
P.O. Box 951, Beverly Hills, CA 90210. Parties and matchmaking. Parties about $12. Matchmaking: $500 for 3 matches.

Fellowship of Christian Singles
(213) 656-5600
A branch of *Young Executive Singles.*

Jewish Association of Professional Singles (J.A.S.P.) (310) 305- 8889 (eventline), 656-7777 (office). Orange County: (714) 771- 0771. Parties and activities. Branch of *Young Executive Singles.*

Jewish Singles Hotline (JASSLINE)
(818) 783-6868. Orange County (714) 956-JASS, Los Angeles (310) 278-6868. Call for recorded activity information.

Sierra Singles: Join the Sierra Club (213) 387-4287 for $35. The schedule of activities booklet you receive contains current *Sierra Singles* information and phone numbers.

The Single Gourmet (310) 271-7088/ 1-800-DINE
Dinners at LA's *nicer* restaurants. This fast growing group (1,300+ members) costs $99 to join, plus about $50-60 for most dinners. In business 3 years. Most members 30's and 40's.

Westside Singles Cycling Club
(310) 364-4616
P.O. Box 88251, LA 90009. Membership is $60 per year. Monthly newsletter. Sister club to *California Singles.*

Young Executive Singles (Y.E.S.)
(213) 650-7100 (event line) 650-1353 office. Address: 270 N. Canon Dr., Suite 1430, Beverly Hills, CA 90210. Large hotel parties, etc. $10 for 6 months, $15 one year. Age 20's-40's. Low event charge for parties, more for cruises, white water rafting, etc.

Note: See write ups on most of the above listings in Part III, Singles Activities. For more information on singles events, check your newspaper for singles listings, such as the *Los Angeles Times* Sunday Calendar of Events under the Singles heading. Also pick up publications like *COSI* magazine with its calendar of events, or the *National Singles Register* listings of singles groups.

videodating

Great Expectations (310) 477-5566
1640 S. Sepulveda Blvd., Suite 100, West LA.

Great Expectations (818) 788-7878
17207 Ventura Blvd., Encino.

Great Expectations (909) 985-2733
450 N. Mountain, Suite B, Upland.

Great Expectations (714) 476-1986
18818 Teller Ave., #110 Irvine.

See write up on *Great Expectations* in Part V, Videodating.

matchmakers/introduction services

Dianne Bennett (see above under singles activities).

Bonnie Bull, Ph.D. (818) 792-4120
595 E. Colorado Blvd., Pasadena.
Personality tests aid this therapist in her matchmaking. Cost: $500 for an open-ended membership.

Lunch Dates (213) 737-6021
For single professionals. $495 for one year and 24 introductions. Potential matches talk on the phone and set up their own lunch. In business 3 years.

Patricia Moore Group, Ltd.
(310) 859-8828, (818) 888-2537, (714) 722-1725. P.O. Box 6972, Beverly Hills, CA 90212
Upscale matchmaker. About $4,500 for 8-12 introductions.

Christine O'Keefe, Ltd. (310) 271-9394
141 El Camino Dr., Suite 207, Beverly Hills. Upscale matchmaker. $5,000 for two year search.

Selectra Date (818) 346-3366, (800) 232-3283 National computer dating company started 25+ years ago. $35 for minimum of 5 matches. Both parties are given each other's names and phone numbers. They talk by phone and decide whether they want to meet. LA office covers Santa Barbara to San Diego.

Singles Connection (714) 528-2588 Anaheim, (818) 332-1776 Covina, (909) 882-2800 San Bernadino
Actually a private personals register more than a matchmaker. $35 for 3 months, $60 for 6 months. A list of personals is mailed to you once a month (your ad is on the list). Response via people's phone numbers (rather than a 900# voice mail).

J. Wingo International (800) 688-6282
2121 Avenue of the Stars, LA 90067. Very upscale. For more information see San Francisco listing.

Debra Winkler (310) 553-7000 or (714) 760-6600
1901 Avenue of the Stars, Suite 241, LA, CA 90067.
Upscale matchmaker who is also the co-founder of *Young Executive Singles* (*Y.E.S.*). $1000-5000 for 5-15 introductions in a year.

Note: For additional information on many of the above listings see Part IV, of the book, Matchmakers and Dating Introduction Services.

Note: For singles listings for Southern California (including those of you in Riverside, San Bernadino, San Louis Obispo, Santa Barbara, Ventura, and San Diego counties), look for the *Singles Guide to Southern California* by Rich Gosse. You can order it yourself for $12 from Marin Publications, 4 Highland Ave., San Rafael, CA 94901 (415) 459-3817. We don't vouch for everything Rich has to say about being single, but the local directories are extensive.

MERCED
Merced Sun Star (209) 722-1511
(N) N&P.

MODESTO
Modesto Bee (209) 521-7777
(N) 900#.

singles activities
Professional Guild (800) 870-7072
Gives local singles parties, see S.F. listing for more info.

MONTEREY
Monterey Herald (408) 372-3322
(N) 900#.

NAPA
Napa Register (707) 226-3711
(N) 900#.

PALM SPRINGS
Desert Sun (619) 322-8889
(N) 900#/N&P Tue, Fri, Sat. About 100 personals per week.

REDDING
Redding Record Searchlight
(916) 243-2424
(N) 900#/N&P.

SACRAMENTO
Sacramento News & Review
(916) 737-1234
(A) 900#/N&P free weekly (Thur).
Major: 700 per week.

Sacramento Bee (916) 321-1234
(N) 900#. Major: about two pages of
personals.

Suttertown News (916) 448-9881
(A) 900# free weekly (Tue).

singles activities
Professional Guild (800) 870-7072
Gives local singles parties, see SF
listing for more information.

videodating
Great Expectations (916) 927-2700
2277 Fair Oaks Blvd., Suite 195.

SALINAS
Salinas Californian (408) 424-2221
(N) N&P.

SAN BERNADINO
San Bernadino Sun (909) 889-9666
(N) 900#.

SAN DIEGO
San Diego Union-Tribune
(619) 293-1482
(N) 900# Thur, Sun. Major: 1000+
personals per week - one of the
nation's largest. Look for personals
under Possibilities in the Sunday
Current section.

San Diego Reader (619) 235-8200
(A) 900# free weekly (Thur). Major:
200-300 personals per week.

Single Magazine
(619) 296-6948/292-8049
(S) bimonthly. Free at stores, $.50 at
newsstands. Major: several hundred
personals. Lists singles events.
Address: *Single Magazine*, Box 5709,
San Diego, CA 92165.

La Jolla Light (619) 459-4201 La Jolla
(N) N&P. Same personals appear in
the *University Light*.

singles activities
Young Executive Singles (Y.E.S.)
(619) 272-1600
See Los Angeles listing for more
information.

Athletic Singles Association
(619) 530-2114
See Los Angeles listing for more
information.

Singles Event Info Line (619) 571-5054
Events for people age 30-49.

Jewish Singles Club Hotline
(619) 273-1111.

videodating
Great Expectations (619) 283-6400
3465 Camino Del Rio South, Suite 300.

**matchmakers/introduction
services**
Patricia Moore Group, Ltd.
(619) 234-2002
(see Los Angeles listing for more
information).

J. Wingo International (619) 558-6934
or (800) 688-6282
(see San Francisco listing for more
information).

Jim Soules, Ph.D. (619) 275-2030
1049 Cudahy Place (619) 275-2122
information line. "Dr. Jim" reports he has
been counseling singles for 25 years. His
matchmaking service costs $500-2000 for
one year (less for hardship cases). 6-25+
introductions per year. He says he only
signs you up if he thinks he can help you.

SAN FRANCISCO
San Francisco Bay Guardian
(415) 255-4600
(A) 900#/N&P free weekly (Wed).
Major: 800-900 personals.

SF Weekly (415) 541-0303
(A) 900#/N&P free weekly (Wed).
Major: 500 personals.

East Bay Express (510) 540-7400
Berkeley
(A) 900#/N&P free weekly (Thur).
Major: 200-300 ads per week.

SF Chronicle & Examiner
(415) 777-1111
(N) 900# Fri, Sun. Major: 200 personals.

San Francisco Focus Magazine
(415) 553-2800
(CN) 900#/N&P monthly. This isn't
your usual city-named magazine. It's
the publication of KQED-TV, but is
also available on newsstands. About a
dozen personals.

Trellis Magazine (415) 941-2900
(S) 900#/N&P. Major: several hundred
personals. Comes out every three
months, free in bookstores. Major
sponsor/lister of singles events.
Address: *Trellis Magazine*, 1260
Persian #6, Sunnyvale, CA 94089.

Pacific Sun (415) 383-4500 Mill Valley
(A) 900#/N&P free weekly (Wed).
About 100 personals per week.

Marin Gazette (415) 457-4888
San Rafael
(N) 900# weekly (Wed). Carries one
page of ads. Most of the same personals
are in the *Sonoma Gazette*, and are
distributed over a five county area.

Palo Alto Weekly (415) 326-8216
Palo Alto
(A) 900 Wed, Fri. About 25 personals.

singles activities
Professional Guild (510) 937-4744,
(800) 870-7072
Similar to *Young Executive Singles* in
Los Angeles. They put on parties at
large hotels in the Bay Area. Also do
ski trips, white water rafting, etc.
Onetime $29 membership fee plus $10-
20 event fee. In business for 10 years,
they call themselves "northern California's
largest singles organization." Offices in
Sacramento, Modesto, Stockton.

Sierra Singles: join the Sierra Club
(415) 776-2211 for $35. The schedule
of events information they send you
includes Sierra Singles activities/
phone numbers for the Bay Area. Also
see write up in Part III Singles
Activities, includes success story of a
couple who met and married through
Sierra Singles, Oakland.

Young Unattached Professionals
(*Y.U.P.S.*) (510) 947-6700
Walnut Creek. Give large parties at
upscale hotels. Ages 25-45.

Note: Also see *Trellis Magazine*
(listed above) for singles events/
listings, the *Bay Guardian's* Singles
Event Line (900) 407- 4504 ($.99 per
minute charge, separate listings for
the East Bay, S.F., Marin, San Mateo).

videodating
Great Expectations (415) 332-2353
330 Pine St., SF.

Great Expectations (415) 964-2985.
2085 Landings Dr., Mountainview.

Great Expectations (510) 944-4900
1280 Civic Drive, Suite 300,
Walnut Creek.

Video Introductions (510) 676-2399
1950 Market, Concord. The East Bay
alternative to *Great Expectations*,
since 1977. Fee up to $1,495 for 3
years with unlimited number of
selections. Or their Passive Plan costs
just $50 - you do a video and are on
file, but can only be selected, not
make selections (a popular choice for
women). They're very forthcoming
over the phone, including giving cost.

matchmakers/introduction services

How About Lunch (415) 281-5845
Covers SF, East Bay, Marin, Peninsula
catering to the proverbial "busy
professional." $400 for one year, with 6
meetings over lunch. You interview in
person, they match you, you both agree,
they set up lunch, you pay dutch.

Patricia Moore Group, Ltd.
(415) 777-9752
Box 31130, SF 94131. Upscale
matchmaker: $4,550 for 8-12 matches.

Perfect Match (510) 947-6006
1501 N. Broadway, Walnut Creek. East
Bay matchmaking service is less
expensive than the above upscale
matchmakers. $950 for 18 months and
9 matches minimum, but usually 18-
24. For college grads in 30's, 40's (into
50's for men). In business 2+ years.

Selectra Date (800) 232-3283
Computer dating service. $35 for a minimum
of 5 matches. You two talk on the phone
and decide whether to meet in person.

J. Wingo International (415) 274-9620
or (800) 688-6282
180 Montgomery, SF 94104. *Very*
upscale ($6000+) matchmaker.

SAN JOSE

Metro (408) 298-8000
(A) 900# free weekly (Thur). Major: 200
personals, which are also in the
*Cupertino Neighbor, Los Gatos Weekly
Times, San Jose City Times, Saratoga
News, Sunnyvale Sun, Willow Glen Resident.*

San Jose Mercury News (408) 920-5000
(N) 900# Fri, Sun.

matchmakers/introduction services

Together Dating Service
(408) 371-6190, or (415) 340-9930
3190 S. Bascom Ave., Suite 270.

SAN LOUIS OBISPO

New Times (805) 546-8208
(A) 900#/N&P free weekly (Wed).
100 personals per week.

SANTA BARBARA

Santa Barbara News Press
(805) 963-4391
(N) 900#/N&P Sun.

Santa Barbara Independent
(805) 965-5205
(A) 900#/N&P free weekly (Thur).
50-90 personals per week.

SANTA CRUZ

Good Times (408) 476-3101
(A) 900#/N&P free weekly (Thur).
125-150 personals per week.

SANTA ROSA

The Paper (707) 527-1200
(A) N&P out every other Thursday.

Santa Rosa Press Democrat
(707) 546-2020
(N) 900#/N&P.

SONOMA

Sonoma Gazette (415) 457-4888
(N) 900#. Most of the same personals
as the *Marin Gazette.*

STOCKTON

Stockton Record (209) 943-1112
(N) 900# Wed, Sun. 3/4 of a page of
personals.

singles activities

Professional Guild (800) 870-7072
Gives local singles parties, see SF
listing for more information.

VENTURA
Ventura County Coast Reporter
(805) 658-2244
(N) 900#.

VISALIA
Visalia Times Delta (209) 739-1637
(N) 900#/N&P.

COLORADO

BOULDER
Daily Camera (303) 442-1202
(N) 900#. A page of personals daily
under People Meeting People.

COLORADO SPRINGS
Spring Gazette Telegraph
(710) 632-5511
(N) 900#. Major: 250 personals a
week.

DENVER
Westword (303) 296-7744
(A) 900#/N&P free weekly (Wed).
Major: 500+ personals.

Denver Post (303) 820-1010
(N) 900#. Major: 250+ personals. Look
for personals under Partners and
Friends in the Sunday classifieds.

Rocky Mountain News (303) 892-5149
(N) 900#/N&P. About 80 personals.

singles activities
La Clef D'or (303) 321-1668
469 S. Cherry. Private club for singles
30's, 40's, 50's. Holds parties and
other events. No cost quotes over the
phone.

videodating
Great Expectations (303) 321-1516
400 S. Colorado Blvd., Suite 200.

**matchmakers/introduction
services**
MatchMaker International
(303) 321-2700
3773 Cherry Creek N., Suite 685.

Together Dating Service
(303) 759-2400
4100 East Mississippi Ave., Suite 303.

Newchoices (303) 355-7223
Psychologically based matchmaking
via several tests. They set up lunch
between you and your match. Fee:
$450 for 6 months, $600 for one year.
No guaranteed minimum of matches,
but they say the average is 1-3
matches per month.

FORT COLLINS
Get-Two-Gether (303) 221-4544
(S) 900#/N&P every two months.
Major: 200-250 ads statewide.

PUEBLO
Pueblo Chieftan (719) 632-3520
(N) 900#. About 100 personals.

CONNECTICUT

BRIDGEPORT
The Post (203) 333-0161
(N) 900# Fri, Sun.

DANBURY
**matchmakers/introduction
services**
Introductions, Inc. (203) 790-4403
Look under Hartford listing for more
information.

The Singles Network (203) 730-9669
35 Padanaram Rd. See Stamford listing
for more information.

HARTFORD
Hartford Advocate (203) 232-4501
(A) 900#/N&P free weekly (Wed).
Major: 200+ personals. Same ads
appear in a series of regional
Advocates: *Fairfield County Advocate*
and *New Haven Advocate* (Conn);
Springfield Advocate and *Valley
Advocate* (Mass).

Hartford Courant (203) 241-6200
(N) 900# Thur. A page of personals.

singles activities

Singles Alternatives (203) 633-0600
Put on large singles parties throughout the state of Conn for about an $8
entry fee. Look for ads in local papers
like the *Hartford Advocate* and
Courant, or call for information.

videodating

Great Expectations (203) 257-3336
2189 Silas Deane Highway, Rocky Hill.

matchmakers/introduction services

Jewish Dating Service (203) 561-3250
New England Dating Service
(203) 561-3250
The *Jewish Dating Service* and the
New England Dating Service are two
arms of the same dating service. They
have been in business for 12 years,
and boast 2-3 marriages per month for
the combined services. Fees: $400 for
6 months, up to $800 for 2 years, with
a minimum of one match a month.
Very forthcoming over the phone with
information and prices. No hard sell.
New England *Dating Service* is in
Hartford only, but the *Jewish Dating
Service* also has interviewers in
Springfield, Mass; New Haven and
Stamford, Conn; White Plains, NY, and
in Bergen County and Piscataway, NJ.

Together Dating Service
(203) 677-2534
790 Farmington Ave., Farmington.

Introductions, Inc. (203) 257-4000
This introduction service is similar to
Together and *MatchMakers International* - no photos, videos or computers. They do not give price quotes
over the phone. However, they say
they are less expensive than the two
national chains. Branches in Danbury,
Conn; Springfield and Pittsfield Mass;
and Albany, Binghamton, Glenn Falls,
Poughkeepsie, Syracuse, and Utica, NY.

Connect (203) 257-7207
Did not respond to our request for
information.

MILFORD

matchmakers/introduction services

The Singles Network (203) 878-2700
99 Cherry St. See Stamford listing for
more information.

NEW HAVEN

New Haven Register (203) 789-5200
(N) 900# Fri. A page of personals.

New Haven Advocate (see under
Hartford Advocate).

matchmakers/introduction services

Jewish Dating Service (203) 561-3250
See under Hartford for more
information.

NEW LONDON

The Day (203) 442-2200
(N) 900#. A page of personals in
Thursday Weekender section.

STAMFORD

The Advocate (203) 625-4400
(N) 900# Fri, the Meeting Place.

matchmakers/introduction services

The Singles Network (203) 327-3280
110 Prospect St. Cost: 6 months $600
for 9 introductions. One year $850 for
18 introductions. 900 members, in
business 13 years. Also in Danbury,
Milford, White Plains (Hartsdale), NY.

Jewish Dating Service (203) 561-3250
See under Hartford for more information.

SOUTHINGTON

Southington Stepsavor (203) 628-9645
(S/C) N&P free classifieds weekly
(Tue). A page of personals.

WESTPORT

Fairfield County Advocate
(203) 226-4242
(A) 900#/N&P free weekly (Thur).
Major: about 300 personals.

DELAWARE

WILMINGTON
Wilmington News Journal
(302) 324-2424
(N) 900# daily. About 1/2 page of personals.

matchmakers/introduction services
Judy Yorio's Compatibles
(302) 655-1421
Matchmaking. Cost in "upper hundreds."

MatchMaker International
(302) 478-0511, or (302) 735-1515
3505 Silver Side Dr., Dover.

DISTRICT OF COLUMBIA

Washingtonian (202) 296-7580
(CN) 900#/N&P. Glossy upscale monthly. Major: 400-450 personals (more personals than any other city-named magazine).

City Paper (202) 628-6528
(A) 900# free weekly (Fri). Major: 200-300 personals per week.

Washington Post (202) 334-6000
(N) 900#. Major: 350+ personals. Look for personals in Sunday classifieds, Friday Weekend section and Thursday's paper.

Washington Times (202) 636-3120
(N) 900#/N&P. About 85 personals per week.

videodating
Great Expectations, (703) 847-0808
8601 Westwood Center Dr., Vienna, VA.

Georgetown Connections, Inc.
(202) 333-6460
1656 33rd Street NW. Videodating service. About 500 members. Say no hard sell. Cost: $1,000 for a year, with no limit on the amount of people you can select.

matchmakers/introduction services
Together Dating Service
(703) 827-9090
1595 Springhill Rd, Suite 320, Vienna, VA.

Together Dating Service
(301) 984-0926
152 Rollings Ave., Rockville, MD.

Ann Wood, the Matchmaker
(202) 234-0670

Jewish Singles (703) 385-1101 ext. 5
Call for recorded message. Will mail you information.

Leora Hoffman Associates
(301) 493-8444
Upscale matchmaker. Chevy Chase, MD.

FLORIDA

FORT LAUDERDALE
Fort Lauderdale Sun-Sentinel
(305) 360-7111
(N) 900#/N&P.

GAINESVILLE
Gainesville Sun (904) 372-4222
(N) 900#/N&P.

JACKSONVILLE
Folio Weekly (904) 260-9770
(A) 900#/N&P free weekly (Tue).
About 100 personals a week.

Singles Serendipity (904) 731-7111
(S) 900#/N&P. Out every two months.
Major: 300 personals per issue.
Personals cover Orlando, Daytona, east coast of Florida and southern Georgia.
Report available in a 1000 retail stores.
Address: *Singles Serendipity,* Box 5794,
Jacksonville, FL 32247.

Florida Times Union (904) 359-4310
(N) N&P.

videodating
Great Expectations (904) 292-9977
4348 Southport, Suite 210.

MIAMI

Miami Herald (305) 376-2828
(N) 900#. Major: 300+ personals under
Getting Personal.

New Times (305) 372-0004
(A) 900#/N&P free weekly (Wed).
Major: 400 personals.

The Flyer (305) 232-4115
(S/C) 900# free weekly (Wed)
classifieds publication.
Major: 500 personals per week.

Community News (305) 665-8214
(N) 900# Mon, Wed, Fri. About 200
personals a week.

Singles Choice (305) 270-9468
(S) Did not respond to requests for
information.

Miami Jewish World (305) 576-9500
(N) N&P. Same personals also appear
in two other weekly papers, the
Brower Jewish World, and *Palm Beach
Jewish World*.

The Bachelor Book (305) 563-4771
(S) N&P/900#. Glossy *national*
PHOTO personals publication for men
who run personals for women to
respond to. See also under the National
heading at end of the Directory, along
with *The Bachelorette Book.*

videodating

Great Expectations (305) 936-1910
20803 Biscayne Blvd., Suite 102.

Great Expectations (407) 393-6666
4800 N. Federal Hwy., Suite B103,
Boca Raton.

matchmakers/introduction services

*A Singles Resource Center Choices
Unlimited* (305) 448-5683
Upscale matchmaking using PHOTOS.
In business for 10+ years. No price
quotes by phone.

ORLANDO

Orlando Sentinel (407) 420-5179
(N) 900#.

videodating

Great Expectations (407) 788-0009
2101 W. State Rd. #434, Suite 201,
Longwood.

*Friends Connection Video &
Introductions, Inc.* (407) 831-3800
283 N. Lake Blvd. Did not respond to
request for information.

matchmakers/introduction services

Together Dating Service
(407) 788-9400

PALM BEACH

West Palm Beach Post (407) 820-4100
(N) 900# Fri, under TGIF.

Palm Beach Jewish World
(407) 833-8331
(N) N&P weekly paper.

SARASOTA

Sarasota Herald (813) 957-5438
(N) 900# Wed, Fri, Sun. About a page
of personals.

TAMPA-ST. PETERSBURG

Creative Loafing (813) 286-1600
(A) 900#/N&P free weekly (Thur).
Major: 400-500 personals.

Tampa Tribune (813) 272-7500
(N) 900#/N&P Fri, Sat, Sun. Major:
three pages of personals.

The Flyer (813) 626-9430
(S/C) 900# free weekly classifieds
publication (Tue). About 100
personals per week under Friend
Finder.

St. Petersburg Times (813) 893-8111
(N) 900# daily 1/2 page of personals.

singles activities
Bay Area Winners Circle Video Dating Club
See their activities under their
videodating listing below.

Gulf Coast Singles
See their activities under their
videodating listing below.

videodating
*Bay Area Winners Circle Video Dating
Club* (813) 282-0382
1410 Westshore Blvd. N. Video
matchmaking done for you with mutual
agreement before you meet in person.
Also sponsor parties open to non-
members. Membership fee: 6 months
$300, one year $500. 400 members.

Great Expectations (813) 538-9331
15950 Bay Vista Dr., Suite 150, Clearwater.

Gulf Coast Singles (813) 576-5800
9500 Koger Blvd., St. Petersburg.
Videodating by mutual selection. $250
for 4 months, $420 for one year. In
business 3 years, 450 members. Also
have a social club which sponsors
singles events. Can join for $100 for
one year without joining videodating.
Can try one event before joining.

**matchmaking/introduction
services**
Date Mate (813) 265-2100
Like videodating but by color PHOTO
and member profile. $125 for 10
introductions. You choose matches
yourself. 1,000 members, in business 7+
years (report 324 weddings in that time).

Talahasse
Talahasse Democrat (904) 599-2219
(N) 900# Tue, Fri, Sun. About 3/4
page of personals.

GEORGIA

ALBANY
Albany Herald (912) 888-9333
(N) 900# Tues, Fri, Sun. About 50
personals.

ATLANTA
Creative Loafing (404) 688-5623
(A) 900#/N&P free weekly (Wed).
Major: 500+ personals per week. Also
lists events for singles.

Atlanta Singles (404) 636-2260
(S) 900#/N&P. Glossy quality singles
publication available on newsstands
every two months ($2.00). Major: 300
personals per issue. Extensive guide to
singles activities/groups. *One of the nicest,
classiest singles publications in America.*

Atlanta Journal-Constitution
(404) 526-5151
(N) 900#/N&P daily. Major: 350+ in the
Sunday classifieds under Let's Talk.

singles activities
See the Guide to Groups and
Activities in *Atlanta Singles* (listed
above). Also see *Heart to Heart* below
in matchmakers.

Singles Outdoor Adventures (SOA)
(404) 242-2338
Dayhikes, backpacking, canoeing,
biking, etc. Did not supply us with
information on cost.

videodating
Great Expectations (404) 956-9223
320 Interstate North, Suite 110.

Heart to Heart See below under
matchmakers.

**matchmakers/introduction
services**
Classey Connection (404) 496-4301
No response to our information request.

Cupid's Arrow Dating Service
(404) 256-6108 Marietta
PHOTO optional matchmaking. No
price quote over the phone. 800
members, in business 4 years.

Heart to Heart (404) 980-1994
Choice of PHOTO or video services.
Sponsor singles events. Report 2,000
members. No price quotes by phone.

Jewish Dating Network (404) 252-0251 130 W. Wieuca Rd. NW. No response to our information request.

Southeast Singles Assoc.
(601) 872-1717
Membership $35 for 4 months, $70 for one year. 10 introductions for $120, 20 for $180. Cover GA, Miss, AL, LA and northern Florida. See Biloxi, Miss listing for more information.

Together Dating Service (404) 953-4700 Marietta.

Together Dating Service (404) 263-6400 Gwinnett.

Together Dating Service (404) 266-0300 Buckhead.

Traditional Matchmakers
(404) 237-8593
Matchmaker Beatrice Gruss charges $85 for an initial interview (usually free with most matchmakers), and $595 for 5 matches. The 5 matches only count if you actually go on to meet, and if you have no matches after 3 months she refunds your money.

AUGUSTA
Metropolitan Spirit (706) 738-1142
(N) 900#.

COLUMBUS
The Dynamic Dime (706) 571-3463
(S/C) 900#/N&P free weekly (Thur) shoppers guide.

Columbus Ledger & Enquirer
(706) 324-5526
(N) 900# Fri, Sun. Same personals in the *Ft. Benning Leader.*

MACON
Macon Telegraph News (912) 744-4200
(N) 900# Tue, Fri, Sun.

Bulletin Board (912) 750-1800
(S/C) N&P weekly classifieds publication. 20-50 personals.

SAVANNAH
Savannah News-Press (912) 236-9511
(N) 900# Mon, Tue, Fri. 50 personals per week.

HAWAII

HONOLULU
Honolulu Star Bulletin & Honolulu Advertiser (808) 525-8000
(N) 900# Mon, Wed, Sun. About 250 personals under It's a Date.

Honolulu Weekly (808) 528-1475
(A) 900#/N&P free weekly (Wed). About a dozen personals.

videodating
See *Compudate* (below under matchmakers/introduction services).

matchmakers/introduction services
Compudate (808) 926-3283
Two different services. Computer introductions: cost $175 for one month and 3 introductions, or $465 for 6 months and 12 introductions. Videodating: cost $1,500 for 6 months with 5 introductions per month. Compudate does all the matching.

MAUI
Maui News (808) 244-3981
(N) 900# Mon, Wed. About 50 personals.

IDAHO

BOISE
Idaho Statesman (208) 377-6200
(N) N&P daily. About a dozen personals.

matchmakers/introduction services
Single Expectations (208) 344-6988
PHOTO matchmaking. $60 for 3 months (no restriction on number of matches). In business 3+ years.

IDAHO FALLS
Post Register (208) 522-1800
(N) 900#.

LEWISTON
The Tribune (208) 743-9411
(N) N&P.

POCATELLO
Idaho State Journal (208) 232-4161
(N) 900#/N&P daily. About a 1/4 page
of personals.

ILLINOIS

AURORA
Beacon News (708) 844-5811
(N) 900#.

BLOOMINGTON
The Pentagraph (309) 829-9411
(N) 900# Wed, Fri, Sun.

CARBONDALE
Southern Illinoian (618) 549-3326
(N) 900#/N&P.

CHICAGO
Chicago Tribune (312) 222-3232
(N) 900# Tues, Fri, Sun. Major: 350+
personals.

Chicago Reader (312) 828-0350
(A) 900# & N&P, free weekly (thur).
Major: 300+ personals.

Chicago Sun-Times (312) 321-2300
(N) 900# Fri, Sun.

Chicago Magazine (312) 222-8999
(CN) 900# & N&P. Glossy city-named
monthly with less personals than usual
for this type of magazine (about a dozen+).

Chicago Life Magazine (312) 528-2737
(CN) 900# & N&P. Chicago's other glossy
city-named magazine is a good source
for personals (about 60+ monthly).

New City (312) 243-8786
(A) free weekly (Wed). About 50
personals per issue.

Singles Choice (708) 634-7700
(S) 900#/N&P free monthly in stores.
Major: 450 personals. Doesn't list/
sponsor singles events, but some are in
classifieds. Address: *Singles Choice*, 113
McHenry Rd, Buffalo Grove, Il 60089.

Daily Southtown (312) 586-8800
(N) 900#.

Daily Herald (708) 870-3600
Arlington Heights
(N) 900#.

Pennysaver (708) 429-6400
Tinley Park
(S/C) 900#.

singles activities
The Dr. Kate Relationship Center
(312) 337-3377
Puts on singles events for $12-20. For
more information see listing under
matchmakers/introduction services.

Gail Prince (708) 475-7709
Puts on Party Mix singles parties
through the Discovery Center, plus
other singles events.

videodating
Great Expectations (312) 943-1760
350 W. Ontario, Suite 500.

Great Expectations (708) 706-9889
1701 E. Woodfield Dr., Suite 400,
Schaumburg/Woodfield.

**matchmakers/introduction
services**
The Dr. Kate Relationship Center
(312) 337-3377
This therapist does matchmaking plus
singles events (see above under
singles activities). 1) Advanced
Degrees Introductions: PHOTO
dating, $1275 for one year. 2) Intimate
Introductions matchmaking: one year
$1575, two years $1875, 9 intros per
year. 3) Ultimate: top of the line
expensive matchmaking search. In
business 10 years.

Personal Profiles, Inc. (312) 440-0777
Upscale matchmaker in business since
1982. $1950 for 2 year membership in
matching pool. Complete marriage
search (SearchMate) for $3,500 +
$3,500 bonus if they get you married.

Selective Search, Inc. (312) 871-7781
Upscale matchmaker. Fees from $900
on up to be in dating pool, $3,000 on
up for a search. Run by Page Greytok
a former executive headhunter who
now applies her skills to
matchmaking.

It's Just Lunch! (312) 644-9999
$500 for 6 months or 6 lunches. They
set up lunch/match, you meet dutch.
To join your weight needs to be
proportional to your height. Also
located in New York City.

Interactions (708) 963-8833
1315 Butterfield Rd, Downers Grove
(708) 559-8578 801 Skokie Blvd.,
Northbrook. Matchmaking, but
virtually no information given out by
phone. Since 1963.

Together Dating Service (312) 755-1150
54 W. Hubbard.

DECATUR
Prairie Shopper (217) 428-0202
(S/C) N&P.

LA GRANGE
Suburban Life (708) 579-4242
(N) 900#.

LAKE COUNTY
Market Journal (708) 223-3200
(N) 900# weekly newspaper (Wed).

MOLINE
Moline Daily Dispatch (309) 764-4344
(N) 900#.

PREORIA
Preoria Journal (309) 686-3060
(N) 900#.

ROCKFORD
Rockford Register (815) 962-2400
(N) 900#/N&P.

SPRINGFIELD
State Journal Register (217) 788-1374
(N) 900#.

Illinois Times (217) 753-2226
(A) 900#/N&P free weekly (Thur).

INDIANA

BLOOMINGTON
Bloomington Voice (812) 331-0963
(A) 900#/N&P free weekly (Wed).
About 75-85 personals per issue.

ELKHART
The Paper (219) 269-2932
(N) 900#.

FT. WAYNE
Journal Gazette & News Sentinel
(219) 461-8333
(N) 900#.

GARY
Post-Tribune (219) 881-3212
(N) 900#/N&P.

INDIANAPOLIS
NUVO Newsweekly (317) 254-2400
(A) 900#/N&P free weekly (Wed).
150+ personals per issue.

Indianapolis Star News (317) 633-1240
(N) 900#/N&P. 100+ personals.

Indianapolis Magazine (317) 237-9288
(CN) N&P/900#. This glossy upscale
city-named publication contains about
75 personals per month.

Thrifty Nickel (317) 782-8111
(S/C) 900#.

**matchmakers/introduction
services**
MatchMaker International
(317) 844-3283

Together Dating Service (317) 879-9144
8910 Purdue Rd.

videodating
Great Expectations (317) 471-0580
3500 Depaul Blvd., Suite 2070

MUNCIE
Muncie Star & Evening Express
(317) 747-5700
(N) N&P.

SOUTH BEND
Single Today (219) 282-4449
(S) 900#/N&P free monthly. Major:
500-700 personals. Serves north and
central Indiana and southern Michigan
("Michiana"). Includes a few photo
ads. Lists some singles events.
Address: *Single Today,* 2014 S.
Michigan, South Bend, IN 46613

Pennysaver (219) 282-4411
(S/C) 900#.

TERRE HAUTE
Tribune Star (812) 231-4246
(N) 900#/N&P. About 70+ personals.

IOWA

Note: *Solo RFD* carries statewide Iowa
personals and singles events. See
listing under Sioux Falls, S. Dakota.

CEDAR RAPIDS
Cedar Rapids Gazette (319) 398-8211
(N) 900#/N&P.

COUNCIL BLUFFS
Daily Nonpareil (712) 328-1811
(N) 900#.

**DAVENPORT/MOLINE/ROCK
ISLAND**
*Davenport Leader, Moline Dispatch,
Rock Island Argus*
(319) 326-5848
(N) 900#. Same personals appear in
all three.

DES MOINES
Des Moines Register (515) 284-8186
(N) 900# daily. About 100-150
personals.

videodating
Selective Singles (515) 270-1000
Report 600 members and in business
10 years. No price quotes by phone,
but they call it "very reasonable."

**matchmakers/introduction
services**
Together Dating Service
(515) 221-9191
1309 W. 50th Street.

SIOUX CITY
Sioux City Journal (712) 279-5092
(N) N&P.

KANSAS

JUNCTION CITY
Daily Union (913) 762-5000
(N) N&P. Can also run personals in sister
papers: *Fort Riley Post, Wamego Smoke
Signal, Daily Union Plus, Chapman
Advertiser, Lindsborg News Record.*

KANSAS CITY
The Squire (913) 384-6397
(N) 900# free weekly.

Overland Park Sun (913) 381-1010
Overland Park
(N) 900#. The personals run in all Sun
papers: *Shawnee Sun, Lenexa Sun,
Prairie Village Sun, Leawood Sun,
Merriam Sun, Mission Sun, Roeland Park
Sun, Mission Hills Sun, Fairway Sun,
Stanley Sun, Lake Quivira Sun, Stillwell
Sun, Country Side Sun, Westwood Sun.*

videodating
Great Expectations (913) 451-3711
7501 College Blvd., Suite 110.

**matchmakers/introduction
services**
Together Dating Service (816) 753-6699
3100 Broadway.

MatchMaker International
(913) 642-5700
7121 W 95 Street, Overland Park.

LAWRENCE
Journal World (913) 843-1000
(N) 900#.

MANHATTAN
Manhattan Mercury (913) 776-2200
(N) 900#/N&P.

OLATHE
Olathe Daily News (913) 764-2211
(N) 900#.

SALINA
Salina Journal (913) 823-6363
(N) 900#.

TOPEKA
Topeka Capital Journal (913) 295-1126
(N) 900#.

WICHITA
Wichita Eagle (316) 268-6000
(N) 900#.

KENTUCKY

LEXINGTON
Lexington Herald-Leader
(606) 233-7878
(N) 900#/N&P. About 1/2 page of
personals.

**matchmakers/introduction
services**
MatchMaker International
(606) 266-4611
120 Todds Road Cir.

LOUISVILLE
Louisville Courier-Journal
(502) 582-2622
(N) 900#/N&P. Major: 250+ personals
in the Meeting Place.

Louisville Eccentric Observer (*LEO*)
(502) 895-9770
(A) 900# free weekly (Wed). About
30-50 personals.

Singles Choice (502) 896-2105
(S) Did not respond to our request for
information.

**matchmakers/introduction
services**
MatchMaker International
(502) 423-0401

Together Dating Service (502) 429-9500

LOUISIANA

BATON ROUGE
Morning Advocate (504) 383-0111
(N) 900#. About 1/2 page of personals.

**matchmakers/introduction
services**
Together Dating Service (504) 926-2080
7916 Wrenwood Blvd.

LAFAYETTE
The Advertiser (318) 235-8511
(N) 900#.

The Times of Acadiana (318) 237-3560
(A) 900# free weekly (Wed). 70+
personals a week.

MONROE
News-Star (318) 362-0204
(N) 900#. About 60 personals.

NEW ORLEANS
Gambit (504) 486-5900
(A) 900#/N&P free weekly (Tue).
About 100 personals.

Times-Picayune (504) 826-3598
(N) 900#.

**matchmakers/introduction
services**
MatchMaker International
(504) 455-5600
3100 Kingman, Metaire.

Professional Introductions
(504) 524-4576
Introductions using PHOTOS and
profile sheets. No cost quotes by
phone. In business 6 years.

Lunch Partners, Inc. (504) 866-1712
They do the matching. Cost: $150 for
3 intros in 6 months. Only about 40
members currently, so call and ask if
they've grown.

Southeast Singles Assoc. (601) 872-1717
For more information see Biloxi, Miss
listing.

SHREVEPORT
Shreveport Times-Journal
(818) 459-3200
(N) 900#. About 1/2 page of personals.

MAINE

AUGUSTA
Kennebec Journal (207) 623-3811
(N) 900#/N&P Mon, Fri, Sat. Up to
100 personals a week (somewhat
seasonal with more personals in the
summer). The same personals also
appear in the *Waterville Sentinel.*

BANGOR
Bangor Daily News (207) 990-8020
(N) N&P daily.

The Weekly (207) 942-2913
(N) N&P free newspaper (Thur).

BRUNSWICK (Topsham)
The Maine Times (207) 729-0126
(A) 900#/N&P free weekly (Wed).
50-75 personals (somewhat seasonal
with more personals in the summer).

LEWISTON
The Sun Journal (207) 784-5411
(N) 900# Fri, Sun. 50+ personals a week.

PORTLAND
Maine Telegram (207) 780-9100
(N) 900# Sun. 100+ personals.

Casco Bay Weekly (207) 775-6601
(A) 900#/N&P free weekly (Thur).
Major: 250-350 personals.

Note: Also see *Dateline New England*
singles magazine under Durham, New
Hampshire, which carries Portland
area personals.

WATERVILLE
Waterville Sentinel (207) 623-3811
(N) 900#/N&P. Same personals as
Kennebec Journal.

MARYLAND

ANNAPOLIS
The Capitol (410) 268-5000
(N) 900#.

BALTIMORE
City Paper (410) 523-2300
(A) 900#/N&P free weekly (Wed).
Major: 300+ personals per issue.
Sponsors monthly singles parties.

Baltimore Magazine (410) 752-3577
(CN) 900#/N&P. About 50-80 per issue
in this glossy city-named monthly.
Sponsors singles parties announced in
classifieds.

The Baltimore Sun (410) 332-6000
(N) 900#. About one page of personals.

Jewish Times (410) 752- 3504
(N) 900#/N&P weekly (Fri).

Baltimore Messenger (410) 337-2410
(N) 900#. About a page of personals
which also appear in 12 other
suburban newspapers: *Columbia
Flyer, Jeffersonian, Laurel Leader, Free
Press, N.E. Times Booster, N.E. Times
Reporter, Cloving Mills Times, Fort
Mead Sound, Howard County Times,
Catonsville Times, Arbudus Times,
Towson Times.*

singles activities

Baltimore Magazine and *City Paper* (both listed above) sponsor singles parties. Look for announcements in classifieds/personals.

videodating

Great Expectations (410) 938-8989 40 York Rd., Suite 500, Towson.

Great Expectations (703) 847-0808 8601 Westwood Center Dr., Tysons Corner, Vienna, VA.

matchmakers/introduction services

Together Dating Service (410) 561-3283 9690 Deereco Rd, Timonium.

Together Dating Service (410) 838-2286 Bel Air.

Together Dating Service (410) 730-0290 10227 Wincopin Cir, Columbia.

Together Dating Service (410) 544-3636 Severna Park.

CUMBERLAND

Cumberland Times News (301) 722-4600 (N) 900#.

HAGERSTOWN

Hagerstown Herald Mail (301) 733-5131 (N) 900#.

LANHAM

Prince Georges Journal Express (301) 459-3131 (N) 900#. Same personals appear in the *Montgomery Journal* and in Virginia papers the *Arlington Journal, Alexandria Journal, Fairfax Journal.*

WALDORF

Waldorf Recorder (301) 373-8000 (N) 900#. Package deal with same personals in the *Maryland Indepen-dent, Calver County Recorder, South County Currant, Inquirer Gazette, Flightliner, Charles County Weekend, Enterprise.*

MASSACHUSETTS

BOSTON

The Boston Phoenix (617) 859-3200 (A) 900#/N&P weekly (Thur). Major: 400 personals per issue.

Boston Magazine (617) 262-9700 (CN) 900#/N&P. One of the best glossy city-named magazines for personals with 150-200 ads per month.

Boston Herald (617) 423-4545 (N) 900#. One page Friday under Singles Scene.

Boston Globe (617) 929-2480 (N) 900#. Calendar section Thursday.

The Jewish Advocate (617) 367-9100 (N) 900#/N&P weekly (Fri). Up to 200 personals (one of the top Jewish papers in the country for personals).

Boston Journal (617) 254-0334 (N) 900# free weekly. The same ads appear in *Auston Brighton Journal* and *Brookline Journal.*

Daily Transcript (617) 487-7200 Deedham (N) 900#. Same personals are in other Boston area community papers: *Needham Chronicle, Newton Graphic, Parkway Transcript.*

Dating Page (508) 535-6660, (S) 900#/N&P. Free and published every three weeks. Major: 600 personals. Available at convenience stores and other outlets in New England. Personals from throughout New England, but mostly Mass, NH and RI. Does not sponsor/list singles events. Address: *The Dating Page*, Box 310, Lynnfield, MA 01940.

The Singles Scene (203) 261-2908 (S) 900#/N&P monthly ($2.95). About 50 personals. Extensive singles events calendar. Address: *The Singles Scene*, P.O. Box 299, Boston, MA 02134.

singles activities
The Post Club (see below under videodating).

New England Singles Network (617) 259-1165, or for recorded events line call (617) 259-1118. Sponsor singles dances at hotels with $5-10 entry fee.

videodating
Great Expectations (617) 332-7755 29 Crafts St., Suite 550, Newton.

Mazel Dating Service (617) 431-8473 25 First St., Cambridge. Jewish dating service. Video and non-video options. Videodating cost: $700 per year for passive membership (can be selected, but not select); $800 5 selections per month; $900 unlimited selections. Non-video matchmaker introductions: 6 months for $350 with a minimum of 10 intros. In business 11+ years. Owner Allison Sherman promises no hard sell (and also teaches a course on how to get married in a year). Sponsors annual Mazel Ball singles event on Christmas Eve.

The Post Club (617) 332-2582 Videodating with 50-60 selections per year. Also sponsors 10-12 singles events a month, including progressive singles dinners and parties. Member controlled, with a $1,000 onetime membership fee, and $26 per month dues.

matchmakers/introduction services
Gentlepeople (617) 492-1200 Values oriented matchmaking. People looking for marriage. No smokers, light drinkers only.

LunchDates (617) 254-3000 general information for Boston area. In Downtown Boston (617) 254-2534; Brighton, Brookline, Newton, Cambridge (617) 254-3000; Quincy, South Shore (617) 471-2700, Framingham (508) 620-1211; Burlington (617) 229-7710.

First you do an in-person interview. They set up matches and lunches (or weekend brunches) for you. You do not talk to each other in advance. Fees: one year $850 for 20 intros (ask for the Yellow Pages discount price of $680); 6 months $595 for 10 introductions minimum (Yellow Pages discount $476).

Lunch Couples (617) 449-7164 Interview is done by phone and you mail in a photo to help them make matches. As opposed to LunchDates, you contact each first and set up lunch yourselves. Three months $275, 5 intros minimum; 6 months $350, 10 intros; one year $425, 20 intros. They promise at least one intro every 3 weeks. Also put on some singles events.

Mazel Dating Service (see above under videodating).

Together Dating Service (617) 536-6711 Boston.

Together Dating Service (617) 232-4800 Chestnut Hill.

Together Dating Service (617) 935-4798 Woburn.

Together Dating Service (617) 749-6700 Hingham.

Together Dating Service (508) 879-8641 Framingham.

BROCKTON
The Enterprise (508) 586-6200 (N) 900#/N&P.

HATFIELD
Valley Advocate (413) 781-1900 (A) 900#/N&P free weekly (Thur). Major: 300+ personals per issue. Sister publication of the *Springfield Advocate*. Many of the same personals are in both, and also in Connecticut's Hartford *Advocate*, New Haven *Advocate*, and *Fairfield County Advocate*.

NEW BEDFORD
Standard Times (508) 997-7411
(N) 900#. About a 1/2 page of personals.

PITTSFIELD
Berkshire Eagle (413) 499-3478
(N) N&P (but may go 900#).

matchmakers/introduction services
Introductions, Inc. (413) 447-8332
See under Hartford, Conn for more information.

SPRINGFIELD
Springfield Advocate (413) 781-1900
(A) 900#/N&P free weekly (Thur). 150+ personals. See additional information above under Hatfield.

matchmakers/introduction services
Introductions, Inc. (413) 732-1544
See under Hartford, Conn for more information.

Jewish Dating Service (413) 734-7200
See under Hartford, Conn for more information.

WORCHESTER
Worchester Magazine (508) 832-7133
(A) 900# free weekly (Wed).

Worchester Telegram & Gazette
(508) 793-9393
(N) 900#.

singles activities
24 hour Singles Dance Line
(508) 485-7113
Call for information on their large (several hundred people) singles dances for central Mass. Low event fee (e.g. $5).

MICHIGAN

DETROIT
Metro Times (313) 962-5277
(A) 900#/N&P free weekly (Wed).

Detroit News & Free Press
(313) 222-6400
(N) 900#/N&P Sun, Fri. About one page of personals.

Oakland Press (313) 332-8181 Pontiac
(N) 900# daily. About one page of personals.

Sincere Singles (313) 476-6110
Ann Arbor/Detroit
(S) 900#/N&P monthly ($2.00). Major: about 250 ads which also appear in *The Orbit, Spirit.* Covers mostly southeast Michigan. Doesn't list/sponsor singles events. Straightforward personals publication - no cheesy/corny photo on the cover. Address: *Sincere Singles,* Box 1719, Ann Arbor, MI 48106.

Singles Network (313) 645-5100
Detroit Suburbs
(S) 900#/N&P. Monthly ($2.00). Major: 450+ personals. Serves Oakland, Macomb, Washtenaw, Wayne counties. This is a straightforward very good personals publication. Not at all tacky. Doesn't sponsor/list singles events. Address: *Singles Network,* Box 970, Birmingham, MI 48012.

singles activities
Tri-County Singles & Entertainment, Inc. (313) 842-7422
6921 Bulwer. Sponsor singles parties and dances at nice locations such as country clubs.

matchmakers/introduction services
MatchMaker International
(313) 258-1515
30400 Telegraph, Bingham Farms (near Birmingham).

Interactions Dating Service
(313) 559-8500
27305 Southfield Rd., Lathrup Village (near Oak Park).
Advertise as the oldest and largest in the area. In business 30 years. Do psychological testing for matching. No photos/videos. No price quotes by phone.

videodating
Great Expectations (313) 354-3210
25925 Telegraph Rd., Suite 145,
Southfield.

GAYLORD
Northern Star (517) 732-5125
(S/C) 900#. Personals will also appear
in six other papers: *Action Shopper,
Community Shopper, Heron Shores
Buyers Guide, Alpina Advertiser, The
Lakeland, E. N. Eastern Buyers.*

GRAND RAPIDS
Single File Magazine (616) 774-8100
(S) 900#/N&P. Monthly, $2.00 at
newsstands. Major: 250+ personals,
mostly Grand Rapids area. Lists and
sponsors singles parties. Address:
Single File Magazine, Box 6706,
Grand Rapids, MI 49516.

**matchmakers/introduction
services**
Executive Search (616) 774-8100
Serves west Michigan. Dating service
sponsored by *Single File Magazine*
(see above). Sign up sheet in
magazine. Cost: $50 for 6 months.

LANSING
Lansing State Journal (517) 377-1105
(N) 900#/N&P.

LAPEER
Lapeer County Press (313) 644-0811
(N) 900#.

MONROE
Monroe Evening News (313) 242-1100
(N) 900# Thur, Sun.

Monroe Guardian (313) 243-3545
(N) 900#. About one page of personals.

PORT HURON
Times Herald (313) 985-7171
(N) 900# Sun, Fri. Personals also
appear in the *Penny Pincher.*

SAGINAW
Saginaw News (517) 776-9638
(N) 900#.

TRAVERSE CITY
Record Eagle (616) 964-2000
(N) 900#.

Note: For those in southwestern
Michigan see *Single Today* listing in
Southbend, Indiana.

MINNESOTA

DULUTH
Duluth Daily News Tribune
(218) 723-5200
(N) 900#/N&P Tue, Fri, Sun.

MINNEAPOLIS-ST. PAUL
City Pages (612) 375-1015
(A) 900#/N&P free weekly (Wed).
Major: about 200 personals. Also
sponsors singles functions.

Twin Cities Reader (612) 591-2500
(A) 900#/N&P free weekly (Wed).
Major: about 200 personals. Sponsors
singles parties and events.

Minneapolis Star-Tribune
(612) 673-4000
(N) 900#/N&P Tue, Fri, Sun.

St. Paul Pioneer Press (612) 222-5011
(N) 900# Wed, Fri, Sun.

videodating
Great Expectations (612) 835-9590
3300 Edinborough Way,
Suite 300 Edina.

**matchmakers/introduction
services**
Computer Dating Service (Comdates)
(617) 333-8088
No information given out by phone,
only by mail. Since 1964.

Better Way Referral Service
(617) 430-2967 St. Paul, (617) 332-
8506 Minneapolis. Report 90% of
clients are college grads. Since 1976.

Sensational Results (617) 927-9070
6950 France Ave., South Edina. Photo/
profile dating. You do the selecting (up
to 12 per month). Since 1987. 2,000
members. No price quotes by the phone.

Together Dating Service
(617) 831-3322 Minneapolis,
(617) 631-1100 St. Paul., 3300
Edinborough Way, Suite 419, Edina.

ROCHESTER
Post-Bulletin (507) 285-7777
(N) 900#. Same personals in a local
weekly, the *Expressline.*

ST. CLOUD
St. Cloud Times (612) 255-8738
(N) 900#.

Note: *Solo RFD* carries personals
statewide and lists singles events. See
under Sioux Falls, S. Dakota.

MISSISSIPPI

BILOXI
**matchmakers/introduction
services**
Southeast Singles Association
(601) 872-1717
Membership $35 for 6 months, $70 for
one year. Publish magazine with 300
personals (900#/N&P). Also have an
introduction service: 10 intros for $120,
20 for $180. Serve Miss, GA, LA, AL and
northern Fla. Give "mixers" in Biloxi.

JACKSON
The Clarion Ledger (601) 961-7000
(N) 900#/N&P daily.

MISSOURI

JOPLIN
Joplin Globe (417) 623-3480
(N) 900#.

KANSAS CITY
New Times (816) 753-7880
(A) 900#/N&P free every two weeks.
About 150 personals.

Pitch (816) 561-6061
(A) 900#/N&P free weekly (Thur).
About 100 personals.

Kansas City Star (816) 234-4095
(N) 900#.

Singles Choice (816) 833-3283
(S) 900#/N&P personals. Did not
supply any additional information.

videodating
Great Expectations (913) 451-3711
7501 College Blvd., Suite 110, KS.

**matchmakers/introduction
services**
MatchMaker International
(913) 642-5700
7121 West 95th Street, Overland Park, KS.

Together Dating Service (816) 753-6699
3100 Broadway.

SPRINGFIELD
Pennypower (417) 887-6539
(S/C) 900#.

Springfield News-Leader
(417) 836-1100
(N) 900# Tue, Fri.

ST. JOSEPH
St. Joseph News Press (816) 233-6181
(N) 900#.

ST. LOUIS
Riverfront Times
(314) 231-6666
(A) 900#/N&P free weekly (Wed).
Major: 250+ personals. Excellent
source for singles event information.

St. Louis Post-Dispatch (314) 621-6666
(N) 900# daily.

singles activities
Note: Look for ads in personals/
classifieds in the *Riverfront Times* (see
listing above) for singles parties/events
sponsored by them and by others. It's
an *excellent* source for singles events.

The Heart to Heart Introductions
Recorded singles group/event
information line (314) 822-4700.
See listing below under matchmakers/
introduction services.

The Meeting Group Party
(314) 878-2215
Put on large singles parties at hotels
in 26 major cities around the country.
About $15-20 per event. In St. Louis
look for party ads in the *Riverfront
Times*, or call above phone#.

The Relationship Center (314) 878-0808
Sponsors 15-10 singles events a year
open to non-members. See listing
below under videodating.

videodating
Great Expectations (314) 291-6789
2458 Old Dorsett Rd., Suite 200,
Maryland Heights.

The Relationship Center (314) 878-0808
12747 Olive Blvd. No cost quotes over
the phone. Videodating incorporating
personality testing to check for
compatibility. Report they screen clients
carefully. Have staff psychologists to aid
in counseling at no extra cost. Sponsor
15-20 singles events a year which are
also open to non-members.

**matchmakers/introduction
services**
MatchMaker International
(314) 275-2200
2300 Westport Plaza Drive.

Heart to Heart Introductions
(314) 822-4700
13100 Manchester. Promise price
quotes by phone and no hard sales.
Also sponsor singles events. In
business since 1981.

B Meyer & Associates (314) 542-3050
Bernice Meyer runs a matchmaking
service for people seeking marriage. Very
forthcoming over the phone. Cost: $5,000
($1,500 upfront for one year, with $3,500
due only if she gets you married). Clients
must have a college degree, weight
proportional to height, be non-smokers,
and "emotionally available." No
guaranteed minimum amount of people
you will meet. Since 1986.

MONTANA

BILLINGS
Billings Gazette (406) 657-1212
(N) 900#.

GREAT FALLS
Great Falls Tribune (406) 791-1420
(N) 900#.

HELENA
The Adit (406) 443-3690
(S/C) 900#. Weekly shoppers guide.

MISSOULA
The Missoulian (406) 721-6200
(N) 900#/N&P.

ST. IGNATIUS
Sweetheart (406) 745-4209
(S) 900#/N&P. About 100 (lengthy)
personals, including some PHOTO ads.
This family operation - Charlie James,
wife Cupcake(!) and daughter Lise - pride
themselves on personalized service.
Charlie also does some matchmaking at
much less cost than his urban counter-
parts. *Sweetheart* Serves Montana, the
Dakotas, Idaho, etc. has personals from
cowboys and cowgirls from California to
Maine. They also sponsor singles parties
and activities. Address: *Sweetheart*, Box
514, St. Ignatius, Montana 59865.

NEBRASKA

GRAND ISLAND
Grand Island Independent (308) 382-1000
(N) 900#.

LINCOLN
Lincoln Journal Star (402) 473-7451
(N) 900# Thur, Fri, Sat, Sun. About 1/3
page.

**matchmakers/introduction
services**
Together Dating Service (402) 467-4846
210 Gateway Green Tree Ct., Suite 245.

**OMAHA
videodating**
New Beginnings Video (402) 333-0300
13937 Gold Circle. In business 14
years. $995 for an open-ended
membership.

**matchmakers/introduction
services**
Together Dating Service (402) 697-9797
11930 Arbor St.

Note: *Solo RFD* carries personals
statewide. See listing under Sioux
Falls, S. Dakota.

NEVADA

CARSON CITY
Penny Saver (702) 883-4322
(S/C) 900#. Shoppers guide mailed to
homes free (Wed).

LAS VEGAS
Las Vegas New Times (702) 871-6780
(A) 900#/N&P free weekly (Fri).
About one page of personals. Also
sponsor singles parties and events.

Las Vegas Review-Journal
(702) 383-0383
(N) 900# Sun. Same personals appear
in the *Las Vegas Sun.*

Thrifty Nickel (702) 457-5500
(S/C) 900# Thur. Two pages of personals.

videodating
Executive Introductions (702) 732-7544
1631 E. Desert Inn. In business 10
years. Promise no hard sell. No price
quote by phone.

Comp-U-Match (702) 732-3283
1555 E. Flamingo Rd., Suite 109.
Matching by computer and video.
They pre-screen and send you tapes
by mail (or you can come by in
person). No limit on number of
matches. Cost of program from $399
to $2,000 (for a 3 year membership).

**matchmakers/introduction
services**
Together Dating Service (702) 791-3377
20001 Flamingo Rd., #103.

Perfect Match (702) 227-3300
1771 E. Flamingo. No price quotes by
phone.

RENO
Reno Gazette Journal (702) 788-6401
(N) 900# daily.

**matchmakers/introduction
services**
Matchmakers Network, Inc.
(702) 826-2232
PHOTO matchmaking (you can see
photos before you meet). $200 for
one year. Minimum of 15-20 matches.
400 members.

NEW HAMPSHIRE

EXETER
Exeter News Letter (603) 772-6000
(N) 900#. Same personals appear in
the *Hampton Union, Kingstonian,
Raymond Times, Plaistow-Hamstead
News.*

MANCHESTER
Dateline New England
(S) See listing under Portsmouth for
more information.

videodating
Videodates (800) 464-3283
See listing under Nashua for more
information.

matchmakers/introduction services
Together Dating Service (603) 624-4552
721 Chestnut St.

NASHUA
Nashua Telegraph (603) 882-2741
(N) 900# Thursday.

videodating
Videodates (603) 886-3283 or
(800) 464-3283
Six month membership for $745. Six
month passive membership (they call it
"one way" - you do a video and can be
selected but not select) for $470. Report
they run background checks on would-be
clients. 1,000 members, in business 5 years.

matchmakers/introduction services
LunchDates (603) 881-7000
For more information see Boston listing.

Together Dating Service (603) 882-8732
6 Trafalgar Sq.

PORTSMOUTH
Dateline New England (603) 868-2222
(S) 900#/N&P. Free monthly. About 200
personals. Serves mostly New Hampshire
but also southern Maine. Sponsors
singles activities and has excellent list of
singles organizations throughout New
England. Address: *Dateline New England*,
P.O. 100, Durham, NH 03824.

matchmakers/introduction services
Together Dating Service (603) 436-3906

SALEM
matchmakers/introduction services
Together Dating Service (603) 893-9293
120 Main St.

NEW JERSEY

Note: See *Jewish Singles News*
newspaper (under New York City) for
northern NJ singles activities listings.

videodating
Visual Preference (201) 488-3371
Hackensack. Serves NJ, Conn, NY. No
cost quote by phone. $50 fee for first
interview (applied toward membership).
They send you potential videocassette
matches by mail. Since 1974.

matchmakers/introduction services
Jewish Dating Service (201) 833-2211
Bergen County,
(908) 463-2233 Piscataway. See
Hartford, Conn listing for details.

Mandy's Matchmaking (201) 265-1300
River Edge

MatchMaker International
(201) 592-5900 Fort Lee

MatchMaker International
(201) 471-3100 Clifton

Solution For Singles (201) 944-6171
Fort Lee
PHOTO and profile dating. $795 for 6
months and 6 choices; $1,195 for one
year and unlimited choices; up to $1,395
for 2 year unlimited selections. Owner
gets involved in process and helps things
along. No high pressure sales.

Note: Commuters can also check
Philadelphia and New York City listings.

ASBURY PARK
Asbury Park Press (908) 922-6050
(N) 900#.

ATLANTIC CITY
The Press of Atlantic City (609) 272-1010
(N) 900#.

CAMDEN
Camden Courier Post (609) 663-6000
(N) 900# daily.

CHERRY HILL
videodating
Great Expectations (609) 667-6673
One Cherry Hill, Suite 600.

matchmakers/introduction services

MatchMaker International (609) 231-4500
496 Kings Highway, Suite 203.

Together Dating Service (609) 663-7222

HACKENSACK
Bergen Record (201) 488-3100
(N) 900# Wed.

JERSEY CITY
Jersey City Reporter (201) 798-7800
(N) 900#. Same personals appear in
seven other papers: *Hudson Reporter,
Hoboken Reporter, Weehawken
Reporter, Secaucus Reporter, North
Bergen Reporter, North Hudson
Reporter,* and *Hudson Current.*

MORRISTOWN
The Daily Record (201) 428-8900
(N) 900#.

NEWARK
Newark Star-Ledger (201) 877-4242
(N) 900#.

PASSAIC
North Jersey Herald (201) 365-3000
(N) 900#.

PRINCETON
See Trenton listings.

TOMS RIVER
The Reporter & The Observer (908) 349-3000
(N) 900#.

PERTH AMBOY
News Tribune (908) 442-0400
(N) 900#.

RAHWAY
The Atom Tabloid (908) 574-1200
(N) N&P.

SUMMIT
Independent Press (908) 464-1025
(N) 900#. You can pay extra and have
your personal appear in up to 15
other North Jersey papers in Passaic
County, Bergen County, etc.

TRENTON
Trentonian (609) 989-7800
(N) 900#/N&P daily.

Trenton Times (609) 989-7870
(N) 900#.

matchmakers/introduction services
MatchMaker International
(609) 231-4500
Mt. Laural.

Together Dating Service (609) 452-0393
5 Independence Way, Princeton.

VINELAND
Daily Journal (609) 691-7770
(N) 900#.

WESTFIELD
Suburban News (908) 396-4500
(N) 900# weekly paper (Wed).

WHIPPANY
Daily Record (201) 428-8900
(N) 900#.

NEW MEXICO

ALBUQUERQUE
Albuquerque Tribune (505) 823-4444
(N) 900#.

Albuquerque News Express
(505) 344-8818
(N) 900#.

Albuquerque Journal (505) 823-3342
(N) 900# Thur, Fri, Sun. About 1/2
page of personals.

On the Scene (505) 299-4401
(S) 900#/N&P. Free monthly available
in stores. About 150-200 personals.
This singles magazine reports it's
broadening its appeal, including
adding entertainment coverage. Lists
singles activities.

matchmakers/introduction services

Perfect Match (505) 275-3333
Introduction service based in Las Vegas, Nevada. No limit on the number of intros, no price quotes by the phone.

Together Dating Service (800) 926-8343

SANTE FE

Sante Fe Reporter (505) 988-5541
(A) N&P free weekly (Wed).

The New Mexican (505) 983-3303
(N) 900#.

NEW YORK

ALBANY

Metroland (518) 463-2500
(A) 900#/N&P free weekly (Thur).
About 50 personals.

Jewish World (518) 459-8455
(N) N&P weekly (Thur).

matchmakers/introduction services

Introductions, Inc. (518) 456-3456
See under Hartford, Conn for more information.

BINGHAMTON

Binghamton Press Sun (607) 798-1234
(N) 900#. Option for your personal to also appear in the *Ithaca Journal*, *Utica Observer Dispatch*, and *Elmira Star Gazette*.

matchmakers/introduction services

Introductions, Inc. (607) 723-9592
See Hartford, Conn for more information.

BUFFALO

Buffalo News & Evening News
(716) 849-3456
(N) 900#.

matchmakers/introduction services

MatchMaker International (716) 835-4046
331 Alberta Dr.

Sincere Dating Service (716) 833-1501
PHOTO dating service. Most clients in their 30's-40's. $245 per year. Average of receiving one match per month. In business 10 years.

ELMIRA

Star Gazette (607) 733-8365
(N) 900#. Your personal can also appear in the *Ithaca Journal*.

**GLENS FALLS
matchmakers/introduction services**

Introductions, Inc. (518) 798-2811
For more information see Hartford, Conn listing.

ITHACA

Ithaca Times (607) 277-7000
(A) 900# free weekly (Thur). Option for your personal to also appear in the *Elmira Star Gazette*.

Ithaca Journal (607) 273-2321
(N) 900#.

MIDDLETOWN

Middletown Times Herald Record
(914) 343-2181
(N) 900#.

**MT. KISCO
matchmakers/introduction services**

Together Dating Service (914) 666-7770
10 Moger Ave.

NEW YORK CITY (& Long Island)

New York Magazine (212) 880-0700
(CN) 900#/N&P weekly. 200+ personals in this excellent publication. It's more of a newsweekly than other city-named magazines.

The Village Voice (212) 475-3300
(A) 900#/N&P weekly (Wed). Major: 400+ personals.

New York City Press (212) 941-1130
(A) 900#/N&P free weekly (Wed).
Major: 400+ personals. (They actually
use a local exchange not a 900# for
their voice mail personals).

Daily News (212) 949-2000
(N) 900# daily.

New York Post (212) 815-8315
(N) 900# Tue, Wed, Fri, Sat. About a
page of personals.

Jewish Singles News (212) 348-1755
(S) 900#/N&P. Monthly ($2.00) quality
singles newspaper with *extensive*
singles events listings for New York
City area, plus 150 personals. Address:
Jewish Singles News, P.O. Box 1053,
NY, NY 10028.

Jewish Week (212) 921-7822
(N) N&P weekly (Fri).

Manhattan Spirit (212) 947-5511
(N) 900# free weekly (Thur). Same
personals appear in *Our Town*.

Brooklyn Heights Press (212) 608-1384
Brooklyn
(N) 900#. Same personals are in
Cobblehill News, Daily Bulletin.

City Sun (718) 624-5959 Brooklyn
(N) 900# weekly paper (Wed).

Queens Tribune (718) 357-7400
Queens
(N) 900# free weekly (Thur).

Staten Island Advance (718) 720-6000
Staten Island
(N) 900#.

Marketeer Islander (718) 980-4848
Staten Island
(S/C) 900# free weekly shoppers
guide (Sat).

Newsday (516) 454-2020
(N) 900#/N&P Tue, Thur, Sun. One
page of personals.

Suffolk County Life (516) 369-0800
Riverhead
(N) 900#/N&P free by mail weekly (Wed).

Beacon (516) 587-5612 Babylon
(N) 900# Thursday. Limited number of
personals.

Pennysaver (516) 698-8400 Medford
(S/C) 900# free by mail weekly (Thur).

South Shore Tribune (516) 431-5628
Island Park
(N) 900# weekly (Thur).

South Bay Newspaper (516) 226-2636
Lindenhurst
(S/C) 900# Wed.

singles activities
See *Jewish Singles News* (listed above)
as an *excellent* source for events.

Jewish Singles party line
(914) 725-2551, or (914) 725-7540
Major parties at hotels and other
activities for professionals in their
20's, 30's, 40's.

**matchmakers/introduction
services**
Denise Winston (212) 593-4843,
(212) 935-9350
Upscale matchmaker. Individual relationship
search for $5,000 on up. Or you can register
for the dating pool: $500 for 2 years.

Abby Hirsch (212) 245-7175
Upscale matchmaker.

Kathryn Hason, Inc. (914) 723-1868
Upscale matchmaker. Scarsdale and
Manhattan locations.

It's Just Lunch (212) 644-0022
120 E. 56 Street. $500 for 6 months or
6 lunches. They arrange matches/
lunches. You meet and go dutch.
Clients required to have their weight
be proportional to their height.

Lunch Dates (212) 259-9348
$495 for one year and 18 introduc-
tions. The matches set up their own
lunch meeting. The original Lunch
Date is in Los Angeles, and has been
in business 3+ years.

Together Dating Service (212) 697-7684
52 E 42 St., Manhattan.

Together Dating Service (914) 963-1414
6 Xavier Dr., Yonkers.

Together Dating Service (516) 731-7900
3601 Hempstead Turnpike, Levittown.

Together Dating Service (516) 541-6400
627 Broadway, Massapequa.

Together Dating Service (516) 829-4454
134 Middle Neck Rd., Great Neck.

PLATTSBURGH
Plattsburgh Press Republican
(518) 561-2300
(N) 900#.

POUGHKEEPSIE
Poughkeepsie Journal (914) 454-2000
(N) 900# daily.

**matchmakers/introduction
services**
Introductions, Inc. (914) 485-8033
For more information see Hartford,
Conn listing.

PUTNAM COUNTY
Putnam Courrier News (914) 225-6397
(N) 900#. Same personals also appear
in nearby Connecticut papers for no
extra charge, including the *New
Milford Times, Brookfield Journal,
Litchfield Inquirer.*

ROCHESTER
City Newspaper (716) 244-3329
(A) 900#/N&P free weekly (Thur).

**matchmakers/introduction
services**
Better Beginnings (716) 227-8400
550 Latona Office Campus Bldg.
B-200. They make introductions for
you. No photos or videos. $150 for 4
month membership and up to 13
introductions. In business 18 years.

Date-Mate (716) 424-4244
PHOTO matching, $195 for 3 months
and 6 introductions. Non-photo
matching $185 for 6 months. They
pick appropriate matches for you,
then you make final decision. In
business 10 years.

Heart to Heart (716) 467-4456
PHOTO and profile. You choose your
matches. $100 for 6 months, $15 for
each selection you actually meet. $25
for a second 6 months.

SYRACUSE *Syracuse New Times*
(315) 422-7011
(A) 900#/N&P free weekly (Wed).
250+ personals. Also lists and
sponsors singles events.

*Syracuse Post Standard, Herald
Journal & Herald American*
(315) 470-0011
(N) 900# Fri in the *Post Standard*,
Thur in the *Herald Journal*, Sun in the
Herald American.

**matchmakers/introduction
services**
Introductions, Inc. (315) 453-9134
See Hartford, Conn for more information.

UTICA
Utica Observer (315) 735-7511
(N) 900#.

**matchmakers/introduction
services**
Introductions, Inc. (315) 768-4210
See Hartford, Conn for more information.

WHITE PLAINS
Reporter Dispatch (914) 694-5111
(N) 900#.

Jewish Dating Service (914) 684-6060
See Hartford, Conn listing for information.

The Singles Network (914) 921-3828
(Hartsdale)
See Stamford, Conn listing for more
information.

Together Dating Service (914) 948-8380
280 N. Central Ave., Hartsdale.

NORTH CAROLINA

ASHEVILLE
Green Line (704) 251-1333
(A) N&P free monthly.

Asheville Citizen-Times (704) 252-5611
(N) 900#.

CHARLOTTE
Creative Loafing (704) 375-2121
(N) 900#/N&P free weekly (Wed).
Major: 300 personals per week.
Also sponsor some singles events.

Charlotte Observer (704) 377-5555
(N) 900#/N&P (Wed) in the Break
magazine.

Metrolina Singles Magazine
(704) 542-4747
(S) 900#/N&P. Glossy quality monthly
singles publication available on
newsstands ($2.00). Major: 150-200
personals. Also runs personals sections
for the *Charlotte Observer, Watauga
Democrat, Charlotte Pennysaver,* etc.

**matchmakers/introduction
services**
Together Dating Service (704) 523-8800
5960 Fairview Rd.

FAYETTEVILLE
Fayetteville Observer Times
(919) 323-4848
(N) 900#.

GASTONIA
The Gaston Gazette (704) 864-3291
(N) 900#/N&P.

GREENSBORO
Greensboro News & Record (919) 373-7099
(N) 900#.

**matchmakers/introduction
services**
Together Dating Service (919) 292-8811
Forum VI Shopping Center.

RALEIGH/DURHAM
News & Observer (919) 829-4500
(N) 900#.

The Independent (919) 286-1972
(A) 9003/N&P free weekly (Wed).
About 150 personals.

The Herald Sun (919) 419-6500
(N) 900#.

videodating
Great Expectations (919) 872-4888
3714 Benson Dr., Suite 200, Raleigh.

WILMINGTON
Wilmington Star-News (919) 343-2323
(N)900#/N&P.

WINSTON SALEM
Winston Salem Journal (919) 727-7429
(N) 900.

NORTH DAKOTA

FARGO
The Forum (701) 235-7311
(N) 900# Tues, Sun.

GRAND FORKS
Grand Forks Herald (701) 780-1100
(N) 900#/N&P (Thur 900#, Sat N&P).

Note: *Solo RFD* carries personals
statewide and lists singles events. See
under Sioux Falls, S. Dakota.

OHIO

AKRON
Akron Beacon Journal (216) 996-3333
(N) 900#.

matchmakers/introduction services

MatchMaker International
(216) 869-6688
3090 W. Market St., Fairlawn.

ATHENS

Athens News (614) 594-8219
(A) N&P free twice weekly (Mon, Thur).

CINCINNATI

Everybody's News (513) 651-2606
(A) 900#/N&P free every other week.
Major: 200 personals.

Cincinnati Inquirer (513) 721-2700
(N) 900#. One page of personals.

Cincinnati Post (513) 352-6300
(N) 900# Tue, Sat. One page of
personals.

*Cincinnati Press Community
Newspapers* (513) 242-4300
(N) 900# free weeklies. The same
personals appear in over a dozen
papers in the Cincinnati area,
including the *Milford Advertiser,
Forest Hills Journal, Western Hills
Press, Delhi Press, Hilltop News,
Community Press, Suburban Life
Press, Eastern Hills Journal.*

matchmakers/introduction services

MatchMaker International
(513) 772-7200
11260 Chester Rd.

Together Dating Service (513) 563-3577
4555 Lake Forest Dr.

videodating

Great Expectations (513) 793-7733
8044 Montgomery Rd., Suite 151.

CLEVELAND

Cleveland Plain Dealer (216) 344-4166
(N) 900# Fri, Sun. Major: 900+
personals under Person to Personals -
one of the largest in the country. Also
listings of singles events and
organizations (next to the personal ads).

Cleveland Magazine (216) 771-2833
(CN) 900#/N&P. Glossy quality
upscale monthly city-named publication with about 50 personals.

Free Times (216) 229-1600
(A) 900# free weekly (Wed). About 75
personals a week. They're beginning
to sponsor singles events.

Scene Entertainment Weekly
(216) 241-7550
(A) N&P free weekly (Thur). 75-100
personals.

Ohio's Finest Singles (216) 521-1111
(S) 900#/N&P free monthly, and
available in convenience stores,
grocery stores, etc. Major: several
hundred personals in northern Ohio
area. Sponsors and lists singles events.
Address: *Ohio's Finest Singles*, Box
770610, Cleveland OH 44107.

Cleveland Call & Post (216) 791-7600
(N) 900#.

matchmakers/introduction services

Encounters by Karen (216) 731-6262
25931 Euclid Av. 400 members. $95 to
join for 2 months with 15 introductions. Karen says she's been in
business 20 years.

MatchMaker International
(216) 765-8600
29525 Chagrin Blvd., Pepper Pike.

MatchMaker International
(216) 221-4700
22255 Center Ridge Rd., Rocky River.

videodating

Cupid's Connection (216) 777-7017
4701 Great Northern Blvd.

Great Expectations (216) 642-8855
6300 Rockside Rd., Suite 200, Independence.

singles activities

See *Cleveland Plain Dealer* listing.

COLUMBUS
Columbus Guardian (614) 486-1010
(A) 900# free weekly (Wed). Major:
200 personals. Calendar also lists
singles events. One of three alternative Columbus papers.

The Other Paper (614) 847-3800
(A) 900#/N&P free weekly (Thur).
Major: 200 personals.

Columbus Alive (614) 221-2449
(A) 900#/N&P free weekly (Wed).
About 100 personals.

Columbus Dispatch (614) 461-5042
(N) 900#/N&P.

The Single Scene (614) 476-8802
(S) 900#/N&P published every two
months, and available on newsstands.
About 30 personals (some with
PHOTOS). Sponsors/lists singles
events. Address: *The Single Scene*,
P.O. Box 30856, Gahanna OH 43230.

videodating
Great Expectations (614) 431-8500
1103 Schrock Rd., Suite 101.

Visual Choice International
(614) 885-6414
6660 Doubletree Ave. $795 lifetime
membership with no limit on your
number of selections. 3,000 members.

**matchmakers/introduction
services**
*Bringing People Together Dating
Service* (614) 436-5683
6161 Busch Blvd., Suite 131; or
(614) 866-6423 2020 Brice Rd.
No videos/computers introduction
service. No price quotes by phone,
but report cost is less than national
franchise outlets. You receive
information on a card about the
people they select for you. Then the
two of you talk by phone and decide
whether to meet. In business 14 years.

MatchMaker International (614) 888-0202
6877 N. High St.

DAYTON
Dayton Daily News (513) 225-2026
(N) 900# Wed, Sun.

LIMA
Lima News (419) 223-1010
(N) 900#.

LORAIN
Morning Journal (216) 245-6901
(N) 900#.

NEWARK
The Advertiser (614) 453-0615
(S/C) 900#. The same personals run in
14 papers in Athens County, Delaware
County, Zanesville, etc.

PORTSMOUTH
Daily Times (614) 353-3101
(N) N&P.

STEUBENVILLE
The Herald Star (614) 283-4711
(N) 900#.

**matchmakers/introduction
services**
MatchMaker International (614) 282-4100

TOLEDO
Toledo Blade (419) 245-6428
(N) 900#/N&P.

OKLAHOMA

OKLAHOMA CITY
Oklahoma Gazette (405) 235-0798
(A) 900#/N&P free weekly (Wed).
About 100 personals per issue.

**matchmakers/introduction
services**
Center For Single Adults
(405) 948-7111
3421 NW 50 St. PHOTO/profile
introduction service. No price quotes
over the phone, but say they cost
substantially less than the competition.

MatchMaker International (405) 722-7500
7101 NW Expwy.

Together Dating Service (405) 236-4916
3030 NW Expwy.

Together Dating Service (405) 949-9091
6305 Waterford St.

TULSA
Tulsa World (918) 581-8400
(N) 900#.

videodating
Single Station (918) 252-0003
6808 S. Memorial. In business 14 years.
No price quotes over the phone, but
they say it's less than *Great Expectations*, and report 2,900 members.

**matchmakers/introduction
services**
Together Dating Service (918) 254-2182
7666 E. 61 St.

OREGON

EUGENE
The Register Guard (503) 485-1234
(N) 900#. About 75 personals.

Eugene Weekly (503) 484-0519
(A) 900# free weekly (Thur). About 50
personals per issue.

Comic News (503) 344-1922
(A) 900# free. Out every other Thursday.

MEDFORD
The Medford Mail-Tribune
(503) 776-4466
(N) 900#.

PORTLAND
Willamette Week (503) 243-1500
(A) 900#/N&P free weekly (Wed).
Major: 600+ personals. One of the
country's best alternative publications
for personals.

Beaverton Valley Times (503) 684-0360
(N) 900#. Same personals in other
local weeklies: *Lake Oswego Review*,
West Lynn Tidings, *Tiger Times*, etc.

singles activities
Sports Link (503) 224-LINK
Sports/singles activities for the
athletically minded, plus parties (non-
members welcome). $65 for the first 6
months, $40 each 6 months thereafter.
In business 4 years. About 70 members.

videodating
Great Expectations (503) 226-3283
5331 SW Macadam, Suite 225.

**matchmakers/introduction
services**
MatchMaker International
(503) 626-9100
9020 SW Washington Square Dr.,
Tigard.

SALEM
Salem Statesman Journal (503) 399-6776
(N) 900#/N&P.

PENNSYLVANIA

ALLENTOWN/BETHLEHEM
Morning Call (215) 820-6663
(N) 900# Sat. 100+ personals.

Express-Times (215) 867-5000
(N) 900# Fri, Sun.

**matchmakers/introduction
services**
Couple's Dating Service (215) 865-3283
Since 1985. Supply one to three
matches per month. No price quotes
by phone, but say it's "affordable for
most people."

Judy Yiori's Compatibles
(215) 432-3003
Matchmaking. Cost in "the upper
hundreds." In business 18 years.

MatchMaker International
(215) 882-9717
3400 Bethlehem Pike, Bethlehem.

MatchMaker International
(610) 395-5222
107 S. Route 100, Allentown.

Soul Mates (610) 432-7888
1509 Hamilton St., Allentown
Advertise a refund policy and
background checks.

ALTOONA
Altoona Mirror (814) 946-7421
(N) N&P.

**matchmakers/introduction
services**
MatchMaker International
(814) 944-9986

DOYLESTOWN
The Intelligencer (215) 345-3010
(N) 900# Wed, Fri.

EASTON
Easton Express (215) 258-7171
(N) 900# Fri, Sun.

**matchmakers/introduction
services**
MatchMaker International
(215) 258-522

ERIE
The Erie Daily Times (814) 870-1618
(N) 900#.

GREENSBURG
The Tribune Review (412) 834-1151
(N) 900# Fri, Sun.

HARRISBURG
Patriot News & Evening News
(717) 255-8143
(N) 900# Sun.

**matchmakers/introduction
services**
Couples Dating Service (717) 697-5683
Mechanicsburg. No price quotes by phone.
Supply one to three matches per month.

MatchMaker International
(717) 657-3111
4807 Jonestown Rd.

MatchMaker International
(717) 737-0400
355 N. 21 St., Camp Hill.

Together Dating Service (717) 766-8220
5020 Ritter Rd., Suite 203, Mechanicsburg.

INDIANA
Indiana Gazette (412) 349-4949
(N) N&P.

JOHNSTOWN
Tribune Democrat (814) 532-5030
(N) 900#.

matchmaker/introduction services
MatchMaker International
(814) 266-8999

LANCASTER
*The News Era, Intelligencer Journal,
Sunday News* (717) 291-8711
(N) 900#.

**matchmakers/introduction
services**
MatchMaker International (717) 295-9400
3002 Hempland Rd.

MEADVILLE
Meadville Tribune (814) 724-6370
(N) 900#.

NORRISTOWN
Times Herald (215) 272-2500
(N) 900# daily.

OXFORD
Chester County Press (215) 932-2444
(N) 900#/N&P.

PHILADELPHIA and surrounding
area
Philadelphia Magazine (215) 564-7700
(CN) N&P/900#. Upscale glossy city-
named monthly magazine with a
healthy 130-160 personals.

Philadelphia City Paper (215) 735-8444
(A) 900#/N&P free weekly (Thur).
About 100 personals per issue.
Also sponsors some singles events.

Philadelphia Inquirer (215) 854-5411
(N) 900#. Major: 400 personals per
week. Under the Connections heading
in the Sunday classifieds.

Welcomat (215) 563-1234
(N) 900#/N&P free weekly (Wed).

Jewish Exponent (215) 893-5700
(N) 900#/N&P.

The Carrier Pigeon (215) 322-6920
(S/C) 900#/N&P free weekly (Wed).

Northeast Times (215) 355-1234
(N) 900#. Free home delivered weekly
serving northeast Philadelphia.

Review Chronicle (215) 336-2500
(N) 900#/N&P. Free home delivered
weekly serving south Philadelphia.

Progress News Press (215) 632-2700
(N) N&P free weekly (Wed). Same
personals appear in the *Bucks County
Tribune, Citizen Sentinel, Bucks
County Telegraph.*

King of Prussia Courier (215) 688-3000
(N) 900#. Weekly serving the Main
Line. The same personals also appear
in the *Suburban* and the *Advertiser.*

News of Delaware County
(215) 649-7600
(N) N&P. For extra charge personals
will also appear in the *Main Line
Times, Mt. Erie Times Express,
Germantown Courier.*

Bucks County Courier (215) 949-4100
Levitown
(N) 900# Wed, Sun.

Delaware Valley Times (215) 622-8800
Primos
(N) N&P.

videodating
Great Expectations (215) 634-3339
1341 N. Delaware Ave.

Great Expectations (215) 244-9800
9501 Roosevelt Blvd., Suite 312.

Great Expectations (609) 667-6673
One Cherry Hill, Suite 600, Cherry
Hill, NJ.

Great Expectations (215) 768-7000
150 Allendale Rd., Bldg. 3, King of Prussia.

**matchmakers/introduction
services**
MatchMaker International
(215) 885-3585
302 Benjamin Fox Pavilion, Jenkintown.

MatchMaker International
(215) 527-8890
2 Bryn Mawr Ave., Bryn Mawr.

MatchMaker International
(609) 231-4500
496 Kings Highway, Suite 203, Cherry
Hill, NJ.

MatchMaker International
(215) 822-7468
445 Bethlehem Pike, Colmar.

Together Dating Service (215) 687-1900
West Valley Rd., Suite 1201 Wayne.

Together Dating Service (215) 885-2505
Jenkintown.

Together Dating Service (609) 663-7222
Cherry Hill, NJ.

Let's Go Dutch! (215) 732-DATE
Lunch date matchmaking. Cost: $400
for 6 months/6 dates, or $595 for one
year/12 dates. You meet over lunch
with no contact beforehand.

Connections (215) 235-3646
Use a psychologist to aid in
matchmaking. PHOTO option available.
Cost: 6 months $700, one year $1,200. No
guaranteed minimum number of
introductions, but say the minimum
average is one introduction per month.
They report 90% of their clients find a
relationship. In business 19 years.

Introductions, Inc. (2150 331-1777
In business 28 years with 800 members.
They do the matchmaking for you. Cost:
no price quotes by phone, but say they
are less expensive than *Together* or
MatchMaker International.

POTTSTOWN
The Mercury (2150 323-3000
(N) 900#/N&P.

PITTSBURGH
Pittsburgh Post-Gazette (412) 263-1100
(N) 900#. Major: several hundred
personals a week.

In Pittsburgh (412) 488-1212
(A) 900# free weekly (Wed). About
200 personals per issue.

Pittsburgh Magazine (412) 622-1360
(CN) 900#/N&P. About 20 personals per
month in this glossy city-named monthly.

Pittsburgh Quality Singles Lifestyle
(412) 561-2277
(S) 900#/N&P. Monthly available at
newsstands ($1.95). About 100 personals
(including some PHOTO ads). Quality
publication. Good source for area singles
organizations and event listings. Address:
Pittsburgh Quality Singles Lifestyle, 300
Mt. Lebanon Blvd. #210-B, Pittsburgh, PA
15234-1505.

Jewish Chronicle (412) 687-1000
(N) N&P weekly (Thur).

The News (412) 375-6611 Alaquippa
(N) N&P.

singles activities
The Network (412) 431-3222
2224 E. Carson St. Singles club giving
large parties (400-500 people) at nicer
hotels. Also sponsor sports activities.
Cost: $96 for one year; 2,000 members.

Jewish Association Serving Singles
(412) 422-5277
Call this their JASSLINE number for
recorded singles event info.

Check calendar of singles events in
Pittsburgh Quality Singles Lifestyle
(see listing above).

Nancy's Sophisticated Singles
(412) 572-5259
Dances every weekend. 500-800 people.

videodating
Great Expectations (412) 928-5575
Seven Parkway Center, Suite 678.

**matchmakers/introduction
services**
*Greater Pittsburgh Matchmaking
Associates* (412) 271-2900
2007 Noble St. Matchmaker Marvin
Roth advertises more than 1,000 clients
married in 13 years. He uses extensive
personal interviews (be prepared to
give a *detailed* dating history!). You
can see PHOTOS of matches first.
Cost: "in the hundreds not thousands,"
he says. The first visit is free.

MatchMaker International
(412) 372-7600
Monroeville

Together Dating Service (412) 856-1800
Monroeville

Together Dating Service (412) 369-7100
Wexford

READING
Reading Eagle Times (215) 376-1527
(N) 900# Sun.

SCRANTON
Scranton Times (717) 328-9100
(N) 900#.

WARREN
Warren Times-Observer (814) 723-8200
(N) 900#.

WEST CHESTER
Daily Local News (215) 696-1775
(N) 900# Fri, Sat, Sun.

WILLIAMSPORT
Sun Gazette (717) 326-1551
(N) N&P.

**YORK
matchmakers/introduction
services**
MatchMaker International
(717) 757-5777
Kingston Center.

RHODE ISLAND

BRISTOL
Bristol Phoenix (401) 253-6000
(N) 900#. Same personals appear in
the *Barrington Times, Warren Times,*
and *Sakonnet Times.*

PROVIDENCE
Providence Phoenix (401) 273-6397
(A) 900#/N&P free weekly (Thur).
Major: about 200 personals per issue.

Providence Journal (401) 277-7000
(N) 900#.

singles activities
Parties by *Times Remembered, Inc.*
(see listing below under videodating).

videodating
Times Remembered, Inc. (401) 944-7788
Videodating. Cost: "in the low hundreds."
In business 8 years. Also sponsor singles
events at hotels (non-members can attend).

matchmakers/introduction
services
Together Dating Service (402) 467-2131
1345 Jefferson Blvd., Suite 1W,
Warwick.

Two of Hearts (401) 433-6880
1445 Wampanoag Trail. Cost: this
female matchmaker doesn't give price
quotes by phone, but says it's "well
under $1,000."

PAWTUCKET
Evening Times (401) 722-4000
(N) 900#.

WARWICK
See Providence.

WOONSOCKET
Woonsocket Call (401) 766-3400
(N) 900# Fri, Sun.

SOUTH CAROLINA

COLUMBIA
Pennysaver (803) 796-8742
(S/C) 900#. Free home delivered
weekly (Mon).

matchmakers/introduction
services
Together Dating Service (803) 750-0700
201 Executive Center Dr.

Single Professionals, Inc. (800) 832-3095
PHOTO/profile matching handled by
mail. Cost: $25 for one month, $15 for
each month thereafter. Very small
currently, however, with only about 80
members. Call and see if they've grown.

CHARLESTON
Evening Post & News Courier
(803) 577-7111
(N) N&P.

matchmakers/introduction
services
Together Dating Service (803) 571-2600
27 Gamecock Ave.

MYRTLE BEACH
Sun News (803) 626-0200
(N) 900#.

SPARTENBURG
The Paper (803) 583-3858
(N) 900# free weekly (Wed). About
130 personals.

Herald Journal (803) 582-4511
(N) 900#.

SOUTH DAKOTA

ABERDEEN
Aberdeen American News (605) 225-4100
(N) 900#.

RAPID CITY
Rapid City Journal (605) 394-8310
(N) 900#/N&P.

The National Dating Directory 239

SIOUX FALLS
Sioux Falls Argus Leader (605) 331-2200
(N) 900#/N&P.

Solo RFD (605) 335-0900
(S) N&P/900. Published monthly and available (for $1.00) in its own newspaper boxes outside post offices. About 200 personals, mostly from Iowa, Minnesota, South Dakota and Nebraska. Also carries listings for singles organizations and events. While this is a "traditional" singles publication (e.g. on newsprint, not glossy and upscale) you can ask owner Harlan Jacobsen about their new high tech options like "Faxback," which gets you any or all of the magazine by fax. Address: *Solo RFD*, 318 S. Main, Sioux Falls, SD 57102.

YANKTON
Daily Press (605) 665-7811
(N) N&P.

TENNESSEE

KINGSPORT
Times-News (615) 246-8121
(N) 900#.

KNOXVILLE
Knoxville News-Sentinel (615) 637-4111
(N) 900# Sun.

matchmakers/introduction services
MatchMaker International (615) 588-1770
5103 Kingston Pike.

Together Dating Service (615) 691-1100
9724 Kingston Pike.

NASHVILLE
Nashville Tennessean & Nashville Banner (615) 254-1031
(N) 900#. The same personals appear in both papers.

Nashville Scene (615) 244-7989
(A) 900# free weekly (Thur).

videodating
Great Expectations (615) 370-0222
5552 Franklin Pike, Suite 200.

matchmakers/introduction services
MatchMaker International
(615) 269-4500
2505 Hillsboro Rd.

MEMPHIS
Memphis Flyer (901) 521-9000
(A) 900#/N&P free weekly (Wed).
100+ personals per week.

Memphis Commercial Appeal
(901) 529-2700
(N) 900# Fri, Sat, Sun.

matchmakers/introduction services
Together Dating Service (901) 794-4700
6094 Apple Tree Dr.

Singles Register Introduction Service & Social Club (901) 365-3988
5830 Mt. Monah Rd. Put on parties and events for members and has a dating file (PHOTO/profile sheet) for members to use. Cost: up to $699 for 3 years. They also print *Single Today*, their own magazine with personal ads.

MURFREESBORO
Daily News Journal (615) 893-7728
(N) 900#.

TEXAS

AMARILLO
Amarillo Daily News (806) 376-5221
(N) 900#/N&P Tue, Thur, Sun in the Meeting Place.

Thrifty Nickel (806) 376-8663
(S/C) N&P free weekly.

ARLINGTON
Arlington Star Telegram
(817) 548-5400
(N) 900#/N&P Fri, Sun.

AUSTIN

Austin Chronicle (512) 454-5766
(A) 900#/N&P free weekly (Thur).
Major: About 350 personals.

Austin American-Statesman
(512) 445-3500
(N) N&P daily.

videodating

Great Expectations (512) 837-3000
9037 Research Blvd., Suite 100.

Two's Company (512) 345-2333
8400 N. Mo-Pac Expwy. Cost: no price
quotes by phone. Report they have
1,000 members.

VIA Video Dating Service
(512) 454-6754
Since 1979. Cost: $500 for one year, up to
50 video selections. 75% of members in
their 30's or 40's. Also do social events
for members. No hard sell and very
forthcoming over the phone.

matchmakers/introduction services

Together Dating Service (512) 440-1511

CORPUS CHRISTI

Corpus Christi Caller (512) 886-3707
(N) 900#/N&P.

DALLAS/FORT WORTH

Dallas Observer (214) 637-2072
(A) 900#/N&P free weekly (Thur).
Major: about 500 personals per week.
Also sponsors personals singles events
around town.

Fort Worth Star-Telegram
(817) 390-7524
(N) 900#/N&P Fri, Sun.

singles activities

See the *Dallas Observer* (above) for
their singles events.

videodating

Great Expectations (214) 448-7900
14180 Dallas Parkway, Suite 100,
Dallas.

matchmakers/introduction services

Christian Singles Adults Dating Service
(817) 457-8050
6451 Brentwood Star Rd., Ft. Worth.

MatchMaker International
(214) 385-8080
12720 Hillcrest Rd., Suite 105, Dallas.

Singles Plus of Fort Worth
(817) 589-2262
1050 W. Pipeline Rd., Ft. Worth.
Reluctant price quote and not terribly
impressive over the phone. Cost:
$50-$100 to start, $60 per month
thereafter.

Together Dating Service (214) 233-8860
14643 Dallas Parkway, Suite 328, Dallas.

Together Dating Service (214) 419-6600
13610 Midway, Suite 236, Dallas.

HOUSTON

Houston Press (713) 624-1400
(A) 900# free weekly (Thur). Major:
about 600 personals per week. Sponsor
singles events ("Singles Mingles").

Houston Single File (713) 966-5694
(S) 900#/N&P. Glossy *quality* free
monthly singles magazine (found in
restaurants, drug stores, etc. in 400
locations). 125+ personals per month.
Also lists single events. Address:
Houston Single File, 2476 Bolsorer #608,
Houston TX 77005.

Houston Post (713) 840-5600
(N) 900#. Thursday classifieds, Sunday
Calendar section.

Houston Chronicle (713) 224-6868
(N) N&P Sun classifieds under People
Meeting People.

Public News (713) 520-1520
(A) 900#/N&P free weekly (Wed).
About 200 personals. A caution: these
personals tend to be sexually explicit
rather than people looking for a
"lasting relationship."

Uptown Express (713) 520-7237
(N) 900#/N&P free New Age monthly
(look for it in bookstores). About 30
personals.

Houston Green Sheet (713) 655-3300
(S/C) 900#. Free weekly. 3-4 pages
of personals.

singles activities

See *Houston Singles File* magazine
(see above listing) for their guide to
singles organizations and activities.

Say Gourmet (713) 621-7003
A singles restaurant group which meets
in a variety of local restaurants. $75 for
one year, plus the cost of meals.

videodating

Great Expectations (713) 623-6495
50 Briar Hollow Suite Dr., Galleria.

matchmakers/introduction
services

First Kiss Introductions (713) 355-5477
Introductions with a PHOTO option.
Cost: $75 for first 3 months, $35 every
other month thereafter. 4 introductions every 3 months. Say they run a
background check on clients. They're
planning to start singles events.

Together Dating Service (713) 621-7788
1900 W. Loop, Galleria.

Together Dating Service (713) 922-5200
10909 Sabo, Clear Lake/Pasadena.

Together Dating Service (713) 872-6767
650 N. Sam Houston Pkwy, Greenspoint.

LUBBOCK

Lubbock Journal (806) 762-8821
(N) 900#/N&P Tue, Wed, Fri, Sun in
People Meeting People.

PASADENA

Pasadena Citizen (713) 477-0221
(N) N&P.

SAN ANTONIO

San Antonio Current (210) 828-7660
(A) 900# free weekly (Thur). About a
dozen personals per week.

San Antonio Express-News
(210) 225-1666
(N) 900# Wed, Fri, Sun.

San Antonio Singles (210) 520-7800
(S) 900#/N&P. Free monthly available
at outlets like convenience stores.
About 75 personals. Report they are
currently changing format to become
a quality, glossy publication. Address:
San Antonio Singles, 9033 Aero, Suite
207, San Antonio, TX 78217.

videodating

Great Expectations (210) 979-7500
8131 IH 10 West, Suite 225.

matchmakers/introduction
services

Together Dating Service
(210) 525-7965
9311 San Pedro Ave.

WACO

Waco Tribune Herald (817) 757-5757
900#.

UTAH

OGDEN

Standard Examiner (801) 394-1677
(N) N&P.

PROVO

Daily Herald (801) 373-6450
(N) 900#/N&P.

Utah County Journal (801) 226-1983
Orem
(N) N&P.

SALT LAKE CITY

Salt Lake Tribune (801) 237-2779
(N) 900#. Fri Entertainment section,
Sun classifieds. Major: 600 personals
under the heading Personally Speaking.

Private Eye (801) 575-7003
(A) 900#/N&P free weekly (Wed).
About 150 personals per issue. Lists
singles events and singles groups.

singles activities
See *Lifestyles* listing immediately below.

**matchmakers/introduction
services**
Lifestyles (801) 266-4939
495 4500 South, Suite 250. Introduction service using PHOTOS/profiles to
matchmake. Cost: $199 one time
membership fee plus quarterly dues
of $30. There is also an option for a 3
month $99 membership. You get 5
introductions per month (an
introduction being when both people
agree to meet). They also put on
parties and other events non-members
can attend.

Let's Do Lunch (801) 266-5600
262 E 3900 South St. Three services
are available: 1) meeting dates for
lunch, 2) social activities, 3) a
newsletter featuring personals. The
lunch dating involves using PHOTOS.
You do the selecting, and talk on the
phone before lunch. Cost: $117 for 3
months with no limit on the number
of selections (and participation in
activities and receipt of newsletter).
1,500 members counting all 3 services.
Promise no hard sell. Very forthcoming and friendly on the phone.

LDS Singles (801) 531-9888
205 W. 700 South.

VERMONT

BURLINGTON
Burlington Free Press (802) 863-3441
(N) 900# Thur Weekender section.

Vermont Times (802) 985-2400
Shelburne
(A) 900#/N&P free weekly (Wed).
About 100 personals.

RUTLAND
Rutland Herald (802) 775-5511
(N) N&P.

Note: For New England personals
check *Dating Page* under Boston,
Mass; and *Dateline New England*
under Portsmouth, NH.

VIRGINIA

**ALEXANDRIA/ARLINGTON/
FAIRFAX**
Alexandria Journal (703) 560-4000
(N) 900#. The same personals appear
in the *Fairfax Journal, Montgomery
Journal, Prince Georges Journal.*

videodating
Great Expectations (703) 847-0808
8601 Westwood Center Dr., Vienna.

**matchmakers/introduction
services**
Together Dating Service (703) 827-9090
1595 Springhill Rd., Vienna.

Note: Those living near Washington
D.C. can also check listings under
District of Columbia.

BRISTOL
Bristol Herald-Courier (703) 669-2181
(N) 900#/N&P. Look for Telepersonals section.

FREDERICKSBURG
The Free Lance Star (703) 373-5000
(N) N&P.

CHARLOTTESVILLE
Daily Progress (804) 978-7202
(N) 900#.

C-Ville Review (804) 980-8000
(A) N&P. Free every two weeks.
About 20 personals.

**NEWPORT NEWS/NORFOLK/
PORTSMOUTH**
The Daily Press (804) 247-4692
(N) 900#.

Norfolk Virginia Pilot, Ledger Star
(804) 446-2000
(N) 900# in the Meeting Place.

RICHMOND
Richmond Times-Dispatch (804) 649-6000
(N) 900# Wed, Fri, Sun.

Style Magazine (804) 358-8949
900#/N&P. Several pages of personals
appear in this free entertainment
weekly (Tue).

**matchmakers/introduction
services**
Lunch Dates (804) 740-3321
See Los Angeles, CA listing for details.

Together Dating Service (804) 273-9500
3951 Westerre Pkwy.

Selective Introductions (804) 273-9419
Paxton Square 3108 Parham Rd.
Introductions with a PHOTO
option. They do the selecting. In
business 10 years. Say 80% of clients
get involved enough with someone to
"go on hold" with their membership.
Cost: "in the hundreds to thousands."

ROANOKE
Times & World News (703) 981-3100
(N) 900#/N&P. Look for 900#
Possibilities section Wed, Fri.

WASHINGTON

BELLINGHAM
The Echo (206) 671-0679
(S/C) 900#. This classifieds publication
comes out every two weeks with 80-
100 personals.

BREMERTON
The Sun (206) 377-3711
(N) 900#/N&P. Look for the Friendly
Connection section.

EVERETT
Daily Herald (206) 339-3080
(N) 900# Fri, Sun. Look for Possibili-
ties section.

OLYMPIA
The Olympian (206) 754-5479
(N) 900#.

SEATTLE
Seattle Weekly (206) 623-0500
(A) 900#/N&P weekly (Wed). Major:
about 200 personals per issue.
The same personals appear in
Eastsideweek, a free weekly (Wed)
serving the Kirkland-Bellevue area.

Seattle Times & Post-Intelligencer
(206) 624-7355
(N) 900#. Recently began running
personals. Look for them under
Getting Acquainted in the Sun
classifieds (about 150 ads). Also see
Fri in the Tempo section of the Times,
and Fri in the What's Happening
section of the Post-Intelligencer.

Seattle Magazine (206) 284-1750
(CN) N&P. Published eight times a
year this magazine has a limited
number of personals compared with
other city-named magazines.

Journal American (206) 453-4200
Bellevue
(N) 900#. The same personals are in
the Valley Daily News.

The Journals (206) 775-2400
(N) 900#. The same personals appear
in 7 papers in the Seattle area.

videodating
Great Expectations (206) 454-1974
10900 Northeast 8th St., Suite 230, Bellevue.

**matchmakers/introduction
services**
MatchMaker International (206) 646-8700
155 108th Ave., NE, Suite 794, Bellevue.

Selective Singles (206) 633-2348,
(206) 347-5133 A one-woman
personalized matchmaking service.
Tina, the owner, reports she has been
in the business 14 years, and is very
forthcoming over the phone. Cost:
$400 for an open-ended membership.

SPOKANE
Spokane Review (509) 459-5000
(N) 900#/N&P. Look for in the
Meeting Place.

TACOMA
The Ranger (206) 584-1212
(N) 900#.

Tacoma Tribune News (206) 572-9511
(N) 900#. See the Personal Line section.

**matchmakers/introduction
services**
Intros (206) 474-4240
15 Oregon Ave., Suite 304. PHOTO
and profiles dating. You do the
selecting. No limit on number of
selections (other than 5 per visit).
Cost: no price quotes by phone.

VANCOUVER
The Columbian (206) 696-1664
(N) 900#.

WASHINGTON, D.C.
See under District of Columbia.

WEST VIRGINIA

BECKLEY
Beckley Register Herald (304) 255-4400
(N) N&P.

CHARLESTON
Daily Mail & Gazette (304) 348-5140
(N) 900#/N&P Wed, Thur, Sun look
for 900# Meeting Place section.

HUNTINGTON
Huntington Herald Dispatch
(304) 526-4002
(N) 900# Fri, Sun in the In Touch section.

WHEELING
Wheeling News Register & Intelligencer
(304) 233-1011
(N) 900# Tue, Fri, Sun.

WISCONSIN

APPLETON
The Bulletin (414) 733-3460
(N) 900# weekly paper.

The Post Crescent (414) 733-4411
(N) 900#.

Appleton Buyers Guide (414) 725-6391
(S/C) 900#. Same personals appear in
14 other *Buyers Guides* (see also
Oshkosh listing).

EAU CLAIRE
Leader Telegram (715) 833-9208
(N) 900#/N&P.

FOND DU LAC
Action Advertiser (414) 922-8640
(S/C) 900#/N&P. Free home delivered
weekly.

GREEN BAY
Green Bay Press Gazette (414) 431-8300
(N) 900#.

KENOSHA
Kenosha News (414) 657-1500
(N) 900#.

The Bulletin (414) 656-1102
(N) 900#.

LACROSSE
LaCrosse Tribune (608) 782-0060
(N) 900#.

MADISON
Isthmus (608) 251-5627
(A) 900#/N&P free weekly (Thur). 75+
personals per issue. Also sponsors
personals singles parties.

Wisconsin State Journal
(608) 252-6320
(N) 900#/N&P.

MILWAUKEE

SingleLife (414) 271-9700
(S) 900#/N&P. Published every other month, we recommend this glossy quality magazine available at newsstands ($2.50). Major: 200+ personals. They also sponsor subscriber singles parties. Address: *SingleLife*, 606 W. Wisconsin Ave., Suite 703, Milwaukee, WI 53203.

Milwaukee Journal & Sentinel (414) 224-2121
(N) 900#/N&P Thur Weekend section in the *Journal*, Fri *Sentinel's* Let's Go section, Sun *Sentinel's* Lifestyle and Reach sections.

Shepherd Express (414) 276-2222
(A) 900#/N&P free weekly (Thur).

Singles Choice (414) 272-8700
(S) 900#/N&P. Published monthly, and free at convenience stores, etc. Major: 300+ personals. Also sponsor parties. Address: *Singles Choice*, P.O. Box 454, Milwaukee, WI 53201.

Bargain Express (414) 446-3933
(S/C) 900# free home delivered weekly.

singles activities

See *SingleLife Magazine* (listed above) for their parties.

videodating

Great Expectations (414) 796-5100
16650 W. Blue Mound Rd., suite 100, Brookfield.

Modern Love (414) 453-3997
2130 N. Mayfair Rd., Suite 11. Give you a choice between video and photo dating. 1/3 of members choose video, 2/3 photos. Cost: $249 for one year with 3 choices per month. 400 members.

Single Attractions, Inc. (414) 774-7764
In business 10 years. Cost: $495 for one year (with a limit on number of selections); $695-$795 for one year with no selection limit. Report they do videodating with a personal touch, and have had "hundreds" of marriages.

matchmakers/introduction services

Computer Dating (414) 444-4800
312 E. Wisconsin Ave. No information by phone, only by mail.

Together Dating Service (414) 257-4433
2401 N. Mayfair Rd., Suite 210.

OSHKOSH

Oshkosh Northwestern (414) 235-7780
(N) 900#/N&P.

Buyers Guide (414) 725-6391
(S/C) 900#. The same personals appear in 14 other Buyers Guides: *Appleton, Anigo, New London, Rhinelander, Clintonville, Marshfield, Seymour, Stevenspoint, Wapaca*, etc.

RACINE

Journal Times (414) 634-3111
(N) 900#. The same personals appear in the *Pennysaver*, a free home delivered weekly shoppers guide.

SHEBOYGAN

Sheboygan Express (414) 457-7711
(N) N&P.

Shoreline Chronicle (414) 459-8820
(S/C) 900#. Free home delivered weekly shoppers guide.

WYOMING

CHEYENNE

Wyoming Tribune Eagle (307) 634-3361
(N) 900# Fri, Sat, Sun. About 25 personals.

NATIONAL PERSONALS

The Bachelor Book (305) 565-4771 (S) N&P. This quality national glossy personals publication is published in the Miami, Florida area. It runs *long* bios of men from around the country with PHOTOS (some in color) for women to respond to. There were about 50 bios in the issue we checked, plus additional non-photo personals at the back of the magazine. For women personals advertisers publisher Mindi Rudan is now publishing the *Bachelorette Book* for men to respond to. Address: *The Bachelor Book* or *The Bachelorette Book*, 8222 Wiles Rd., Suite 111, Coral Springs, FLA 33067. Check your newsstands or call to subscribe.

Cinema Liaisons (800) 827-6001 (N&P) For film buffs to meet other film buffs. Newsletter includes personals from members. $65 for a six month membership. Address: P.O. Box 990, NY, NY 10113-0990.

The Nation (212) 242-8400 N&P. There are a limited number of personals in this weekly political affairs magazine.

National Review (212) 679-7330 N&P. Published every two weeks, there are a limited number of personals are in this conservative political affairs magazine.

New York Review of Books (212) 757-8070 (N) N&P. This weekly book review newspaper is available at bookstores and newsstands around the country. 100+ personals featuring an eclectic and intellectual mix. Address: *New York Review*, 250 W. 57th Street, NY, NY 10107.

Single Women and Gentlemen Magazine (919) 659-1100 (S) 900#. Published in North Carolina this is a national personals publication similar to *The Bachelor Book*, but it's for men *and* women. It's a glossy quality magazine featuring about 100 men and women from around the country, with bios and color PHOTOS. Address: Mail Sort, Inc, 3880 Vest Mill Rd., Suite 100, Winston-Salem NC 27103. Check your newsstand or call to subscribe.

Smoking Singles Magazine (212) 969-8624 (S) 900#/N&P. Available at newsstands in NY and by subscription nationally. Features 40-50 national personals from smokers who don't want smoking to be an issue in dating. Address: 331 W. 57th Street, Suite 165, NY, NY 10019.

The Sun (212) 490-0172 (N) N&P. Weekly tabloid newspaper with 100+ personals (however, a number of them are from correctional institution inmates - both male and female!).

Sweetheart This Montana based singles magazine has many national personals. For more information see under Montana listings.

USA Today (703) 276-3400 (N) 900#. Prints sample personals and the rest are accessed by plugging in using your area code.

Glossary of Personal Ad
Terms:

A Asian
B Black
W White
H Hispanic
NA Native American
S single
WW widowed
D divorced
F female
M male
J Jewish
C Catholic

P professional
NS non-smoker
ND no drugs
ISO in search of (only in certain publications)
Bi bisexual
G gay
LTR long term relationship (only in certain publications)
BBW big beautiful woman (very overweight)
WLTM would like to meet (only in certain publications)

Personals terminology can vary from one publication to another. You don't want to use "ISO" if you don't see anyone else using it, because no one will know what you are talking about. However, most of these abbreviations are standard. If you see an abbreviation in a personal you don't understand, call the publication's classifieds department and ask about it.

ACKNOWLEDGMENTS

We would like to thank some of the people who contributed to the finished book you hold in your hands. Cherilyn Parsons, who did copy-editing early on and offered invaluable suggestions. Janice Roberts at Mike the Printer for formatting from Wordperfect to Macintosh with consummate skill. Laura Sjoberg at Griffin Printing for being so helpful. Steve Simpson and his associates for an excellent cover. Lynn Dowling for the Laurel Canyon Press logo. John Flaa at Microvoice for supplying his personals publications client list.